# Labour in the Clothing Industry in the Asia Pacific

The clothing industry provides employment for 60 million workers worldwide. More than a quarter of these workers are employed in the Asia-Pacific region, where the industry is based on subcontracted production on behalf of international buyers. Rapid movements of manufacturing activity from country to country in search of cost advantages make clothing workers part of a globalizing labour market where they increasingly suffer from job insecurity.

This book presents carefully researched case studies, which highlight the ways in which labour is informalized, fragmented and made disposable by the globalization of production. Chapters address issues pertaining to rights and citizenship, and new forms of activism and organization in conjunction and coordination with diverse support groups, consumers and wider global campaigns. Contributors further examine the role of the nation state, government regulatory bodies, as well as independent monitoring systems such as the International Labour Organization. Although there has been considerable effort directed to understanding how firms operate across multiple countries – in studies of the organization of global production networks, and the implications for complexities of scale, (de)territorialization and state development projects – there has been far less focus on how these processes produce precarious labour and reshape worker consciousness.

Offering new insights into the understanding and support of workers in the global textile and garment industry, this book will be of interest to academics in a variety of disciplines including Asian studies, sociology, political economy, development, human rights, labour and gender.

**Vicki Crinis** is Associate Researcher with the Law, Humanities and Creative Arts Faculty at the University of Wollongong, where she previously held a Post-doctoral Fellowship as part of an Australian Research Council Discovery Project on the garment industry in the Asia-Pacific.

**Adrian Vickers** holds a personal chair at the University of Sydney, and researches and publishes on the cultural history of Southeast Asia.

# Routledge Studies in the Growth Economies of Asia

123 **Economic Growth and Employment in Vietnam**
*David Lim*

124 **Asian Financial Integration**
Impacts of the global crisis and options for regional policies
*Edited by Yiping Huang and Shiro Armstrong*

125 **Informal Labour in Urban India**
Three cities, three journeys
*Tom Barnes*

126 **Business Leadership Development in China**
*Shuang Ren, Robert Wood and Ying Zhu*

127 **Women, Labour and the Economy in India**
From migrant menservants to uprooted girl children maids
*Deepita Chakravarty and Ishita Chakravarty*

128 **Negotiating Financial Agreement in East Asia**
Surviving the turbulence
*Kaewkamol Karen Pitakdumrongkit*

129 **Managing Cyber Risk in the Financial Sector**
Lessons from Asia, Europe and the USA
*Edited by Ruth Taplin*

130 **Chinese Economic Diplomacy**
Decision-making actors and processes
*Shuxiu Zhang*

131 **China's Iron Ore Boom**
*Luke W. L. Hurst*

132 **Economic Change in Asia**
Implication for corporate strategy and social responsibility
*Edited by M. Bruna Zolin, Bernadette Andreosso-O'Callaghan and Jacques Jaussaud*

133 **China's Economic Culture**
The ritual order of state and markets
*Carsten Herrmann-Pillath*

134 **Labour in the Clothing Industry in the Asia Pacific**
*Edited by Vicki Crinis and Adrian Vickers*

# Labour in the Clothing Industry in the Asia Pacific

Edited by Vicki Crinis and
Adrian Vickers

LONDON AND NEW YORK

First published 2017
by Routledge
2 Park Square, Milton Park, Abingdon, Oxon OX14 4RN

and by Routledge
711 Third Avenue, New York, NY 10017

*Routledge is an imprint of the Taylor & Francis Group, an informa business*

© 2017 Vicki Crinis and Adrian Vickers

The right of the editors to be identified as the authors of the editorial
matter, and of the authors for their individual chapters, has been asserted
in accordance with sections 77 and 78 of the Copyright, Designs and
Patents Act 1988.

All rights reserved. No part of this book may be reprinted or reproduced or
utilized in any form or by any electronic, mechanical, or other means, now
known or hereafter invented, including photocopying and recording, or in
any information storage or retrieval system, without permission in writing
from the publishers.

*Trademark notice*: Product or corporate names may be trademarks or
registered trademarks, and are used only for identification and explanation
without intent to infringe.

*British Library Cataloguing in Publication Data*
A catalogue record for this book is available from the British Library

*Library of Congress Cataloging in Publication Data*
Names: Crinis, Vicki, editor. | Vickers, Adrian, 1958– editor.
Title: Labour in the clothing industry in the Asia Pacific / edited by Vicki
Crinis and Adrian Vickers.
Description: New York : Routledge, 2016. | Series: Routledge studies in
the growth economies of Asia ; 134 | Includes bibliographical references
and index.
Identifiers: LCCN 2016027965| ISBN 9781138125704 (hardback) |
ISBN 9781315647326 (ebook)
Subjects: LCSH: Clothing workers–Asia. | Clothing workers–Pacific Area.
| Labor and globalization–Asia. | Labor and globalization–Pacific Area.
Classification: LCC HD8039.C62 A784 2016 | DDC 331.7/687095–dc23
LC record available at https://lccn.loc.gov/2016027965

ISBN: 978-1-138-12570-4 (hbk)
ISBN: 978-1-315-64732-6 (ebk)

Typeset in Times New Roman
by Wearset Ltd, Boldon, Tyne and Wear

**The book is dedicated to Melanie Beresford our colleague and friend**

# Contents

| | |
|---|---|
| *List of figures* | ix |
| *List of tables* | x |
| *Notes on contributors* | xi |
| *Acknowledgements* | xv |
| *List of abbreviations* | xvi |

**1  Introduction: dis-organizing labour in the clothing industry in the Asia Pacific**   1

VICKI CRINIS AND ADRIAN VICKERS

**2  The fragmentation of the clothing and textile trade union movement in Malaysia**   23

VICKI CRINIS

**3  Scrutinizing the effectiveness of trade unions in post-socialist Vietnam**   43

ANNE COX

**4  Before Rana Plaza: towards a history of labour organizing in Bangladesh's garment industry**   60

DINA SIDDIQI

**5  Migrant workers in the clothing industry: networking in Christian spaces**   80

VICKI CRINIS AND ANGIE NGỌC TRẦN

**6  China's migrant workers and the global financial crisis**   97

KATE HANNAN

viii *Contents*

**7 Workers in the Indian export garment industry: surviving neoliberal reforms** 119

RUCHIRA GANGULY–SCRASE

**8 Child labour and gender discrimination in the garment industry of Kong Pisei, Cambodia** 142

MELANIE BERESFORD, IVAN CUCCO AND LAURA PROTA

**9 Asian women doing home-based garment manufacturing in Sydney, Australia** 169

ELISSA SUTHERLAND

*Appendix* 190
*Index* 192

# Figures

| | | |
|---|---|---|
| 4.1 | Workers' federations: a partial count | 68 |
| 8.1 | Graph plots of female and male garment workers' current age against first employment age | 154 |
| 8.2 | Incidence (per cent) of child labourers, young workers and ceased workers per year (1995–2010) | 155 |
| 8.3 | Percentage distribution of average weekly overtime hours for young and adult workers | 156 |
| 8.4 | BFC reported percentage of non-compliant monitored factories on childcare provision from October 2006 to April 2012 | 158 |
| 8.5 | BFC reported compliance levels of maternity leave from October 2006 to April 2012 | 159 |
| 8.6 | BFC reported percentage of non-compliant monitored factories on gender discrimination from October 2006 to April 2012 | 160 |
| 8.7 | Job cessation and birth of first child | 161 |
| 8.8 | Job cessation and birth of last child | 162 |

# Tables

| | | |
|---|---|---|
| 1.1 | Clothing export value of major Asian producers | 5 |
| 3.1 | Interview distribution of the case studies | 50 |
| 7.1 | Workers recruited from ten exporter companies | 131 |
| 8.1 | Child labour detected in Cambodian garment factories | 151 |
| 8.2 | Reasons for quitting garment factory work | 161 |
| A1.1 | Vietnamese worker interviews conducted in Batu Pahat and Johor in 2008 | 190 |
| A1.2 | Vietnamese and Nepalese worker interviews conducted in Penang in 2009 | 190 |
| A1.3 | Vietnamese worker interviews conducted in Batu Pahat in 2010 | 190 |
| A1.4 | Nepalese and Vietnamese worker interviews conducted in Kuala Lumpur in 2010 and 2013 | 191 |

# Contributors

**Melanie Beresford** was a leading scholar of Southeast Asia political economy. She taught History of Economic Thought at Macquarie University and she was the recipient of numerous research projects funded by the Australian Research Council (ARC). Her research interests included: Southeast Asian economic transition from plan to markets, gender, environmental issues and development. She investigated these themes through the lens of class analysis. Her most recent publications were 'Emerging class relations in the Mekong Delta of Vietnam: a network analysis' (*Journal of Agrarian Change*, 2012); 'Layoffs in China's city of textiles: adaptation to change' (*Journal of Contemporary Asia*, 2012); 'The factory hierarchy in the village: recruitment networks and labour control in Kong Pisei District of Cambodia' (*Institutions and Economies*, 2012) Melanie died suddenly in 2013.

**Anne Cox** is a senior lecturer at the University of Wollongong, Australia. She researches and publishes in three main areas, namely the transfer of multinational companies' industrial relations/human resource management (IR/ HRM) policies and practices across borders, the transformation of IR/HRM systems in developing countries and gender equity. Her book *The Transformation of HRM and Industrial Relations in Vietnam* was published by Oxford Chandos Publishing in 2009.

**Vicki Crinis** is Associate Researcher with the Law, Humanities and Creative Arts Faculty at the University of Wollongong, where she previously held a Postdoctoral Fellowship as part of an Australian Research Council Discovery Project on the garment industry in the Asia-Pacific. Her research focuses on the global clothing industry, trade unions and migrant workers in Malaysia, and she has published some book chapters and journal articles on female labour, sweatshops in the clothing industry, NGOs and trade unions, CSR labour rights and human rights.

**Ivan Cucco** is a Postdoctoral Research Fellow in the Department of Economics and Statistics at the University of Naples 'Federica II'. His current research project brings theoretical and methodological insights from social network analysis to the field of innovation studies. Recent empirical applications xii *Contributors*

include evaluation of network-based innovation policies in Italian technological districts and the analysis of persisting spatial asymmetries in co-patenting activities across European Union (EU) regions. Ivan obtained his PhD in 2012 at Macquarie University with a neo-Marxist class analysis of inequality in a Chinese new- and high-technology development zone. Beyond innovation and inequality, his research interests include rural development, the transformation of global food regimes and the political economy of alternative food networks. He spent several years doing fieldwork in rural and urban areas of China and (to a lesser extent) Vietnam.

**Ruchira Ganguly-Scrase** is Adjunct Professor at the Globalism Research Centre, RMIT University and was formerly Professor of Anthropology and the National Course Director for International Studies, Australian Catholic University. Her research has specialized on the intersections of forced migration and various development narratives. She is the author of a number of articles and book chapters on migration, the impacts of neoliberal reforms, ethnographic method, childhood and schooling, and gender relations in Asia. Her most recent books include *Rethinking Displacement: Asia Pacific Perspectives* (Ashgate, 2013, co-edited with Kuntala Lahiri-Dutt) and *Globalization and the Middle Classes in India: The Social and Cultural Impact of Neoliberal Reforms* (Routledge, 2009, co-authored with T. J. Scrase). Ruchira is currently completing a major study funded by the ARC on globalization and regional development in South Asia.

**Kate Hannan** has been researching and writing on the topic of contemporary Chinese politics since the Deng Xiaoping government introduced the 1978 programme for economic reform. She has had a particular interest in the 1990s reform of China's state-owned enterprises; the employment conditions of two generations of China's rural to urban migrant workers; and more recently, in China's 'going out' and 'Belt and Road' policies and the effect of these policies on an ever-growing number of developing countries. Her latest publication (with Stewart Firth) is 'Trading with the Dragon: Chinese trade, investment, and development assistance in the Pacific Islands' (*Journal of Contemporary China*, Vol. 24, No. 95). Kate has taught courses on Chinese politics and society, political theory and development studies at a number of universities including Macquarie University (Sydney), the University of the South Pacific (Suva, Fiji) and the University of Wollongong.

**Angie Ngọc Trần** is Professor of Political Economy at California State University, Monterey Bay. She received fellowships from the National University of Singapore, Stanford University, University of Wollongong and the Australian National University and was a Fulbright Professor at Hanoi National University (1999–2000). Her 2013 book, *Ties That Bind: Cultural Identity, Class, and Law in Vietnam's Labor Resistance*, covers labour protests from the French colonial period to the twenty-first-century global market system. Her articles appeared in *Labor Studies Journal, International Journal of*

*Institutions and Economies, Journal of the Asia Pacific Economy, Journal of Business Ethics*, and *Harvard International Review*. Her ongoing research and manuscripts are on migrant workers traversing Vietnam and Malaysia, critical analysis of CSR initiative, Vietnamese state-labour-management relations with attention to the Trans-Pacific Partnership.

**Laura Prota** holds a PhD in Economics from Macquarie University in Sydney, a Master's degree in Economic Development and Cooperation from the University of Bologna and an undergraduate degree (magna cum laude) from the University of Federico II in Naples. She had a post-doctoral fellowship from the Faculty of Economics and Statistics, University of Salerno from 2012–15. Specializing in social network analysis and rural development, she adopts a relational approach to study the configuration of agricultural production and innovation systems under globalization. She published on issues related to the specificity of Southeast Asian market transition with a particular focus on place and path dependent trajectories of local development, land markets, persistent poverty, gender and labour rights. Laura also published methodological articles on positional analysis to study local forms of coordination and to identify the topology and evolutionary trajectory of local innovation systems.

**Dina Siddiqi**, an anthropologist by training, divides her time between the US and Bangladesh where she teaches in the Department of Economics and Social Sciences at BRAC University, Dhaka. She is currently working on a book-length manuscript tentatively entitled *Elusive Solidarities: Islam and Transnational Feminism at Work*. Her most recent publication is 'Scandals of seduction and the seductions of scandal' (*Comparative Studies of South Asia, Africa and the Middle East* 2015).

**Elissa Sutherland** is an Affiliate to the School of Social Sciences at Monash University having been a tenured academic from 2003 to 2014 in Human Geography. Her PhD examined the role of home-based workers in the Australian clothing industry and her research actively engaged with debates and regulatory processes shaping the industry and urban labour markets of inner western Sydney. Dr Sutherland is accustomed to working in cross-cultural contexts. Her key strength is in drawing on the personal histories and experiences of groups and individuals to provide insights to regulators about appropriate governance. Her research addresses labour market restructuring, urban change and social enterprise development. Dr Sutherland has also worked in local government and key research centres and is now also undertaking consultancy work.

**Adrian Vickers** holds a personal chair at the University of Sydney, and researches and publishes on the cultural history of Southeast Asia. He has held a series of ARC grants, the most recent looking at Indonesian art, the Cold War, and labour and industry in Southeast Asia. As part of a linkage grant on the history of Balinese painting, he has created a virtual museum,

xiv  *Contributors*

continuing previous pioneering work in eResearch and teaching. His books include the highly popular *Bali: A Paradise Created* (new edition 2012), *A History of Modern Indonesia* (new edition 2013) and *Balinese Art: Paintings and Drawings of Bali, 1800–2010* (2012). Professor Vickers has recently been a Senior Visiting Fellow at the Asia Research Institute, the National University of Singapore, a Senior Visiting Fellow at the Joint Centre for History and Economics at the University of Cambridge, and a Visiting Fellow at Magdalene College, Cambridge. He is a Fellow of the Australian Academy of the Humanities.

# Acknowledgements

This volume is the outcome of an Australian Research Council (ARC) project 'The Clothing Industry in the Asia Pacific: Managing Constant Change' and a workshop on the effects of the global financial crisis (2008–9) on workers in the clothing industry in the Asia Pacific held at the University of Wollongong. The workshop, which was funded by the Asia Pacific Futures Research Network (APFRN), the Centre for Asia Pacific Social Transformation Studies (CAPSTRANS) at the University of Wollongong, and the Faculty of Arts at the University of Sydney, provided an invaluable forum to discuss how the global economic crisis (GEC), which affected globalized chains of commodity production and consumption also affected workers in the garment industry. Some of the chapters in this volume were presented at the workshop.

My thanks to all our authors for the efforts they have put into their chapters and the anonymous reviewers for their invaluable comments. Special thanks to Sally Weller for academic guidance and editing the introduction and Chapter 4; to Belinda Henwood for her expert copy-editing; Brian Martin for the writing group and Andrew Wells for his motivational support getting the project off the ground. The people who attended the workshop and are not the authors of the book chapters deserve a special mention for their intellectual contribution to the book's framework such as Rowan Cahill, Anita Chan, Leo van Grunsven, Di Kelly, Piyasuda Pangsapa, Rajah Rasiah, Tim Scrase, Helena Spyrou and Sally Weller.

# Abbreviations

| | |
|---|---|
| AAFLI | Asian American Free Labour Institute |
| ABS | Australian Bureau of Statistics |
| ADI | Agricultural Development International |
| AFL-CIO | American Federation of Labour – Congress of Industrial Organizations |
| AIRC | Australian Industrial Relations Commission |
| AL | Awami League |
| ARC | Australian Research Council |
| ASEAN | Association of South East Asian Nations |
| ATC | Agreement on Textiles and Clothing |
| ATO | Australian Tax Office |
| BBC | British Broadcasting Corporation |
| BCWS | Bangladesh Center for Worker Solidarity |
| BFC | Better Factories Cambodia |
| BGMEA | Bangladesh Garment Manufacturers Export Association |
| BGTLWF | Bangladesh Garments Textile & Leather Workers' Federation |
| BIGUF | Bangladesh Independent Garment Workers Federation |
| BLAST | Bangladesh Legal Aid and Services Trust |
| BNP | Bangladesh Nationalist Party |
| BWSC | Bangladesh Welfare Society Campbelltown |
| CAMSA | Coalition to Abolish Modern-day Slavery in Asia |
| CAPSTRANS | Centre for Asia Pacific Social Transformation Studies |
| CCC | Clean Clothes Campaign |
| CEO | Chief Executive Officer |
| CSR | corporate social responsibility |
| DOL | Department of Labour |
| EPW | Economic and Political Weekly |
| EPZ | export processing zone |
| ETI | Ethical Trading Initiative |
| EU | European Union |
| FDI | foreign direct investment |
| FTZ | Free Trade Zone |
| GATT | General Agreement of Tariffs and Trade |

*Abbreviations* xvii

| | |
|---|---|
| GCC | global commodity chain |
| GDP | Gross Domestic Product |
| GFC | global financial crisis |
| GMAC | Garment Manufacturers Association in Cambodia |
| GPN | global production network |
| GUF | Global Union Federation |
| GVC | global value chain |
| GWUF | Garment Workers Union Federation |
| HRM | human resource management |
| ICFTU | International Confederation of Free Trade Unions |
| IFC | International Finance Corporation |
| ILO | International Labour Organization |
| IMA | International Migrant Workers Alliance |
| IMF | International Monetary Fund |
| IR | industrial relations |
| ISA | Internal Securities Act |
| ITGLWF | International Textile, Garment and Leather Workers' Federation |
| IUF | International Union Federation |
| KL | Kuala Lumpur |
| MFA | Multi-Fibre Arrangement |
| MKMA | Malaysian Knitting Manufacturers Association |
| MNC | multinational corporations |
| MOLVT | Ministry of Labour and Vocational Training |
| MOU | memorandum of understanding |
| MTMA | Malaysian Textile Manufacturers Association |
| MTUC | Malaysian Trade Union Congress |
| NAFTA | North Atlantic Free Trade Agreement |
| NAP | National Awami Party |
| NEP | New Economic Policy |
| NGO | non-government organization |
| NIC | newly industrialized country |
| NOHD | National Office of Human Development |
| NSW | New South Wales |
| PTGWU | Penang and Province Wellesley Textiles and Garment Manufacturing Employees' Union |
| RAB | Rapid Action Battalion |
| RMG | Ready Made Garment |
| SAI | Social Accountability International |
| SCOP | Workers Employees Unity Council |
| SME | small to medium enterprise |
| SPARTECA | South Pacific Regional Trade and Economic Co-operation Agreement |
| SSE | small-scale enterprise |
| TAFE | Technical and Further Education |

xviii  *Abbreviations*

| | |
|---|---|
| TATA | Trade Agreement on Textiles and Apparel |
| TCF | textile, clothing and footwear |
| TCFUA | Textile, Clothing and Footwear Union of Australia |
| TWARO | Textile Workers Asia-Pacific Regional Organization |
| UK | United Kingdom |
| UN | United Nations |
| US | United States |
| VGCL | Vietnamese General Confederation of Labour |
| WAO | Women's Aid Organization |
| WTO | World Trade Organization |
| WWW | Women Working Worldwide |

# 1 Introduction

## Dis-organizing labour in the clothing industry in the Asia Pacific

*Vicki Crinis and Adrian Vickers*

The Rana Plaza disaster in Bangladesh in 2013 brought home to an international audience the implications of industrial mobility in the clothing industry. In this event, a substandard building that housed, among others, five clothing factories employing over 3000 workers collapsed, and the lives of hundreds of workers were lost. Estimates put the death toll at between 425 and 1200 (Yardley 2013). These workers died as the result of the operations of an industry that seeks to reduce the margins of labour costs. In addition to low wages and poor working conditions, nowadays contractors also use strategies of transnational mobility. While the reaction in some western countries has been to call for the withdrawal of subcontracted production from Bangladesh, analysts with a better knowledge of conditions in Bangladesh have pointed to the fact that textiles and clothing account for 80 per cent of the country's exports and contribute significantly to the country's Gross Domestic Product (GDP). This growth is underpinned by the pricing of local labour more cheaply than any other Asian country (Chakravarty and Luce 2013). More than 90 per cent of garment workers are women, and almost all of them are migrants who work to support families in perhaps distant rural provinces. The imperative to support families binds these workers to exploitative employment and substandard labour conditions that in turn reflect the subordinate position of Bangladeshi firms in the cost-based system of international competition for work contracts (see Ruwanpura and Wrigley 2011) When the core firms that commission production have the knowledge and the market power to extract favourable deals that minimize production costs (Gereffi *et al.* 2005), local manufacturers meet these demands by threatening workers and extracting concessions from them (Collins 2007: 145). The essays in this collection reveal logics intended to fragment labour, but show that in practice the consequences of the resulting change processes are complicated, uneven and often unpredictable.

The unexpected onset of both the 1997 Asian economic crisis and the 2007–8 trans-Atlantic economic crisis have shown how quickly patterns of world trade can change. This book demonstrates how such changes affect workers by showing how one of the most important industries in the Asia Pacific, the manufacture of clothing, is subject to massive fluctuations in production volume and employment numbers as the global demand for clothing waxes and wanes and the cost relativities of different production locations alter (see Stalker 2000: 35). Because clothing purchases can be deferred when times are hard, this sector is vulnerable to the economic cycle. Yet, the clothing industry provides employment for 60 million workers worldwide. More than a quarter of these workers are employed in the Asia-Pacific region, where the industry is based on subcontracted production on behalf of international buyers. In 2014 to 2015 there were 4.2 million mostly women employed in the clothing industry in Bangladesh; ten million in China; 600,000 in Cambodia; 12 million in India; 102,120 in Malaysia and two million in Vietnam. These figures listed in the formal production sector statistics, do not include the large numbers of informal workers in countries such as in India. It is estimated that in India at least 60 per cent of garment workers are employed in the informal sector. In Australia where the wages are high, large numbers of home-based workers more than double the 40,000 workers employed in the formal sector work as home-based workers.[1] Rapid movements of manufacturing activity from country to country in search of cost advantages make clothing workers part of a globalizing labour market where they increasingly share the experience of job insecurity.

After 2008, as orders from Europe and the United States (US) declined in the wake of the financial crisis, thousands of workers in the Asia Pacific were retrenched as garment companies closed down or moved to locations with cheaper labour costs. It is estimated that 11 million of those jobs never returned.[2] In China, where city industrial workers do not have residents' rights (*hukou*), migrant workers who lost their factory jobs left the cities and returned to their rural areas of origin. In 2008, the United Nations Development Fund for Women found that 700,000 clothing and textile workers in India and 30,000 – mostly female – garment industry workers in Sri Lanka and Cambodia lost their jobs at that time. In such countries, where clothing production is a major contributor to export earnings, these job losses adversely affected their entire national economies (United Nations Development Fund for Women 2010: 155). Sometimes these jobs were replaced by new ones in other locations, employing new groups of vulnerable workers. As Bangladesh has been one of the 'beneficiaries' of this movement in attracting garment factories, it suggests that cost minimization has been a major motivation for relocation.

Governments use taxation breaks and other incentives, including the establishment of 'special economic zones', to lure investment and entice global firms to establish production facilities. Governments justify the incentives they offer to attract foreign companies – such as tax concessions, infrastructure and discounted water and energy – in terms of the benefits of direct employment creation and the indirect employment created when local contractors take over parts of the production sequence. Global production processes are inherently unstable because each fashion trend requires different types of skills, different inputs and different machinery, which implies selecting the factory most appropriate to the particular production task (Weller 2007). In addition, labour productivity is changeable, with countries that invest in education and training (for example, China) increasing their capacity to absorb a more complex range of production tasks (see Gereffi and Sturgeon 2009). The lowest wage sites are also those where the least complex tasks are carried out (for example, sewing t-shirts). Global core companies are driven by profit-seeking, which is passed down through the production chain via subcontractors, with decisions about where to locate a particular production task based on a combination of labour productivity (that is, output relative to wage costs), quality and skill requirements, although the overall economic environment and infrastructure are also important. Over time, where trust has been established, relationships develop between preferred suppliers. The leading firms in global garment production are not interested in industrial upgrading or improving workers' rights and conditions – their strategies are better described as being about the informalization and dis-organization of labour (Wills 1998). These terms refer to the ideas of removing labour from processes regulated and scrutinized by government and unions, and also to the idea of disempowering those organizations, largely unions, that have historically supported the collective interests of workers.

It is not surprising, therefore, that the globalization of capital and production systems has generated the parallel globalization of protest and industrial action, but in a new form (Waterman and Wills 2001). In places where union activity is weak or is suppressed by the state – as is the case in a number of Asian locations – voluntary organizations working outside the production system and workplace have become central sites of opposition and mobilization. In the Asia-Pacific region, consumer-based non-governmental organizations (NGOs) have emerged as advocates of workers' rights. These NGOs have sought to expose the exploitative processes inherent in global commodity chains, showing the links between brand names and the factories that exploit workers, thus opening spaces where consumers become active participants in the chains. Larger coalitions of these organizations, such as the International Labor Rights Forum and the Worker Rights Consortium, have developed connections among labour activists, unions and academics. Although based in the US, the chief consumption end-point for many commodity chains, they build on the accountability-based models developed in human rights activism and use the internet to mobilize their followers in coordinated responses to crises (Collins 2007: 405). As the tactics of consumer-based NGOs infiltrate the logics of mobile capitalism and exploit fashion brands' vulnerability to adverse publicity, they have created voluntary, firm-based international codes of conduct (Collins 2007: 407–8). We will return to this issue later.

This book documents and analyses these processes of dis-organization, by providing case studies of the different policies, processes and actions that keep labour divided, and hence controlled. Avoiding the strong US bias of other studies,[3] this volume focuses on Australia, Bangladesh, Cambodia, China, India, Malaysia and Vietnam, all of which illustrate particular combinations of state management, liberalization and labour regulation and conditions. Each of the case study countries has features that make it distinctive, but also allow us to pursue connections between them, contributing to the larger picture of labour in the clothing industry in the Asia-Pacific region.[4] The Asia-Pacific region

4  *V. Crinis and A. Vickers*

produces over 60 per cent of the world's garments, with China alone producing nearly one-third of the world's clothing exports (see Table 1.1).

In 2004, the 30-year clothing regulatory system known as the Multi-Fibre Arrangement (MFA) under the auspices of the General Agreement of Tariffs and Trade (GATT) ended. During the MFA period that Australia was not a signatory, the MFA directed production to locations with quota, which meant that the US Department of Trade decided where production would be.

The MFA was replaced by the World Trade Organization (WTO) Agreement on Textiles and Clothing of 2004, which has permitted the gradual expansion of exports from Asia into the core US and European markets. The dismantling of the MFA's quota restrictions after 2004 allowed buyer firms to source garments from any supplier, but the realities of production costs and productivity – as well as the proximity to textiles and accessories production sites – have resulted in increasing concentration of production in China (Appelbaum 2008). More recently, Chinese labour costs have increased relative to other Asian locations and the Chinese government has committed to repositioning the Chinese economy towards high value-added, more technologically sophisticated industries. Although this process was interrupted by the 2007 financial crisis, it is likely that China will increasingly become a purchaser of production capacity in other parts of Asia, rather than a direct producer. For core sourcing firms in the US and European Union (EU), the financial crisis altered cost relativities between imports from Asia and from adjacent production centres (in Mexico and East Europe). Agreements like the North Atlantic Free Trade Agreement (NAFTA) are designed to support capital-intensive textile production and have made these sites in the agreement cost-effective for the production of high-value garments made using local cloth. In addition, as Smith *et al.* (2002) have demonstrated in their work on the Slovakian clothing industry, by sourcing closer to the market, buyers save time and transport costs, and control the quality production of the garments.

## Modes of analysis: networks and chains

The cases presented in this book highlight the ways labour is informalized, fragmented and made disposable by the globalization of production. Although there has been a considerable effort directed to understanding how firms operate across multiple countries – in studies of the organization of global production networks, and the implications for complexities of scale, (de)territorialization and state development projects – there has been far less interest in how these processes produce precarious labour and reshape worker consciousness (Cumbers *et al.* 2008).

Labour relations must be located in production systems. Three related analytical approaches have been used to study the clothing industry's form of internationalized organization: these approaches focus on global commodity chains (GCCs), global production networks (GPNs) and global value chains (GVCs). Scholar-activists have mobilized these related frameworks to reveal links

*Table 1.1* Clothing export value of major Asian producers (US$ million)

| | 1990 | 2000 | 2008 | 2009 | 2010 | 2011 | 2012 | 2013 | 2014 |
|---|---|---|---|---|---|---|---|---|---|
| World | 108,129 | 197,363 | 363,621 | 315,516 | 351,464 | 416,521 | 422,686 | 459,662 | 483,280 |
| China | 9669 | 36,071 | 120,405 | 107,264 | 129,838 | 153,774 | 159,614 | 177,414 | 186,607 |
| Hong Kong | 15,406 | 24,214 | 27,908 | 22,826 | 24,049 | 24,505 | 22,573 | 21,922 | 20,510 |
| Re-exports | 6140 | 14,279 | 25,041 | 22,248 | 23,632 | 24,145 | 22,317 | 21,708 | 20,310 |
| India | 2530 | 5965 | 10,968 | 12,005 | 11,246 | 14,672 | 13,833 | 15,542 | 17,742 |
| Bangladesh | 643 | 5067 | 10,920 | 12,525 | 14,855 | 19,213 | 19,948 | 23,501 | 24,584 |
| Vietnam | ... | 1821 | 8724 | 8540 | 10,390 | 13,149 | 14,068 | 17,148 | 19,544 |
| Indonesia | 1646 | 4734 | 6285 | 5915 | 6820 | 8045 | 7524 | 7692 | 7670 |
| Thailand | 2817 | 3759 | 4241 | 3724 | 4300 | 4561 | 4275 | 4100 | 4129 |
| Cambodia | ... | 970 | 2981 | 2419 | 3041 | 3600 | 4294 | 5025 | 5869 |
| Malaysia | 1315 | 2257 | 3624 | 3126 | 3880 | 4567 | 4563 | 4581 | 4766 |
| Pakistan | 1014 | 2144 | 3906 | 3357 | 3930 | 4550 | 4214 | 4549 | 4991 |
| Sri Lanka | 638 | 2812 | 3437 | 2991 | 3491 | 4211 | 4005 | 4517 | 4919 |

Source: WTO 2013–15.

between producers and consumers in consumer campaigns opposing labour exploitation (O'Rourke 2003; Bair 2005; Rainnie *et al.* 2011). As their titles suggest, each has a different emphasis.

The first, GCCs, focuses on the flows of commodities from production sites to end consumers. It developed from world systems theory (Wallerstein 1989), linking the different elements in a dynamic but structured global system through the threads of commodity flows. Research from this perspective has tended to characterize the garment industry as a buyer-driven commodity chain (Gereffi and Korzeniewicz 1995) which relies on multiple tiers of subcontractors but is controlled by a central buyer firm (Gereffi *et al.* 2005; Donaghu and Barf 1990; Tsing 2009). Accounts from peripheral sites recognize the complexity of the power relationships, the importance of intermediaries and the effects of regulatory and political contexts and territorial divisions.

The second variant, GPNs, more than the commodities, focuses on the forms of industrial organization through which commodities are produced. It therefore focuses on relationships among firms, but it encompasses the state interventions, regulations and labour market conditions which influence firms' locational and strategic decision-making. GPN analyses have contributed to understanding the erratic changes in production locations as contexts and trading rules change. GPN stretches the commodity chain into a network form by including firms that contribute to the production system but do not handle the commodity (for example, designers and accountants), and contextual factors that reside outside the production system, such as state regulation and labour market issues (Dicken *et al.* 2001; Henderson *et al.* 2002; Coe *et al.* 2008; Smith and Pun 2006; Weller 2006). Henderson *et al.* (2002) argue for a return to seeing these 'niches' as operating in networks that are much more fluid than allowed by the mechanical models of Gereffi and his associates. Such networks create a form of reterritorialization, as they 'constitute and are reconstituted by the economic, social and political arrangements of the places they inhabit' (Henderson *et al.* 2002: 446).

The third variant, GVCs, includes all the sites or 'nodes' along a chain of actors that add value to a commodity (Bair 2009). This orientation is better able to focus on the contribution of labour to the final product and assess the relative contribution of different contributors, including (often) women's low-paid labour (Kelly 2009). The GVC approach gives more emphasis to agency along the chain, rather than at its end-point. Researchers are now using GVCs to question the benefits at each link in the chain, including for labour (Barrientos 2002; Jenkins *et al.* 2002; Barrientos and Kabeer 2004).

One issue on which these analyses agree is that the 'vertically disintegrated' subcontracting arrangements used by global firms deliver 'value' and profits to those who orchestrate the chains and networks by producing commodities more cheaply than would be possible in a regulated and unionized workplace close to the boutiques where the end products are sold. Vertically disintegrated, subcontracted production relies on numerically and temporally flexible workforces. Firms working as contractors engage labour for the duration of the contract only. Contractual deadlines and cost pressures inject a sense of urgency, while the changeable demands of the work – with each new contract – require workers to also have an adaptable set of skills.[5] One of the reasons for the low pay in the clothing industry is the lack of social recognition of sewing skills, which women learn in the home and which are ubiquitously considered inborn. Socially constructed conceptions of 'skill' reinforce workplace-based division between skilled male and unskilled female workers (Phillips and Taylor 1980; Coyle 1982; Collins 2001; Tran 2004).

Many economists expect that the developmental trajectories of western economies and Japan and South Korea will be replicated in the poorer countries of Asia, and that production firms in Asia will move 'up' the value chain as they adopt innovations from the West and develop innovations themselves. As this occurs, skills will improve accordingly and so will labour standards. There is some evidence of this process in China, where clothing industry wages have increased significantly since the 1980s. Much GCC research in development studies has sought to understand the conditions that encourage such upgrading (for example, Gereffi and Sturgeon 2009). Understandings of the conditions that stimulate this type of growth, however, remain elusive. The relationships between engagement with GPN and labour markets are relatively under-researched. Where these processes do occur, however, the benefits tend to accrue to those with power over resources. In the clothing industry, historically, managers have mostly been men and workplace technologies have almost always been controlled by male workers (Elson 1986; Wajcman 1990). In almost all factories across the clothing industry in Asia, sewing machine technicians and cutters are male workers, while machinist and other jobs on the factory floor are allocated to women. (There are also numbers of male machinists, however, in Malaysia and Vietnam.) In many countries government-funded mechanic apprenticeship schemes also play a role in reinforcing this gendered division of labour. In the majority of 'cut-make-and-sew' factories, upgrading and up-skilling are rare, as the work is menial rather than skill enhancing (Morris *et al.* 2009). Computerized technologies have expanded to replace pattern makers and cutters – skilled occupations on which industrial action once hinged (if the cutter stopped cutting, work would stall). This means that some jobs are deskilling, but others are being created which demand new and more complex skills. The divisibility of tasks in the clothing production sequence makes it easy to separate highly skilled workers – like designers and production schedulers – from the factory environment.

The clothing industry has always operated using subcontracted and informal labour, but with intensified globalization, flexibilization has led to greater labour informalization and dis-organization, but also to different employment conditions for different types of workers. Along with gender, ethnicity and race have become points of labour differentiation, especially as labour mobility has increased (Lee and Eyraud 2008; Arnold and Pickles 2011: 1599). A surplus precarious labour force is produced, ordered, segmented and racialized in the employment of the migrant labour forces that are the mainstay of clothing production in Asia: Indonesian, Vietnamese and Nepalese workers in Malaysia, and

Burmese, Laos and Cambodian workers in Thailand, as will be discussed later. In Vietnam, factory workers are recruited to cities from poorer central regions, usually from minority ethnic groups. Such processes of racialization and fragmentation have important implications for how we theorize 'social and surplus' labour (Arnold and Pickles 2011: 1598).

The issue of skill reveals a series of problems when analysing the complexities of the GVC, both in terms of positing agency, and identifying power at different levels. Tsing argues that the kind of 'niche-based capitalism' along the chains is, in itself, disorganized (2009: 172). The demise of the clothing industry in Fiji, as Weller (2006) argues, shows that insecurity can be passed up the chain, although in this case the role of governments in sponsoring industry is significant. A global view of the clothing industry shows that it is not just the Walmarts that have influence. Powerful supply corporations, equal in power to the western buyers, exist in Asia. Weller (2007), for example, shows that Hong Kong traders were more powerful than Australian buyers in orchestrating China–Australia commodity flows. Taiwanese, Korean and Hong Kong trading corporations and subcontractors have design and manufacturing centres in China to service large retailers (Appelbaum 2008). The clothing industry has become more complex as China has risen to dominate the global production of garments and textiles and fashion accessories. Western nations no longer control all the design, marketing and advertising in fashion wear. Developing countries no longer only cut, make and sew garments. Across the world, governments are positioning fashion as a leading industry in service-oriented economic transformations, sometimes at the same time regenerating local production using migrant labour. The structures of garment production are changing. Is it possible, in the future, that higher costs for fossil fuels will reinvigorate local production?

Kelly (2002) and Collins (2007) argue that the notion of 'deterritorialization' can be useful in understanding the ways labour is both dispersed and disorganized across commodity chains. For them, the workforce can no longer be divided into skilled core and unskilled peripheral workers, since the flexibilization of work is spread everywhere. The deterritorialized and reterritorialized spaces of production are complex and challenge existing theories. The call by Henderson *et al.* (2002) for a reconsideration of network theory, combined with Tsing's (2009) appeal for a complex way of viewing people within the diversity of supply chain hierarchies, provide clues to developing new ways of mapping out local actions and situations. In this book, we apply such approaches to the lives of workers in Asia.

## States, export manufacturing, flexible workers and trade union demise

It is not possible to understand the global clothing industry without also understanding the ways that it is governed and regulated. The relatively recent emergence of regulation via codes of conduct and their external monitoring was justified and supported by NGOs and others on the basis that the governments of the countries where export factories have been established were either unwilling or unable to establish and police adequate labour laws. When they bypass governments, codes of practice both assume and affirm the exclusion of the state from the operations of industries such as clothing production. This implies a rescaling of governance, so that local factory managers are monitored by global prefects, but without a national and local oversight of their activities. There is no place for democratic processes in this arrangement.

Nonetheless, globalization scholars argue that social life is embedded in the global system, so that what happens in any given nation is shaped by its interconnectedness with other geographical regions (Sklair 1997). From this viewpoint, nation states can no longer be a complete unit of analysis. However, all places have always been interconnected in more or less dense networks of interaction. The issue is this: the uneven landscape produced by national territorial boundaries produces the uneven valuations of production factors, which feed capitalist profit making (see Harvey 1989). As Smith concludes:

> Uneven development is both the product and the geographical premise of capitalist development … as the premise of further capitalist expansion, uneven development can be comprehended only by the means of a theoretical analysis of the capitalist production of nature and space. Uneven development is social inequality blazoned into the geographical landscape and it is simultaneously the exploitation of that geographical unevenness for certain socially determined ends.
>
> (1984: 155)

Uneven economic development has important implications for competition, which is a crucial determining factor in the drive to accumulate (Rainnie 1984). Elson's (1986) earlier study of the clothing and textile industry demonstrated that small firms in the clothing industry do not operate alone but are linked by dense networks to include various forms of cooperation. Subcontracting emerged as an effective means to manage the seasonal and business cycle volatility of garment markets (Rainnie 1984).

In the market-based global system envisaged by the WTO, states would be concerned principally with the export of goods and resources and charged with protecting the rights of private capital within their jurisdictions. In the clothing industry, this view contributed to the dismantling of the GATT MFA and its replacement by the market-opening WTO Agreement of Textiles and Clothing in 2004 (Rai 2002; Bakker and Gill 2003: 29–32).

In Asia, especially since the Asian crisis of 1997, national governments have been induced to adopt the policies associated with the Washington Consensus of free trade in order to qualify for loans from the World Bank and the Asian Development Bank. Such policies advocate zones where unions are not allowed to operate, or the passing of legislation that restricts the powers of unions and their rights to withdraw labour and bargain collectively. The repressions associated with these measures have disorganized existing national labour movements and inhibited the development of labour opposition. Asian states have generally resisted the emergence of western-style trade unionism. By the 1970s, Japanese firms were promoting enterprise unions in their operations in other parts of Asia. Prior to 1998, authoritarian governments in Indonesia introduced a form of corporatism to industrial relations to suppress and curb labour activism. In the workplace the unions' primary role was to control workers rather than to represent them (Ford 2009), so that labour activists began organizing outside the official union structures (Broadbent and Ford 2008: 16). In Thailand, where authoritarian governments forced the labour militant movement underground, unions did not reappear until the 1990s (Pangsapa 2007: 34). The 1997–8 Asian financial crisis, however, undermined the position of unionized garment workers, despite a temporary increase in labour militancy. The relocation of factories to new economic zones near the borders of Thailand and consequent job losses quelled any organized resistance. Less than 4 per cent of Thai workers are now members of trade unions (Arnold and Pickles 2011: 1615). Crinis, in her chapter here on Malaysia, attributes the decline in trade union density in the clothing industry to both capital relocation strategies and the state's role in promoting in-house unions to provide a 'stable' workforce for the manufacturing industries. The Malaysian state allowed the recruitment of transnational migrant workers and, until recently, these migrant workers were outside union jurisdiction (Crinis 2008). In the socialist state of Vietnam, as Cox's chapter in this volume shows, the government has favoured export processing policies and official state-sponsored unions. Due to lack of trust and confidence these are often bypassed by workers. The union's role in foreign-owned factories is designed to keep workers happy rather than lobby for their rights. Migrant workers participate in wild-cat strikes outside state union jurisdiction to address their workplace problems (Tran 2008). In order to challenge these employer strategies some labour activists have moved beyond shop-floor activism to campaigns building alliances with unions across the global garment chains, as well as adopting the strategy of trade unionism in industrial clusters. If carried out on a broader scale, the actions outlined above would have a positive influence on labour rights in the garment industry. It would be naïve, however, to assume that this can happen in the short term. Social conventions, including formidable patriarchal and hierarchical forms of authority and submission, may well be an important element in understanding women garment workers' unwillingness to unionize, alongside their tendency to be involved in casual labour.

Ong has attempted to account for the shifting balance of state and capital power through her model of graduated sovereignty (2000: 57). She argues that in certain instances the state is strong and protects its citizens, with the notable exception of places that are open to international capitalism, notably free trade zones. Ong's view of these areas as spaces where the state withdraws its power to protect workers does not take full account of the positions of mobile workers who are not citizens or who labour outside the free trade zones. A more complex view comes from Arnold and Pickles' (2011) analysis of new systems of regime management and social regulation based around a precarious, flexible workforce.

Arnold and Pickles' (2011) study of clothing production networks along state borders disputes the view that states are weak and global capital strong, highlighting the reterritorialization of power at the borders between local, national and regional interests. The state allocates border areas or special zones where workers are made disposable through immigration and amended industrial laws. The result is a global/state development site involving 'complex networks of social relations that extend beyond actual state borders and operate at multiple scales' (Arnold and Pickles 2011: 1599). These zones act as a magnet attracting clothing suppliers and surplus minority workers made docile through the threat of state violence.

## Commodification and consciousness

The debates about commodity chains, the demise of organized labour and the role of the state demonstrate that the global scale of study cannot adequately account for gender differences, or make visible vulnerable workers buried deep in the subcontracting structure. Top-down views of chains and networks tell us little about how people understand their situation and their options. Lately, workers have increased levels of resistance in Bangladesh, Cambodia and Malaysia. How should we take account of these new kinds of expression of consciousness among the women who labour in the clothing industry?

It is questionable whether the class-based analysis of clothing production developed in Euro-American labour history applies to the Asian manufacturing context. Many economies in the Asia-Pacific region have developed without state welfare and without a traditional urban working class seeking full-time employment. Their manufacturing industries have developed 'permanent temporary' arrangements using contract workers, migrants, temporary workers or other forms of outsourcing (Standing 1999; Burgess and Connell 2007; Lee and Eyraud 2008). Workers are mobile, and mobility leads to a new despotism where workers' continued employment depends on the factory's success in obtaining orders. Employers are able to mobilize workers' consent because the factory workers understand they are competing against other factories and other workers. As workers struggle to earn a living, and as their employment is informalized and fragmented, fractures and clashes between labour and management become more multifaceted than in earlier forms of union-led struggle.

This, we argue, gives rise to a new consciousness hinging on the gendered nature of these work arrangements, in structures through which employers exploit and divide workers whose vulnerability arises from their household responsibilities, differing cultural expectations and the physical isolation in the factory environment. Feminist analysts have shown how female workers in the clothing industries in Asia develop a class consciousness, but one that differs from those identified in Euro-American labour studies (Ong 1987; Wolf 1996; Mills 1999; Tran 2002; Pangsapa 2007; Derks 2008). In Thailand, Pangsapa identifies four categories of consciousness: accommodation, alienation, acquiescence and resistance (2007: 11). She argues that levels of militancy differ between women who work in factories that were isolated and women who work in factories close to other factories, and which share transport and eating facilities. Women in the networked factories were more likely to discuss conditions in their factories and compare them to other workers in other factories. In these factories militant women workers believe that the higher the factory output, the more suffering workers would have to endure. This breeds militancy and often increases the struggle between capital and worker. The women who mobilize against capital, however, were often dismissed and harassed. In extreme cases they have been subject to violent attacks leading to injury and even death. On other occasions labour militancy has led to improvement and increased wages, but this has usually occurred after NGOs, church and student groups become involved (Pangsapa 2007).

Worker resistance, however, is complex and relates to the types of women involved and the structure of the production process as shaped by the demands of the local and global markets. In the labour trade union general consensus, most believe that if women are left to fend for themselves their social commitment towards one another diminishes. Women who work in isolation from other women in other factories believe that the harder they work the better the factory output and the more money they will earn on piece-rates, and so they agree to work hard. If a factory or subcontractor supplies the minimum basic needs, these workers are more than likely to be compliant and productive than those in factories that do not provide wages that cover the minimum basic needs. After the Asian financial crisis, some workers in Pangsapa's (2007) study felt that because they relied on their jobs to feed their families, the larger issues of worker solidarity and struggling for better wages and conditions were not so important.

Transnational migrant workers share similar experiences of a consciousness that accepts minimal conditions. According to clothing suppliers in Malaysia, migrant workers recruited from rural areas almost always work overtime when requested, 'they will put up with the hard work so they can return home with some money' (Crinis 2010: 601). This is largely because they need the money to send remittances to families back home and pay off interest on recruitment debts. When viewed from a global perspective that focuses on women's income-pooling strategies and running households, the situation of migrant workers in the remittance economy connects the global political economy to the household (Douglass 2012). Douglass (2012) found that working people are finding it harder to achieve a living income. Similarly, Lindquist (2009), in a study of Indonesian migrants in Batam and Singapore, talks about the demands of migration, of sending money home and of Indonesian migrants' experiences of failure when they cannot earn enough to remit to their families. Women's own financial management and the increasing tendencies towards consumerism of both workers and families at home leave the worker more vulnerable to loan sharks (Lim and Oishi 1996). In times of economic recession work is less secure. In some cases workers who lose their jobs are required to return to their country of origin with debts still outstanding; in other cases, the perceived shame of failure discourages workers from returning home. These conditions force migrant

Workers, especially female workers, to make decisions in a moral economy that celebrates economic success. Not all experiences are negative. Tran demonstrates in her earlier work that Vietnamese workers use their cultural and kinship network bases to organize and support each other as well as to protest (Tran 2008: 59–60).

## Places and spaces in the new moral economy

Contributors to this book extend these analyses by explicitly invoking the notion of moral economy. Although work in the GCC and GPN approaches has implicit moral positions about exploitation, there arguments are grounded in political-economic considerations rather than moral economies. Their scope of interest is restricted to matters that are included in traditional GDP-based definitions of economic activity, an approach that excludes household production, social interaction and community cohesion. The migration flows that fuel factory employment are also beyond their purview. We want to bring these practised realities into the story of clothing workers employed in GCCs. To do this we need to first show how firms control physical spaces and the activities permitted in those spaces. Second, we will show how agency operates when commodity chains are viewed from below. As well as the issues of 'value' raised by the economics of production, we will show that value for workers is related to a moral economy.

Although 'the precise combination or configuration of practices itself varies across space' (Kelly 2002: 398), the control of workers in a physical space is the principal means of control. For example, factories in industrial enclaves have become like prisons, secure environments where gates are controlled by guards who prevent outsiders from entering – such spaces are quite separate from their surroundings in the local industrial suburbs (Crinis 2010). For Kelly, (2002), the bringing together and control of groups of mobile workers, and then the channelling of worker mobility into confined and controlled spaces, exerts power over labour. These processes are a material expression of reterritorialization processes which dissolve the urban–rural divide and make national boundaries more permeable, but at the same time create more rigid divisions between industrial areas and the general polity.

A second aspect of the control of space within these created enclaves is the removal and exclusion of workplace-based trade unions. Kelly (2002) shows that this strategy does not end contestation, and examines the development of new forms of the capital and labour struggles which operate outside trade unions and in new types of spaces (see also Herod 2001). Kelly (2002) recognizes that in Asia – as in other places – employers are empowered by the strategy of individualizing workers, of isolating the embodied individual and approaching her as though she were an autonomous unit of skill whose market price was open to negotiation. This use of space precludes collective bargaining.

The third means of control is targeting vulnerable workforces. In other contexts, segmented labour market theorists have documented how firms organize their internal employment structure – their division of labour – with the

14  V. Crinis and A. Vickers

characteristics of particular enclaves of labour in mind (Rubery and Wilkinson 1994). In Malaysia, for example, a contractor for a European brand set up a factory in a rural town where the presence of a large palm oil estate employing men created a pool of women available for work. These same logics regulate labour in Asia's garment sector but by targeting particular ethnic communities, often using 'guest worker' programmes to bring workers from distant locations. Migrant labourers without social rights are easily individualized and controlled. Governments facilitate this market-based process, often by omitting to regulate these practices.

The fourth dimension of control is cultural. In earlier Asian societies, particularly rural ones, a 'moral economy' allowed workers and employers to make claims on one another and this provided a shared language for framing those claims (Scott 1985; Collins 2007: 403). In effect, there were cultural rules governing both employee and employer behaviour that ensured social rights were respected. There was no tradition here of western-style unionism, but also no means to negotiate with employers that operate outside the recognized cultural system. In globalized production, workers and employers do not share the same social and cultural space so these shared moral understandings evaporate (Smith and Pun 2006).

NGO scholars take the position that a new kind of political organization is necessary to improve the conditions of workers in factories that operate in global subcontracting chains and networks (Hale and Willis 2005: 9, 2007). This task of organization is difficult because in public discourse, the moral economy that governed traditional social interaction has been displaced by a morally inflected slogan: 'fair trade', which purports to link producers and consumers in a way that empowers consumers to discipline firms by not purchasing the offending products. Embedding production in this distanciated community of interest, it is argued, will induce firms to improve their performance with respect to labour and human rights. At the same time, however, fair trade celebrates market processes and makes (western) consumers the active agents in directing factory-based outcomes, thereby perpetuating the passive positioning of factory labourers. This is not the sort of moral economy the authors seek for clothing workers.

One positive outcome of consumer activism in the clothing sectors has developed from the anti-sweatshop movement (Hale and Willis 2007; Crinis 2010). Since the 1990s, targeting the reputations of leading brand-name buyers has become such a successful strategy that brand companies drive down wages, ignoring child labour and health and safety issues at their peril. These tactics have forced large firms to protect their reputations by instituting 'codes of conduct' which mostly relate to core labour standards set out under the International Labour Organization (ILO). These have been incorporated into 'corporate social responsibility' (CSR) agendas and triple bottom line (economic, social and environmental) accounting. Brand-name buyers now work with suppliers and stakeholder groups in highly publicized displays of global corporate citizenship (Barrientos 2002). The codes usually state that the firm will comply with local labour laws – which in some places are lax, and in others repressive.

After the codes are agreed, their implementation in factories is not a priority. The multi-level nature of the subcontracting supply chains makes it difficult to monitor compliance, or to expose code violations in the unlicensed factories at the bottom of the production chain (Tran 2011: 146). The marketing value of codes lies in their creation rather than their enforcement, resulting in the establishment of over 10,000 different codes in the clothing and textile industry, many of which use jargonistic legal language to render their content opaque, and many of which fail to adhere to basic ILO principles (Jenkins *et al.* 2002). The codes also often fail to address the needs of the majority female workforce (Barrientos and Kabeer 2004). While many codes stress how employers will recognize and respect the right of employees to free association and collective bargaining, these are boxes for the auditors to 'tick', and even then they are often left empty (DeNeve 2008: 214). Codes of conduct are a top-down method of governing labour relations. Rather than managing workplaces internally – with unions monitoring workplaces via their members and acting in response to actual conditions – compliance with codes of conduct is audited by outside bodies, such as NGOS or accounting firms, in occasional visits to factories. O'Rourke (2003), among others, found that international campaigns raise awareness, but the resulting codes of conduct do not necessarily change working conditions. The proliferation of codes of conduct is a simulation of a moral economy.

## Dis-organizing labour in the Asia Pacific

By placing labour centre stage, the chapters in this book provide a more varied and complex understanding of the clothing industry and its workers. On the one hand, viewed in terms of increasingly complex operations of global capital, 'disposable' workers are the passive end of a commodity chain that terminates in the West or with some elite consumers in Japan, Taiwan, South Korea and parts of China. On the other hand, as Asian agents in production networks grow in scale and importance, the ability of workers to actively carve out positions, in however limited a capacity, becomes more obvious. The changes in the mode of production are bringing about a new kind of moral economy.

Workers acquire agency based on their own understandings of a moral economy. Given the decline of collective struggle in the face of labour fragmentation, both workers and their organizations have looked to other avenues for resistance and collective struggle. While the Crinis chapter highlights the decline of clothing and textile trade unions, it also shows that in response to state and capital containment, national unions have formed alliances with international unions. This has had some success, but the most advantageous support networks for the mostly migrant workers in the clothing factories are the local NGOs, civil society and church group alliances. These new forms of communal support do not take the place of unions, but they have proved to be a useful strategy for the mostly non-citizen workforce.

Cox highlights the tensions that continue to intensify when a socialist government introduces neoliberal economic policies that challenge the clothing and textile trade unions and produce adverse outcomes for workers. In this context, workers shift to everyday acts of resistance when they perceive workplace injustices but unions lack power to act on their behalf. In most cases, these strikes are organized by the workers themselves, with the unions standing by, which makes these strikes illegal, regardless of whether the organizers followed the right procedures and processes. Collective action is limited in some export industries, however workers continue to strike for increased benefits. Through their actions, workers produce new challenges for both government and the global clothing subcontracting industry.

Siddiqi highlights the increase in union registrations in the post-Rana Plaza period after the introduction of government reforms she equates these unions to the company union and calls into question the way neoliberal reforms have played into the hands of the powerful erasing the agency of Bangladeshi garment workers and their rich history of resistance. Through a close reading of a workers uprising in May 2006 that resulted in significant gains for labour, Siddiqi suggests that fundamental contradictions and constraints remain untouched by the kind of reforms made after 2013. Unions, in this case, can play a potentially useful role in containing labour struggles as well as promoting them. It is critical to situate the new international recognition of the need for unions to ensure workers rights in shifting ideologies of neoliberal governance.

Crinis and Tran's chapter demonstrates the mobility of Vietnamese and Nepalese who come to work in Malaysia, and how they have shifted in their image from the older capitalist fantasy of 'docile' young Malay women to a perception that migrant workers are 'disposable'. When these women move from place to place and job to job, however, they bring the prior consciousness of being a worker with them. This chapter examines the forces and networks outside the factory, such as Christian churches, and the extent to which these forces are deployed to redirect workers' consciousness: to discipline themselves in an individualized bipolitics through Christianity, to weaken worker resistance, or to empower them through various forms of migrant worker social networks. Christian outreach groups provide services that migrant workers use for their own purposes. Through these networks migrants develop a sense of commitment to each other and a physical means, in times of distress, to look out for each other. These spaces in the church become an expression of their ethnicity and agency.

There are many ways that workers assert themselves. Hannan's study of China at the time of the global financial crisis (GFC) found that Chinese migrant workers assert their rights by walking away from exploitative factory work – in other words, by withdrawing their labour permanently. For years migrant workers in China have been deprived of basic income levels, support and rights through immigration control and contract-based work arrangements (Chan 2004). Failing to secure a living wage, many simply leave the cities and return to their villages, stating that they will not return unless the wage rates increase: 'it's not worth the effort'. It is becoming increasingly evident that the next generation of Chinese rural workers will not migrate to the cities unless pay and conditions improve. They have developed class-consciousness despite being isolated from a

*Dis-organizing labour in the clothing industry* 17

labour movement. The resulting shortage of workers in production centres combined with rising expectations of standards of living has fuelled worker unrest. In response, export manufacturers have to pay higher wages to attract labour or move to countries such as Bangladesh.

Ganguly-Scrase's chapter shows that in India wages in the factory sector are undermined by the informal sector, which remains on the margins of the economy, despite being central to the structure of the production system. The vast majority of garments are produced by small locally owned enterprises. Despite the textile and garment industries being one of India's largest export production sectors and employing over 35 million people, there remains a high concentration of cheap and flexible labour. In 2005 only 6 per cent of overall clothing production occurred in large factories. Many of the small family-owned operations provide subcontracting arrangements for the few large factories and garment traders. Outsourcing keeps the wages down in the factories, but it also keeps the suppliers dependent on low-paid family labour. Ganguly-Scrase shows that the existence of small-scale cottage industry alongside large-scale industrial production explains the contemporary conditions of workers in India's export garment industry.

The ability of small-scale operators to reduce their costs is strongly linked to the unpaid domestic labour provided by women and children. In the informal sector women's and children's labour is either not accounted for or is given less value in the computation of labour costs compared to adult males (Bakker and Gill 2003). Labour and feminist scholars, however, are divided about the benefits and exploitation of informal work for women. Despite the dismal conditions for clothing workers in Bangladesh, Kabeer (2000) points out that women are better off working in export factories because the alternative of scraping out a living in the informal economy is not as attractive. The informal sector, in particular, discriminates against women. If factory jobs are available in the paid workforce, despite the low wages, women tend to move out of petty production. The constant supply of labour then serves to keep wages low. To address this, activists call for both social clauses in free trade agreements and for a basic wage across the economy that takes into account the costs of living, including food, accommodation, education and health benefits (Bonocich and Applebaum 2003: 351).

Beresford, Cucco and Prota argue that despite the undoubted successes of the monitoring programme in Cambodia, there are indications that Cambodian products are not as 'sweat-free' as has been claimed. These not sweat-free results derive from the conditions of the labour market in Cambodia combined with the gender-specific interaction of paid work with unpaid domestic work. Moreover, there are recent indications that the situation is no longer improving, as it was when the initial codes were established. These authors conclude that sustainable improvement in working conditions requires change that goes beyond the factory floor and beyond the single sector of traded goods. Labour standards and their formal implementation in Cambodia do not go far enough. Rather, gender equality should be addressed in the village society at large in order to effectively improve the working conditions of female garment workers. The provision of

18   *V. Crinis and A. Vickers*

childcare facilities at the factory cannot be a solution for commuters who travel hours on cattle trucks to reach their workplaces. Similarly, the creation of childcare facilities in the village will have to compete with free and available childcare from under-employed relatives.

In another context, work in the informal sector – such as home-based work – is seen as empowering women to balance their productive and reproductive roles and earn money for the family. This is especially important when the cost of childcare is high. Sutherland's chapter on the Australian clothing industry highlights these aspects of the employment of migrant home-based workers. The marginal status of home-based workers coalesces around issues of gender, migration and the fact that work occurs in home-spaces. Exploitation as well as livelihood and empowerment are central themes. In this work we hear the voices of the workers and the difficulties these women face working for low pay, coping with language difficulties and earning money in a foreign country. According to Sutherland, the marginalization of migrant women into a work form considered to be peripheral to the economy proper, given its relatively unregulatable nature, is a context that enables easy exploitation. This outcome is subverted, though, by women's agency in using this work to their own ends.

Overall, the authors of this volume look to a reinvigorated notion of moral economy as the basis for the development of new forms of organization, contestation and negotiation. A moral economy that arises from and is congruent with the cultural mores of working people and which is owned by them, so they become active agents in shaping their employment conditions.

## Notes

1 These statistics were sourced from: Department of Statistics Malaysia Official Portal; Australian Government Department of Industry; International Labour Organization www.ilo. org/dhaka/Whatwedo/Projects/WCMS_240343/lang–en/index.htm; Vietnam Fairwear Foundation Report www.pdf-search.club/VIETNAM-Fair-wear-Foundation.pdf; Industriall www.industriall-union.org/industriall-global-union-supports-cambodian-workers; Facts on India's Garment Industry www.cleanclothes.org/resources/publications/factsheets/india-factsheet-february-2015.pdf; Facts on China's Garment Industry www.cleanclothes.org/resources/publications/factsheets/china-factsheet-february-2015.pdf.
2 See Appendix, interviews Crinis 2009; Barry Naughton (2007: 422); see also 'Migrants' job situation in cities better than expected', *China Daily*, 26 March 2009; and 'China's rural migrant workers top 225 million', *Xinhua*, 25 March 2009.
3 See, for example, Collins (2001); Bair (2002); Bonocich and Applebaum (2003); O'Rourke (2003); Ross (2004); Hale and Willis (2005).
4 The use of the term 'Asia Pacific' refers both to the nations that border the Pacific Ocean and to an 'imagined community' of nations in the Asian region. Our use of the term does imply that we perceive the region as a homogeneous geographical space. See Dirlik (1998).
5 One of the reasons for the volatility of this model at the production site is that buyer firms will direct work to firms with proven capacities in particular tasks (in this industry, mistakes are costly). Production firms that become locked into a particular niche activity (sewing t-shirts) therefore find it difficult to upgrade to more skilled tasks (see Gereffi *et al.* 2005).

# References

Appelbaum, R. (2008) 'Giant transnational contractors in East Asia: emergent trends in global supply chains', *Competition and Change*, 12(1): 69–87.

Arnold, D. and Pickles, J. (2011) 'Global work, surplus labour and the precarious economics of the border', *Antipode*, 43 (5): 1598–624.

Bair, J. (2002) 'Beyond the Maquila model? NAFTA and the Mexican apparel industry', *Industry & Innovation*, 9(3): 203–25.

Bair, J. (2005) 'Global capitalism and commodity chains: looking back going forward', *Competition and Change*, 9(2): 153–80.

Bair, J. (ed.) (2009) *Frontiers of Commodity Chain Research*, Stanford, CA: Stanford University Press.

Bakker, I. and Gill, S. (2003) 'Ontology, method and hypotheses', in I. Bakker and S. Gill (eds), *Power Production and Social Reproduction*, pp. 17–41, London: Palgrave Macmillan.

Barrientos, S. (2002) 'Mapping codes through the value chain: from researcher to detective', in R. Jenkins, R. Pearson and G. Seyfang (eds), *Corporate Responsibility and Labour Rights: Codes of Conduct in the Global Economy*, pp. 61–76, London: Earthscan.

Barrientos, S. and Kabeer, N. (2004) 'Enhancing female employment in global production: policy implications', *Global Social Policy*, 4(153): 153–68.

Bonocich, E. and Applebaum, R. (2003) 'Offshore production', in D. E. Bender and R. A. Greenwald (eds), *Sweatshop USA*, pp. 141–68, New York: Routledge.

Broadbent, K. and Ford, M. (eds) (2008) *Women and Labour Organising in Asia: Diversity Autonomy and Activism*, London: Routledge.

Burgess, J. and Connell, J. (eds) (2007) *Globalisation and Work in Asia*, Oxford: Chandos.

Chakravarty, P. and Luce, S. (2013) 'May Day: reflecting on Bangladesh factory disaster and corporate terror', *Aljazeera* (1 May 2013) www.aljazeera.com/indepth/opinion/201 3/05/201351104516268273.html (accessed 2 May 2013).

Chan, A. (2004) 'In pursuit of labour rights', in R. Appelbaum (ed.), *Introduction to Global Studies Politics and Economics*, pp. 165–83, Dubuque, IA: Kendall Hunt.

Coe, N., Dicken, P. and Hess, M. (2008) 'Global production networks: realizing the potential', *Journal of Economic Geography*, 8(3): 271–95.

Collins, J. (2001) 'Flexible specialisation and the garment industry', *Competition and Change*, 5(2): 165–200.

Collins, J. (2007) 'The rise of a global garment industry and the reimagination of workers' solidarity', *Critique of Anthropology*, 27(4): 395–409.

Coyle, A. (1982) 'Sex and skill in the organisation of clothing industry', in J. West (ed.), *Work, Women and the Labour Market*, pp. 10–26, London: Routledge and Kegan Paul.

Crinis, V. (2008) 'Malaysia: women, labour activism and unions', in K. Broadbent and M. Ford (eds), *Women and Labour Organising in Asia: Diversity, Autonomy and Activism*, pp. 50–65, London: Routledge.

Crinis, V. (2010) 'Sweat or no sweat: foreign workers in the garment industry in Malaysia', *Journal of Contemporary Asia*, 40(4): 589–611.

Cumbers, A., Nativel, C. and Routledge, P. (2008) 'Labour agency and union positionalities in global production networks', *Journal of Economic Geography*, 8(3): 369–87.

DeNeve, G. (2008) 'Global garment chains local labour activism: new challenges to trade unionism in the Tiruppur Garment Cluster South India', *Research in Economic Anthropology*, 28: 213–40.

20 *V. Crinis and A. Vickers*

Derks, A. (2008) *Khmer Women on the Move: Exploring Work and Life in Urban Cambodia*, Honolulu: University of Hawai'i Press.

Dicken, P., Kelly, P. F., Olds, K. and Wai-chung Yeung, H. (2001) 'Chains and networks, territories and scales: towards a relational framework for analysing the global economy', *Global Networks*, 1(2): 89–112.

Dirlik, A. (ed.) (1998) *What's in a Rim? Critical Perspectives on the Pacific Region Idea*, revised edn, Lanham, MD: Rowman & Littlefield.

Donaghu, M. and Barf, R. (1990) 'Nike just did it: international subcontracting and flexibility in athletic footwear production', *Regional Studies*, 24(6): 537–52.

Douglass, M. (2012) *Global Householding and Social Reproduction: Migration Research Dynamics and Public Policy in East and Southeast Asia*, ARI Asia Research Institute Working Paper Series No 188, Singapore: National University of Singapore Press.

Elson, D. (1986) 'The new international division of labour in the textile and garment industry: how far does the "Babbage Principle" explain it?' *International Journal of Sociology and Social Policy*, 6: 45–54.

Ford, M. (2009) *Workers and Intellectuals: NGOs, Trade Unions and the Indonesian Labour Movement*, Singapore: National University of Singapore Press.

Gereffi, G. and Korzeniewicz, M. (1995) 'Commodity chains and global capital', *Social Forces*, 73(3): 1170–2.

Gereffi, G. and Sturgeon, T. J. (2009) 'Measuring success in the global economy: international trade, industrial upgrading, and business function, outsourcing in global value chains: an essay in memory of Sanjaya Lall', *Transnational Corporations*, 18(2): 1–35.

Gereffi, G., Humphrey, J. and Sturgeon, T. J. (2005) 'The governance of global value chains', *Review of International Political Economy*, 12(1): 78–104.

Hale, A. and Willis, J. (eds) (2005) *Threads of Labour: Women Working Worldwide*, Oxford: Blackwell.

Hale, A. and Willis, J. (2007) 'Women working worldwide: transnational networks corporate social responsibility and action research', *Global Networks*, 7(4): 453–76.

Harvey, D. (1989) *The Condition of Postmodernity*, Oxford: Blackwell.

Henderson, J., Dicken, P., Hess, M., Coe, N. and Wai-Chung Yeung, H. (2002) 'Global production networks and the analysis of economic development', *Review of International Political Economy*, 9(3): 436–64.

Herod, A. (2001) 'Labour internationalism and the contradiction of globalisation: or, why the local is sometimes still important in a global economy', *Antipode*, 33(3): 407–26.

Jenkins, R., Pearson, R. and Seyfang, G. (eds) (2002) *Corporate Social Responsibility and Labour Rights: Codes of Conduct in the Global Economy*, London: Earthscan.

Kabeer, N. (2000) *The Power to Choose: Bangladeshi Women and Labour Market Decisions in London and Dhaka*, London: Verso.

Kelly, P. F. (2002) 'Spaces of labour control: comparative perspectives from Southeast Asia', *Transactions Institute of British Geographers*, 27(4): 395–411.

Kelly, P. F. (2009) 'From global production networks to global reproduction networks', *Regional Studies*, 43(3): 449–61.

Lee, S. and Eyraud, F. (eds) (2008) *Globalization, Flexibilization and Working Conditions in the Asia Pacific*, Oxford: Chandos.

Lim, L. L. and Oishi, N. (1996) 'International labour migration of Asian women: distinctive characteristics and policy concerns', *Asia and Pacific Migration Journal*, 5(1): 85–116.

Lindquist, J. A. (2009) *The Anxieties of Mobility: Migration and Tourism in the Indonesian Borderlands*, Honolulu: University of Hawai'i Press.

## Dis-organizing labour in the clothing industry 21

Mills, M. B. (1999). *Thai Women in the Global Labour Force: Consuming Desires Contested Selves*, New Brunswick, NJ: Rutgers University Press.

Morris, J., Wilkinson, B. and Gamble, J. (2009) 'Strategic international human resource management or the "bottom line"? The cases of electronics and garments commodity chains in China', *The International Journal of Human Resource Management*, 20(2): 348–71.

Naughton, B. (2007) *The Chinese Economy*, Cambridge, MA: MIT Press.

Ong, A. (1987) *Spirits of Resistance and Capitalist Discipline, Factory Women in Malaysia*, Albany, NY: State University of New York Press.

Ong, A. (2000) 'Graduated sovereignty in South-East Asia', *Theory Culture and Society*, 17(4): 55–75.

O'Rourke, D. (2003) 'Outsourcing regulation: analyzing nongovernmental systems of labor standards and monitoring', *Policy Studies Journal*, 31(1): 1–29.

Pangsapa, P. (2007) *Textures of Struggle*, Ithaca, NY: ILR Press.

Pangsapa, P. and Smith, M. (2008) 'Political economy of Southeast Asian borderlands: migration, environment, and developing country firms', *Journal of Contemporary Asia*, 38(4): 485–514.

Phillips, A. and Taylor, B. (1980) 'Sex and skill: notes towards a feminist economics', *Feminist Review*, 6: 79–88.

Rai, S. M. (2002) *Gender and the Political Economy*, Cambridge: Polity Press.

Rainnie, A. F. (1984) 'Combined and uneven development in the clothing industry: the effects of competition on accumulation', *Capital and Class*, 4: 141–56.

Rainnie, A. F., Herod, A. and McGrath-Champ, S. (2011) 'Review and positions: global production networks and labour', *Competition & Change*, 15(2): 155–69.

Ross, R. (2004) *Slaves to Fashion: Poverty and Abuse in the New Sweatshops*, Ann Arbor, MI: University of Michigan Press.

Rubery, J. and Wilkinson, F. (eds) (1994) *Employer Strategy and the Labour Market*, Oxford: Oxford University Press.

Ruwanpura, K. N. and Wrigley, N. (2011) 'The costs of compliance? Views of Sri Lankan apparel manufacturers in times of global economic crisis', *Journal of Economic Geography*, 11(6): 1031–49.

Scott, J. C. (1985) *Weapons of the Weak: Everyday Forms of Peasant Resistance*, New Haven, CT: Yale University Press.

Sklair, L. (1997) 'Social movements for global capitalism: the transnational capitalist class in action', *Review of International Political Economy*, 4(3): 514–38.

Smith, A., Rainnie, A., Dunford, M., Hardy, J., Hudson, R. and Sadler, D. (2002) 'Networks of value, commodities and regions: reworking divisions of labour in macro-regional economics', *Progress in Human Geography*, 26(1): 41–63.

Smith, C. and Pun, N. (2006) 'The dormitory labour regime in China as a site for control and resistance', *The International Journal of Human Resource Management*, 17(8): 1456–70.

Smith, N. (1984) *Uneven Development: Nature, Capital and the Production of Space*, Oxford: Blackwell.

Stalker, P. (2000) *Workers Without Frontiers: The Impact of Globalisation on International Migration*, Boulder, CO: Lynne Rienner.

Standing, G. (1999) *Global Labour Flexibility: Seeking Distributive Justice*, London: Macmillan.

Tran, A. N. (2002) 'Gender expectations of Vietnamese garment workers: Viet Nam's re-integration into the world economy', in J. Werner and D. Belanger, *Gender Household,*

## 22   *V. Crinis and A. Vickers*

*State: Doi Mo'i in Viet Nam*, pp. 49–72, Ithaca, NY: Cornell Southeast Asia Program Publications.

Tran, A. N. (2004) 'What's women's work: male negotiations and gender reproduction in the Vietnamese garment industry', in L. Drummond and H. Rydstrom (eds), *Gender Practices in Contemporary Vietnam*, pp. 210–30, Singapore: Singapore University Press and NIAS Press.

Tran, A. N. (2008) 'Contesting "flexibility": networks of place, gender, and class in Vietnamese workers' resistance', in J. Nevins and N. L. Peluso (eds), *Taking Southeast Asia to Market: Commodities, Nature, and People in the Neoliberal Age*, pp. 56–72, Ithaca, NY: Cornell University Press.

Tran, A. N. (2011) 'Corporate social responsibility in socialist Vietnam: implementation, challenges, and local solutions', in A. Chan (ed.), *Labour in Vietnam*, pp. 119–59, Singapore: Institute of Southeast Asian Studies.

Tsing, A. (2009) 'Supply chains and the human condition', *Rethinking Marxism*, 21(2): 148–76.

United Nations Development Fund for Women (2010) 'Facts and figures on women, poverty and economics' www.unifem.org/gender_issues/women_poverty_economics/facts_figures.html (accessed 7 September 2010).

Wajcman, J. (1990) 'Patriarchy, technology and conceptions of skill', *Work and Occupations*, 18: 29–45.

Wallerstein, I. (1989) *The Modern World System Volume 3: The Second Era of Great Capitalist World Economy 1730s – 1840s*, New York: Academic Press.

Waterman, P. and Wills, J. (2001) 'Space, place and the new labour internationalisms: beyond the fragments?', *Antipode*, 3: 305–31.

Weller, S. (2006) 'Networks, commodity chains and crisis: the impact of Fiji's coup on garment production networks', *Environment and Planning*, 38(7): 1249–67.

Weller, S. (2007) 'Power and scale: the shifting geography of industrial relations law in Australia', *Antipode*, 39(5): 896–915.

Wills, J. (1998) 'Taking on the Cosmocorps: experiments in transnational labor organization', *Economic Geography*, 74(2): 111–30.

Wolf, D. (1996) 'Javanese factory daughters', in L. Sears (ed.), *Fantasizing the Feminine*, pp. 141–62, London: Duke University Press.

World Trade Organisation. (WTO) (2013) 'International Trade Statistics 2013', www.wto.org/english/res_e/statis_e/its2013_e/its13_toc_e.html (accessed 20 November 2013).

World Trade Organisation. (2014) 'International Trade Statistics 2015', www.wto.org/english/res_e/statis_e/its2015_e/its2015_e.pdf. (accessed 6 April 2016).

Yardley, J. (2013) 'Grim task of identifying factories' dead overwhelms Bangladeshi lab', *New York Times*, 30 May 2013.

# 2 The fragmentation of the clothing and textile trade union movement in Malaysia

*Vicki Crinis*

The labour movements in Southeast Asia, and Malaysia in particular, have been shaped by colonial legacies, the cold war and the development models of strong state and export manufacturing industries tied to global markets (Ford 2013b). The labour literature from scholars such as Brown and Chatyaweep (2008) and Ford (2013b) argues that Southeast Asian states play a significant role in the de-unionization process to further their development plans. Based on the apparent successes of the newly industrialized countries (NICs) – Singapore, Hong Kong, Taiwan and Korea – Southeast Asian governments have attempted to follow their development patterns of free trade, a strong state institution and weak worker organizations. According to Brown and Ayudhya the tripartite industrial relations system in Southeast Asia is explicitly aimed at promoting an enterprise-focused 'bread and butter' unionism that restricts activities to workplace economic and welfare matters (2013: 105–6). In theory workers' broader social and political objectives would be accommodated by the entrepreneurial business ventures of foreign and local capital and export-oriented industrialization. In this context the state has worked towards the interests of big business and the disorganization of the labour movement. As a result, the labour movement in these countries has been unable to effectively represent workers in general, and in particular those in export-led industries. The absence of trade unions to organize workers in the export processing zones (EPZs) has had an impact on the largely female workforce. These workers, relegated to low-paid, unskilled, repetitive jobs in production assembly lines, have no voice and no political representation. According to Brown they are doubly disadvantaged because they have no voice in the political system, or in the trade union movement because of its male-dominated structure (Brown and Chatyaweep 2008: 101). This is the situation in Malaysia.

In the interest of economic development (GDP) the Malaysian government has undermined the power of trade unions to the systemic demands of capital. Despite the fact that there are textile and garment unions registered in each state in Malaysia, a large percentage of the working class, especially the unskilled workforce in the export factory or home-based work sector, have little if any knowledge of trade unions or the activities of trade unions. The increased competition in the global market has fostered growing hostility to unions in

24   *V. Crinis*

Malaysia, narrowing union bargaining power and effectiveness in representing workers' interests and increasing work insecurity.

This chapter aims to identify some of the factors that account for the weak and marginalized position of trade unions in both Malaysia, and in the clothing and textile industry in particular. It is structured as follows: the first section provides the historical background to the union movement in Malaysia and the political marginalization of unions based on ideologies and racial politics. It outlines the ways scholars have explained how the labour politics are played out by the nation state. The second section highlights how suppliers' relocational strategies managed to undermine textile trade union membership in each state of Malaysia after the 1990s to the point where unions are hardly relevant in the clothing and textile industry.[1] After painting a fairly dismal picture of unionization, the third section focuses on global unions and the bilateral agreements between unions introduced under the umbrella of the ILO. Global and regional responses have had little success in addressing labour rights in Malaysia. Coupled with the increasing numbers of overseas contract workers employed in the manufacturing industries in the last decade, workers in the clothing trade unions have declined even further. Without question some organizations have taken up the slack and helped to fill the gap left by the unions. As Ford (2009) argues, the dis-organization of the labour movements, in general, has often led to new forms of communal organization.

## Malaysian labour history from communism to terrorism

In Malaysia the literature also points to the persistence of colonial legacies in the labour movement and workforce (Todd and Bhopal 2002; Rowley and Bhopal 2006). During the colonial period the workforce consisted of Malays and non-Malay Chinese and Indian workers. The British colonial government brought Chinese and Indian labour to the colony to service the tin-mining and rubber industries. The largest percentage of Malays worked on small family holdings in the rural areas, while others worked in colonial government and service jobs. The non-Malay Chinese and Indians respectively worked in the tin mines and on the plantations and lived in urban areas and on plantation estates. The British divide-and-rule policy created a population segregated by class, ethnicity, religion, language and cultural practices. By the end of the colonial period the non-Malays almost outnumbered the Malays. What was most significant was that the British policy also created a population where the Chinese capitalists outnumbered the Malay capitalists (Jomo 1988). The British had carried out their economic infiltration of the Malay Peninsula (trade and expropriation of natural resources) through the medium of the Chinese entrepreneurial class who were already working the tin mines on the peninsula at the time of British colonization. The Chinese were also divided in terms of class and language. Unlike the Chinese, the Indian population were mostly relegated to a life of poverty in the rubber plantations and surrounding shantytowns. Nevertheless the Indian workers formed a relatively strong plantation workers' union and fought to improve the wages and

## Clothing and textile trade union in Malaysia    25

conditions of plantation workers. Between the 1930s and the late 1940s there was considerable labour unrest as miners and plantation workers protested against the colonial system of labour exploitation (Yuen 1999). These labour activists also played a role in the underground movement that opposed the Japanese during World War II (Jackson 1991). After the war, the same group splintered under the banners of Malay nationalism and Chinese communism.

The British under a new law, the Internal Securities Act (ISA), declared a state of emergency (1948–60) and engaged in a war to prevent communist expansion into the labour movement. At the time communism was considered a form of terrorism. Due to the perceived threat, the British relocated rural villages believed to be harbouring 'fringe' communists and engaged in jungle warfare against the same Chinese who had supported them during the Japanese invasion. The post-World War II Malayan Emergency created a generation of Chinese Malaysians who distanced themselves from the labour movement (Jomo and Todd 1994).[2] After the war, rather than the more militant unions, the British supported Indian-led unionization established under the International Confederation of Free Trade Unions Affiliation (ICFTU) founded in 1949 and favoured by the British and Americans (Gamba 1962).[3]

Funded by the ICFTU, the Malaysian Trades Union Congress (MTUC) was formed in 1949. During the 1960s the government pursued an import-substitution policy and allowed the registration of unions, and a tripartite system was instituted between the state, employer and worker unions. The economic policy failed to provide jobs for the unemployed and culminated in racial violence in 1969, ending in a second state of emergency under the ISA. Then the government sought economic solutions to prevent ethnic tensions between large numbers of unemployed youth, Malay soldiers returning to civilian life and the urban non-Malays. These tensions had been brewing for years, resulting from the uneven economic development created between Malays and non-Malays during the colonial period. The race riots had significant outcomes for the future of unions in Malaysia.

### New economic policy, export manufacturing and unions

After the race riots, the government changed from an import-substitution economic policy to an export-oriented policy under the New Economic Policy (NEP) in 1971 to provide more jobs and to create a class of modern Malay capitalists. After the NEP was introduced it opened up EPZs to accommodate export manufacturing, and the Investment Incentives Act offered generous benefits – such as exemption from company tax, relief from payroll tax, investment tax credit, depreciation allowances, export incentives, tariff protection and exemption from import duty – to approved companies, to encourage more firms to supply clothing and textiles for the export industry. Labour laws were amended to create a stable workforce for foreign capital. According to Jomo and Todd (1994), to accommodate capitalist desires, four pieces of industrial legislation were passed in 1969 that restricted trade union activity in the country, including

26   *V. Crinis*

the EPZs, the Essential (Trade Unions) Regulations, the Essential (Modification of the Trade Unions (Exemption of Public Officers) Order 1967) Regulations and the Essential (Employment) Regulations and the Essential (Industrial Relations) Regulations.

Under the various amendments and exemptions, the government first refused to allow national unions in the clothing and textile industry. Even though it has since relented and lifted the restriction on a national union, the state divisions are too deep and state leaders no longer want a national union (state Textile Union Secretaries, pers. comm., 2007–9). Second, the government initially restricted the registration of garment and textile trade factories to join the state union in the export industry because many textile and garment industries were classed as pioneer industries and the Minister of Labour refused the registration of unions in them. Since then the unions have succeeded in registering the textile and garment unions in each state (Rasiah 1993: 13). In this regard in these early years the state placed a number of obstacles for trade union organizing to reach its full potential in the export sector (Crinis 2003, 2008). According to unionists, even if workers organize into a union and attempt to register with the Industrial Relations Department, it can take years before it is recognized because employers continue to block its registration (Crinis 2010).

Over the next two decades, the 1980s to the 1990s, the Prime Minister of Malaysia, Doctor Mahathir, generated discourses about growth and labour stability. According to Mahathir, any disruption to production was perceived as a threat to economic growth, as evidenced in the 1980s, when the Malaysian Airlines staff and pilots went on strike. The government called a third state of emergency, and under the ISA the airlines union was deregistered and unionists and newspaper editors were arrested and charged with interfering with the stability of the economy and the country (Jomo and Todd 1994). These amendments and subsequent gaol sentences, although vigorously contested, sent a clear message to labour activists that the space to protest in Malaysia was severely limited. Afterwards, amendments to labour laws made it illegal to hold strikes without notifying the Industrial Relations Department at least 42 days before the strike, and to strike altogether in industries considered vital to the country's economy. The tightening of the strike laws in Malaysia showed a strong preference for the concept of compulsory labour arbitration over strike action. As permission to strike was refused, the matter was then relayed to the arbitration courts.

In more recent times (2012) the ISA has been outlawed and replaced by a counter terrorism measure – the Security Offences Special Measures Act. While the new security measures were introduced to fight terrorist acts, they also enable the government to continue to prevent unions finding loopholes to organize workers and/or for unions and workers to engage in strike action (Rajasekaran 2010).

### Trade unions and ethnic and gender issues

The union structure between the Malays and non-Malays also undermined union strength and disorganized the labour movement. What ultimately emerged from the NEP was the policy-mandated state intervention for ethnic affirmative action, on behalf of the Malay community for Malay capital accumulation (Gomez 2009). The state's emphasis on the economic and political development of the Malays eventuated in a Malay middle class, which left the Chinese capitalists and the Indian labour movement out in the cold. Since then unions remain sidelined by the dominant Malay-led political power, with little if any political and economic support.

The well-recognized division between Indian and Malay union leaders lasted until the 2000s (Todd and Bhopal 2002; Rowley and Bhopal 2006). During the import substitution period when garment and textile unions were established, most union leaders were Indians (Rowley and Bhopal 2006). By the 1990s the Malay working class were asserting their position in the labour movement and the Indian-dominated MTUC changed to a Malay leadership with considerable internal upheaval (Rowley and Bhopal 2006). Ethnic divisions across the leadership have declined to some extent as more Malays are elected into the leadership roles and Indian unionists retire, but the divisions between workers have deepened due to government policies that allow employers to recruit workers from other countries in the region. In the past clothing and textile workers were divided between Malays, Chinese and Indian. In 1986 in the 296 factories there were 28,000 Malays, 25,000 Chinese and only 6000 Indians (Crinis 1993). At present the workforce is mostly made up of foreign workers from neighbouring countries; and the factory owners and floor supervisors are mostly Chinese Malaysians.

As already noted, the labour movement has faced problems developing and sustaining effective trade union organizing, first due to its historical connections to the communist movement, and second due to the Malaysian government's capitalist development and affirmative action policies. But trade unions themselves contribute to their declining membership because they have largely failed to represent the interests of female workers (Ariffin 1988, 1989, 1997; Yuen 1999; Todd and Bhopal 2002). Ariffin (1989) argues that the failure of unions to organize female workers is caused by two factors. First is the dominance of male skill-based trade unions, and second is the unsuitability of the largely unskilled and often fragmented female workforce to be organized into unions. Trade unionism in Malaysia is based on the British model whereby association and organizing is central to skilled male workers. Skilled workers are mostly male in the textile industry but also include pattern makers and cutters in the clothing industry – these jobs could only be replaced by other mechanically trained skilled workers, which gave the unions more bargaining power. However, female workers have little 'skill' for unions to bargain with because they can learn on the factory floor and are easily replaced with other female workers. That is not to suggest that sewing is not a skill, but because it is performed by women it has traditionally been seen as something that is natural to the female gender.

Additionally, Elias has pointed out that for female workers local forms of repression, such as employer labour breaches and state-sanctioned anti-unionism, intersect with male domination in the factories (2005: 222). She argues that

28  *V. Crinis*

many factories, especially multinational corporations (MNCs) – although there are few MNCs in the clothing industry in Malaysia – need to be viewed as actors that elaborate and reinvent principles of male and racial superiority (Elias 2005: 222).[4]

This was also highlighted in the literature in the 1980s when large numbers of young women with 'nimble fingers' and 'docile disposition' entered the export-manufacturing workforce. Between 1975 and 1990, women in paid employment almost doubled. As the government sought to persuade manufacturers to employ women from the towns and nearby villages, thousands of females moved to areas near the EPZs and worked for Malaysian supply factories. These mostly Malay workers were new to industrial production. Coming from the rural areas and from an agricultural background, they had no knowledge of trade unions and had few networks to claim a decent wage. In addition, in those days it was difficult for young Malay Muslim women to engage with the mostly male Indian unionists and, vice versa, it was difficult for Indian Malaysian unionists to engage with young Malay women. According to a study by Rose *et al.*, employees lack knowledge about unions, indicating problems with male union leadership being able to reach out to employees, especially female workers (2010: 46). While times have changed and more unionists are Malay women, women may still not be interested in joining unions because trade unions have not traditionally been gender sensitive to women's productive and reproductive roles (Noorlaila Bt Aslah, pers. comm., 2005, 2008). Unless childcare, maternity leave and equal pay are addressed, women may not see any reason to join trade unions and hand over their hard-earned money for fees (Ariffin 1988: 253). While most union bodies recognize the problems unions face in organizing women and are seeking to address this, putting women into leadership roles has been a long-term goal with only moderate success. Malaysian women were more inclined to join feminist or labour NGOs to support female workers in the export industries. While the MTUC called for the government to allow women to join trade unions, there was no real study on how this might be achieved. According to the MTUC, female workers comprised 89.5 per cent of the workforce in garment factories, 55 per cent in electronics factories and 56.8 per cent in textile plants, and should be organized into trade unions. These requests were disregarded, since the incentives to attract foreign investment were low wages and 'stable' working conditions.

The next section looks at the nature of clothing industry production and the subsequent global subcontracting arrangements between buyers and suppliers, which have also had a significant bearing on the decline of clothing and textile union membership.

## Clothing industry restructuring and declining union density

Malaysia's political, economic and social dynamics have facilitated business offensives against union organizing at the level of production. In Malaysia most clothing and textile factories are registered with the Malaysian Knitting

Manufacturers Association (MKMA) and the Malaysian Textile Manufacturers Association (MTMA). During the MFA quota period, these associations were established to mediate for the industry.[5] Between 2003–5 the MKMA had 162 member companies and the MTMA had 174. During the GFC in 2007–8, many companies closed their doors and relocated to countries where production costs were cheaper, while others shut their doors and went out of business. According to the members' directory of 2007–8, the number had reduced significantly. The MTMA had 133 members and the MKMA had 134.

Decreasing numbers of manufacturers usually means one of two things: either buyers have moved countries to source cheaper garments, or suppliers have moved their factories to cheaper locations. For many Malaysian clothing suppliers the ability to relocate to Cambodia, for example, allows them to provide goods at a lower price but deters them from making long-lasting and value-added investments in their Malaysian factory (Rasiah 2009). Some manufacturers, however, invest in technology in their Malaysian factory and employ migrant workers (Crinis 2010). These manufacturers continue to survive the high levels of competition by moving up the value chain. The following are case studies of how trade union density declines under these conditions.

The Penang and Province Wellesley Textiles and Garment Manufacturing Employees' Union (PTGWU) lost 90 per cent of its membership within a decade. In 1992 it had over 5000 members, the majority being female clothing factory workers. However, the numbers started to decline reflecting the increasing levels of competition in the global industry and capitalist relocation strategies in the following decade, as cited in the annual union newsletter (*Penang Union Newsletter*, 1922, 1994). Later in 1992, the PTGWU lost three garment factories with 400 members or 10.8 per cent of its membership. Home Shiffon Garments sacked workers because management was unable to provide work due to reduction in the contract orders, while JP Coats and Terry Prai retrenched workers and re-established production lines outside the state of Penang. Once the factory closed and moved operations to another state, workers were dismissed and the unions lost their members. During this period the unions negotiated and concluded six agreements. They also won the cases against Home Shiffon Garments and Terry Prai for non-compliance with awards, including issues relating to annual leave, retrenchment benefits and annual bonuses. Although the trade union was successful, in both cases the factories relocated and workers lost their jobs.

Large garment factories including Pen Apparel, Oriental Garments, Eastern Garments and Imperial Garments have in-house unions, as does Amtex a local small to medium enterprise (SME) (Mohamed Bin Osman, pers. comm., 2006). These in-house unions are not industry based and do not extend to other workers in other factories. This system originated in Japan and has been a key factor in undermining industry-based unions in Malaysia. As a result, the textile and clothing workers' union in Penang has only five textile factories belonging to the same company listed in the union (Kenneth Perkins, Union Secretary Penang, pers. comm., 2010). The last three garment factories to register with the Penang

Textile Trade Union – Sweet Hearts, MWE and Dora Garments – closed down and apparently, MWE re-opened in the less-developed state of Pahang. DNP also closed operations in Penang and moved to the state of Kelantan. The PTGWU Secretary and committee members are employed by the five textile factories owned by one company, Pen Fabric. When asked why there is only one company registered with the PTGWU, the General Secretary stressed that the bulk of local Chinese Malaysian SMEs do not want workers in the clothing and textile unions (Mohamed Bin Osman, pers. comm., 2010). On the other hand, he said that Japanese textile companies are more advanced in the way they think about workers and union organizations: 'The MNC understands the benefits of worker unions and does not block unions from organizing workers' (Mohamed Bin Osman, pers. comm., 2010).[6] Or it could be that the union does not pose a problem for the company.

The pattern in Penang was repeated in Kuala Lumpur (KL), Selangor. In KL there are no garment factories in the union (A. Sivananthan, pers. comm., 2009). According to the long-serving union leader A. Sivananthan, Executive Secretary, Selangor and Federal Territory Textile and Garment Industry, member numbers declined in KL after the big factories relocated to less-developed states or other countries in the last decade (A. Sivananthan, pers. comm., 1999, 2006, 2009). The industry in Selangor consists of a few large factories and many SMEs as well as a number of home-based workers (Loh-Ludher 1998). The majority of garment-producing companies are Chinese SMEs with a Chinese and Malay workforce or, more recently, a migrant labour force. In 2010 a government survey showed that the textiles and clothing sector has the largest number of SMEs.[7] This in part explains the low union membership in the clothing industry in Selangor. Like Penang, there are Japanese textile factories registered with the union but no clothing factories.

Except in Johor, the situation is much the same in the other states in Malaysia where clothing textile unions are registered. One textile factory is registered with the union in Negeri Sembilan and one thread factory is registered in Malacca (M. Marree, Union Secretary Negeri Sembilan, pers. comm., 2008). In Johor, however, the union has a number of registered clothing factories. Situated in the capital and close to Singapore, these factories are owned and operated by Singaporean and Malaysian companies (although a number of Singaporean companies relocated to China during the GFC and the union in Johor lost members) (Boskco Augustin, Union Secretary Johore, pers. comm., 1999, 2000, 2006, 2010). However, the Johor union has had little success in organizing workers in Batu Pahat, the largest textile- and garment-producing area in Malaysia and where there are a number of Chinese SMEs and many migrant contract workers.

The clothing and textile industry is dominated by Chinese Malaysian SME capitalists, the dominant capitalist class in Malaysia at the time of independence (Jomo 1988). Although there are some exceptions, these suppliers mostly shy away from unions. Some argue that they can look after their own workers and do not need unions to cause 'trouble', while others brush unions off as not being relevant in today's business world. If anything, the managers prefer workers to

*Clothing and textile trade union in Malaysia* 31

join in-house unions or the employers themselves join CSR initiatives and have their factories audited by the buyers. Barrientos (2002) believes that buyers are joining initiatives rather than be exposed by anti-sweatshop activists, which for workers is a step in the right direction. While CSR initiatives protect workers in supply chains, it is a double-edged sword. On the one hand, they can operate to the workers' advantage, but on the other hand, they undermine the role of the trade unions in organizing workers.

As a result, unlike textile factories that are owned by Japanese, Taiwanese and Indian transnational companies where unions have been especially resilient, union membership in the clothing factories is particularly low. This may be explained by the preponderance of male workers in textile factories compared to the high number of female workers in the clothing factories. In recent times, the informalization of the largely female clothing workforce has been exacerbated by transnational migrant workers replacing local workers. During the 1980s middle-class female activists began to play a role in trying to mediate between employers, unions and female workers, and by the 1990s these mediations started to include migrant workers. At the same time, trade unions looked outside the nation state to international unions.

## International union affiliations to global union federations

One strategy to deal with globalization and to meet the challenges associated with union dis-organization is the formation of global unions (Cumbers *et al.* 2008). At the time of writing, Malaysian unions had alliances with International Union Federations (IUFs) and more recently Global Union Federations (GUFs). The GUFs are sectorial federations that operate at the international level and to which regional and sectorial unions belong (Ford 2013a: 272). The clothing and textile unions in Malaysia are affiliates of the Textile Workers Asia-Pacific Regional Organization (TWARO), the regional arm of the International Textile, Garment and Leather Workers' Federation (ITGLWF).[8] TWARO's objectives are to promote unity among textile unions and encourage consciousness of comradeship among all workers in the trades, without distinction of creed or sect. While it functions to benefit all workers, it started with textile workers and is particularly involved with those in countries such as Bangladesh and Cambodia. Recent campaigns include the protection of workers sand-blasting jeans and seeking back pay for those in the carpet industry in Bangladesh. TWARO works under the traditional union model with the same calls to build a strong union, to secure a reduction in hours and to improve wages and conditions for clothing workers. An important TWARO focus is to promote the active participation of women at all union levels. Although, Elias (2010) argues, the real issues for unions and women workers need to be addressed in the actual definition of gender-blind key labour rights.

Clothing and textile unions in Malaysia are also affiliated with the ITGLWF, which addresses the economic issues and spatial realities of the clothing industry.[9] The ITGLWF concedes the need to address workers across commodity chains rather than at a national level. It works with the ILO to set guidelines for corporations seeking to establish minimum wages and decent working conditions in global supply chains. It challenges the precarious employment of clothing workers by calling on international buyers to protect workers in their supply chains through global framework agreements. These agreements between global unions and brand-name buyers have been increasing in the last few years in an attempt to deal with labour abuse in supply factories producing garments for brand-name buyers. The ITGLWF has had some success with the corporate top-down approach. On 15 November 2011 an agreement was made between Mizuno, a Japanese MNC producing sportswear, golf clubs and athletic shoes, and the ITGLWF's Japanese affiliate, UI ZENSEN (ITGLWF 2011). According to ITGLWF President Hisanobu Shimada, this agreement ensures that workers in this supply chain are protected under the eight ILO core labour conventions. The Mizuno Corporation employs 1983 workers in Osaka and Tokyo and thousands more in other countries. The company produces goods at their factories in the United Kingdom (UK), the US, Thailand, China and Japan, as well as through suppliers in several countries in Asia. According to the ITGLWF General Secretary, these agreements should be fully exploited (ITGLWF 2011). In this context unions need to make use of emerging relationships with multinational brands to reconnect with workers at the local level. In the context of Malaysia there are some areas where these relationships could be exploited across borders to address workers' issues, but have not eventuated.

An incident in February 2012 had the potential for cross-border union/worker action. The ITGLWF's website listed Coats (a global UK company) for anti-union behaviour in Bangladesh, locking up union leaders and failing to discuss pay increases with workers and their unions (ITGLWF 2012).[10] The Coats Employees' Union is part of the Bangladesh Garments Textile & Leather Workers' Federation (BGTLWF), an affiliate of the ITGLWF.[11] Coats Thread has a factory in the Malaysian state of Malacca and the BGTLWF called for solidarity from the wider trade union movement. If Malaysian workers joined Bangladeshi workers the unions could have a stronger case against Coats. Although more advantageous for the union movement and the workers involved, cross-border action is outside the reach of most union organizers in the Asia-Pacific region. In Malaysia, for instance, the law states that strike action that also includes going slow or holding up production in a factory, or a section of the factory, is termed illegal unless permission is given by the Director General of Trade Unions to hold or partake in strike action. A strike is also illegal if it has any other objective than the furtherance of a trade dispute between the workman on strike and their employer. At the individual level, workers who have participated in an illegal strike are liable for dismissal and may not be allowed to be members of a union in the future.

The ITGLWF, however, has written to the Chief Executive Officer (CEO) of Coats demanding that the company intervenes and engages in constructive dialogue with the local trade union to resolve the dispute on terms acceptable to the workers. What is significant here is that this type of exposure opens the door for

*Clothing and textile trade union in Malaysia* 33

further negotiating with the company. With some persuasion the CEO and Board of Directors, who are not averse to union organizing evidenced by the fact that their factories are registered with clothing unions in their respective countries, could establish an international framework agreement to cover all factories in the supply chain.

In 2013, ITGLWF and TWARO (formed in the 1970s) were liquidated and replaced by a new GUF. The international union bodies no longer functioned to benefit industry-based workers in supply chains because the workforces became more fragmented. The GUFs are considered more efficient, taking up the fight for better working conditions and trade union rights on a global level with a number of industry-based unions. IndustriALL represents 50 million workers in 140 countries in the mining, energy and manufacturing sectors (IndustriALL 2014). The global union attempts to make global workers a stronger force by linking the solid metal workers' unions with the weaker unions in the clothing industry. The union leadership has recognized that the textile and clothing sectors are a large source of precarious employment consisting of low-paid workers who are predominantly young women, older migrant women and cross-border migrants employed on short-term contracts. Union activists understand that to be successful in addressing global capital and achieving labour rights for women, they must also incorporate the stronger and weaker unions into a global union. The Malaysian affiliates include textile unions and electrical unions as well as rubber, shoe and paper product unions. This brings most of the unions in the export sectors in Malaysia under the umbrella of IndustriALL.

Global unions, such as IndustriALL, have adopted similar website and news reporting strategies using the same language as global corporations. At present, the union is involved in publishing campaigns against multinationals in Bangladesh, Cambodia and Indonesia. Together with the ILO, IndustriALL has coordinated the compensation fund for the families of the women killed and those injured in the building collapse in Bangladesh. The fund is trying to raise US$40 million for the families of the mostly clothing workers who died in the tragedy. IndustriALL has called on consumers to petition brand-name buyers to contribute to the fund; according to IndustriALL Assistant General Secretary Monika Kemperle 'it is time to name, shame and campaign' (*Express Tribune*, online 24 February 2014). IndustriALL also works with Clean Clothes Campaign to pressure nations such as Indonesia to investigate the wages and conditions of clothing workers in supply chains producing for brand-name retailers. But these protests are dependent on consumer actions. Workers at the grassroots level continue to be silenced.

A number of academics and anti-sweatshop activists are writing about other kinds of stakeholder campaigns specific to the clothing industries, some involving unions and some outside unions (Barrientos 2002; Kabeer 2004; Miller 2004; DeNeve 2008). Barrientos (2002), for example, looks at Women Working Worldwide (WWW), a mix of grassroots workers' organizations from the global South and labour activists in the global North. These new forms of political organization for workers are termed 'new labour internationalism'. They seek

34  *V. Crinis*

multi-stakeholder initiatives connecting brand-name designers/retailers with workers, unions and NGOs (Barrientos and Kabeer 2004). They encourage multi-stakeholder partners to improve the lives of women working worldwide. Their aim is to be one stakeholder among many to teach, intervene and monitor the labour standards in supply factories, including the labour standards and rights of subcontractors and home-based workers. Anti-sweatshop activists believe that both the formal and informal sectors must be included in stakeholder initiatives and that workers must have labour intellectuals who can provide the language for the negotiating process between workers and stakeholders. WWW is also involved in establishing multi-stakeholder initiatives such as Social Accountability International (SAI) and Ethical Trading Initiative (ETI), which monitors the corporations' codes of conduct in supplier factories. Most of this work is connected with China, Bangladesh and Cambodia or with Latin American countries.

There is no real focus on Malaysia because the clothing industry pales in significance to the industries in Bangladesh, Cambodia and China, and many activists feel the conditions for workers are worse in these less-developed countries. But Malaysia is a good example of how competition in the industry intensified in the last decade and most SME supply factories in the export market failed to record profits in the global market, making the conditions for workers and unions more difficult. The intense competition after China joined the WTO and the MFA ended in 2004 has provided further hostility to unions in Malaysia, increasing the number of short-term contract workers and the exploitation of these workers.

## Migrant workers in Malaysia

The recruitment of migrant workers has started to be a significant strategy of government and employers. In 2002 the Malaysian government allowed large numbers of foreigners to fill low-cost sewing jobs (Crinis 2010). In the following ten years the government signed memorandums of understanding (MOUs) with a number of neighbouring countries to supply workers. In 2010 there were approximately 1.9 million authorized migrant workers and about 35 per cent of them were employed in the manufacturing industries (Hamid 2010). In 2013 the Home Ministry reported 2.1 million authorized migrants and another 1.3 million unauthorized, a total of 3.1 million migrant workers in Malaysia (*Migration News*, January 2014). At present foreigners make up 16 per cent of Malaysia's 29 million residents and 20 per cent of the 14 million labour force (*Migration News*, October 2013). In the clothing factories migrant workers make up 80 per cent of production workers as well as filling a number of supervisory jobs on the factory floor.[12] Workers consist of a core group of locals plus males from Bangladesh, Indonesia, Nepal, Sri Lanka and Vietnam, and females from China, Cambodia, Indonesia, the Philippines, Vietnam and Myanmar. The totals vary depending on the numbers and ethnicities available at the time of recruitment.

Workers, including migrant workers, are in theory protected under the umbrella of the International Labour Conventions and many anti-unionists agree that both citizen and non-citizen are protected under the law. But while the Employment Act 1955, 1968, 1998, the Workman's Compensation Act 1952, Occupational Safety and Health Act 1994 and Industrial Relations Act 1967 protect both locals and migrants, these laws can be swayed to the advantage of employers. Moreover, there are no efficient measures to monitor this. For example, the Industrial Relations Act 1967 gives employees the right to become a trade union member and to participate in its lawful activities; the Employment Act Restriction 1968 does not allow foreign workers to become a member of an association, which in many cases workers believe, incorrectly, to be a trade union. Even if migrant workers are members of trade unions, which is highly unlikely, the worker is further confused by the contradictory effects of the Employment Act and the Industrial Relations Act 1967. For instance, while migrants have the right to join a trade union, if their contract is terminated for whatever reason, they are not allowed union representation under section 5.10 of the Employment Act Restriction 1968 (Ku Ahmad 2003). In addition, a labour law when applied to migrant workers often trumps another law. Hundreds of workers were dismissed from garment industries in Malaysia in the GFC. According to the government, the Employment Act states that in the event of a financial downturn migrant workers must be dismissed before citizens, and as a result newly recruited workers who had not paid off their recruitment debt were forced to return to their country of origin. However the law does not discriminate between citizen and non-citizen workers: under the Malaysian Constitution, the employer is supposed to dismiss workers on a last-in-first-out basis, not according to citizenship.

According to the MTUC, migrant workers experience more labour breaches than locals, including unfair dismissal, withholding wages, health and safety in the workforce and worker's compensation, as well as sexual harassment, which is rarely reported (Crinis 2010).[13]

### Migrant workers: a site of controversy in Malaysia

Migrant workers have been a site of contention for trade unions since the 1990s. First, government policies of bringing in contract workers created a gulf between the local working class and the guest workers. Most of the calls from the MTUC have been in regards to contract workers and minimum wage legislation. But by 2010 migrant workers became a problem for both employers and the government due to human rights abuses and increasing crime rates in Malaysia, and it was obvious to all concerned that the migrant worker issue had to be addressed. In response, the government wanted to make capital less dependent on migrant workers and to reduce the number of migrant workers in the service sector. The government devised three strategies. The first was to make employers advertise for local workers before applying for guest workers, the second was to bring migrant workers' wages in line with the wages of local workers, and the third was to reduce Malaysian workers from full-time to contract work.

In 2010 the Human Resources Minister proposed amendments to the three major labour laws – the Employment Act 1955, Industrial Relations Act 1967 and the Trade Union Act 1959 – to make locals more attractive to employers. The amendments removed security of tenure for thousands of workers in Malaysia and were deliberately designed to allow employers to remove fixed-term contract workers, especially unionized workers. Even workers who had ten years' service could be placed on a short-term contract and would have no redress in the event of termination (Pekwan 2010). According to the MTUC Secretary Mr Rajasekaran (2010):

> This will have a serious impact on trade unions' right to negotiate on terms and conditions of employment. This will also encourage employers to intensify their efforts to encourage their employees to relinquish their union membership. MTUC is deeply concerned with the Minister's retrogressive step. The proposed amendments, we believe, are done at the behest of multinational corporations and potential investors.

In recent times the government has been forced to introduce a minimum wage to kick-start the economy because growth rates stagnated in the 2000s as employers failed to introduce higher levels of technology and skilled labour. Since 2012 employers must now pay a minimum wage of MR900 (US$235) to both citizen and migrant workers alike. But according to newspaper reports, employers are resuming the practice of recovering the employer levy by deducting this money from workers' wages. The minimum wage increased suddenly from MR600 (US$167) to MR700 (US$183) a month to MR900 (US$234) a month, so employers insist migrant workers pay the levy. If this is the case, their after-levy wages would be lower than for Malaysian citizens.

SMEs in the manufacturing industries have warned of the dire consequences to their businesses if they have to pay the minimum wage to migrants; some even suggesting withholding paying migrants the minimum wage for five years (*Migration News*, April 2014). Others want the government to declare an industry-wide labour shortage in the manufacturing industries and to end the requirement that employers seek local workers first, which is only slowing down the process (*New Straits Times*, 25 June 2014).

The MTUC on the other hand argues that migrant workers should receive the same money as locals and wants the government to temporarily halt the intake of foreigners so as to take stock of the available local labour demand, with the specific aim of reducing the importation of foreign workers altogether (*New Straits Times*, 25 June 2014). According to the MTUC, the minimum wages policy has succeeded in encouraging more locals to seek employment in sectors that were previously monopolized by migrant workers. The MTUC supports the employment of locals. But the notion that locals will work under the same conditions as migrant workers is highly unlikely in the short term and probably in the long term.

*Clothing and textile trade union in Malaysia*   37

### Alternate forms of worker activism

In the last few years there is evidence that the MTUC, sponsored by the ILO and the GUFs, have started to direct attention to the migrant worker issue. The aid has allowed the MTUC to study the situation and commence workshop programmes to educate groups of workers regarding their labour rights and the employer responsibilities in Malaysia. The MTUC also provides union training programmes for migrant workers to understand the work of unions. The MTUC also distributes a Migrant Rights Passbook, a small booklet printed in a number of migrant worker languages with the names and phone numbers of unions in Malaysia. These booklets encourage migrant workers to contact local trade union secretaries when they need help.

Possibly the most important development for migrant workers in supply factories in Malaysia then, is the triangle union suggested by the ILO/GUFs, whereby a three-way relationship develops with the migrant workers' support group and the main union body in the destination and sending countries. The Nepalese Migrant Workers' Support Group was developed under the wings of the MTUC and Nepalese Trade Union Congress (Gefont) in Nepal. Nepalese workers once considered 'docile' by Malaysian standards have organized their own worker support group with 4000 members, of which 300 are women. Gefont appears to be an important step in establishing a migrant-worker movement by involving labour movements across nations. When Nepalese workers need assistance they contact Gefont to file reports to the MTUC, the Nepalese Union in Nepal and, if the complaint is in relation to wages, then a copy is sent to the Labour Office in Malaysia. At present there are cases pending with both individual workers and groups of workers in a number of factories. The complaints range from underpayment, work-related injuries and beatings to other unfair labour practices. At the time of writing, other ethnicities were also using the support group, and the group was networking with other NGOs and support groups in Malaysia (Somasundrum, Foreign Worker Officer MTUC, pers. comm., 2010). The internet and mobile phones have made communication between migrant workers and labour activists easier.

### Conclusion

Reflecting on the restrictions on trade union organizing in industrial zones and the linking of unions with anti-development rhetoric, it is plain to see how unions were pushed to their limits, leaving a small number of under-resourced unionists to keep the unions afloat. Despite these drawbacks, this study has shown that unions are doing all they can to survive and clothing and textile trade unionists continue to represent workers in the labour courts, and continue to pressure the labour department to register unions. But unions must find new ways to address their responsibility towards workers, especially migrant workers.

In the past unionists did not see how they could organize migrant workers and look after local workers at the same time. Unions are now playing catch up.

38　*V. Crinis*

GUFs have attempted to link unions across different industries. But while local unions are able to join forces on a global level, any strike action or support for unions outside Malaysia will be interpreted by the Malaysian government as an illegal activity and workers will face discriminatory action, not to mention the incarceration of union leaders. The state in Malaysia is well rehearsed in ceding to the demands of local investors, so it is hard to imagine that under these circumstances global unions will be able to help local unions reach workers at the grassroots level. The triangle labour union strategy is a step in the right direction and while it is not specific to the clothing industry, garment and textile workers can use the helpline to their advantage to report specific labour abuses. For the future, unions need to address the separation between non-citizen and citizen divisions in the workplace and the persistence of cultural gender divisions and norms in the union movement itself. In addition, there need to be alliances and cooperative actions with NGOs to assist migrant workers in both their recruitment and living and working conditions in the different states in Malaysia. Because of the restrictions placed on trade unions in the workplace and the marginalization of migrant workers in Malaysia, collective activism must be expressed in broader social movement unionism within Malaysia. In this period of late capitalism, against all odds unions must change the focus from attempting to pursue an out-dated union model to something that works in Malaysia.

## Notes

1 My research commenced by comparing lists of state trade unions and the numbers of members in each, including the states of Selangor, Penang, Malacca and Negeri Sembilan, Johor Bahru and Perak, to the lists collated in the 1990s. Although the numbers of union members in all unions in Malaysia have increased, this is largely the result of increases in the white collar union sectors such as banking. The figures show a decline in union membership in the textile and garment trade unions. The chapter is based on past and current research (Australian Research Council (ARC) Grant) including interviews with trade union leaders (past and present), Malaysian workers both unionized and non-unionized, migrant workers, non-government organizations (NGOs) and civil society organizations, including Christian NGOs. The interviews commenced with clothing and textile trade union secretaries in the 1990s, with further interviews in 2007, 2009 and 2010, and concluded with interviews with various NGO representatives in Malaysia. Interviews were also conducted with union committee members in the Malaysian Trades Union Congress (MTUC), including the various leaders of the Women's Committee, as well as interviews with local and migrant workers.
2 In the 1920s the Chinese led the General Union and in 1947 the Chinese dominated the Pan Malayan Federation of Trade Unions (PMFTU) with over 250,000 union members. After the decimation of the Malaysian Communist Party in the 1950s, which included Chinese union leaders, the Chinese distanced themselves from the union movement (Rowley and Bhopal 2006: 100).
3 The International Confederation of Free Trade Unions (ICFTU) was an international trade union. It came into being on 7 December 1949 following a split within the World Federation of Trade Unions (WFTU), and was dissolved on 31 October 2006 when it merged with the World Confederation of Labour (WCL) to form the International Trade Union Confederation (ITUC).

Clothing and textile trade union in Malaysia 39

4 Elias argues that everyday patterns of resistance actually feed into highly localized regimes of workplace control, as company managers argue that 'backward' women from the 'farm' perform acts of resistance for the simple reason they are backward and do not understand the 'progressive' work environment (Elias 2005: 222–4).

5 After the government changed its import substitution policies to export manufacturing to attract foreign direct investment (FDI), Singapore and East Asian clothing manufacturers transferred part of the quota allocated to them to Malaysian suppliers and/or set up their own factories in export processing zones (EPZ). These zones provided an environment for clothing companies to escape organized workforces in their own countries and the pattern has continued (Galenson 1992).

6 Industrial relations scholars have also drawn attention to the ways Japanese multinational corporation (MNC) managers prefer a unionized workforce (Bhopal and Todd 2010).

7 Out of 30,954 small to medium enterprises (SMEs), 22.7 per cent were in the textile and clothing sector and most were situated in Selangor, Johor and Kuala Lumpur (Department of Statistics Malaysia 2010).

8 The Textile Workers' Asia-Pacific Regional Organization (TWARO) has a membership of some 2.4 million textile, garment, shoe and leather workers from 72 affiliated organizations in 21 Asian and Pacific countries. The long-serving Secretary of the Penang and Province Wellesley Textiles and Garment Manufacturing Employees' Union (PTGWU) is also the secretary of TWARO.

9 The International textile, Garment and Leather Workers' Federation (ITGLWF) is an important international body and brings together 217 trade unions from 110 countries with a combined membership of ten million.

10 Management at the Coats thread factory in Bangladesh had failed to reach agreement with trade union negotiators over an increase in wages eventuating in strike action. The management somehow obtained a court order declaring the strike illegal. The workers at Coats are paid poverty wages of only BD Tk.1625 (US$19.80). The trade unions in Bangladesh consider BD Tk.7000 (US$85.29) to be the minimum that could be considered a living wage. Despite trade union compromises the employer refused to bargain in good faith.

11 In 2012 the ITGLWF was liquidated and was affiliated to a global union. IndustriALL is a unification of three former global union federations (GUFs): International Metalworkers' Union, 'International Federation of Chemical, Energy, Mine and General Workers' Union and the ITGLWF.

12 During research I found that except for a factory in Malacca, employers generally prefer migrant workers to Malaysian workers.

13 The increase in the numbers of migrants that chose to become unauthorized challenges the state's policies to control migration for the benefit of capital development. It also allows the state to conduct amnesty and repatriation projects to appease the locals and rid the country of excess labour.

## References

Ariffin, R. (1988) 'Malaysian women's participation in trade unions', in N. Heyzer (ed.), *Daughters in Industry*, pp. 239–65, Kuala Lumpur: Asia Pacific Development Centre.

Ariffin, R. (1989) 'Women and trade unions in West Malaysia', *Journal of Contemporary Asia*, 19(1): 78–94.

Ariffin, R. (1997) *Women and Trade Unions in Peninsular Malaysia with Special Reference to MTUC and CUEPACS*, Pulau Pinang (Penang): Universiti Sains Malaysia (University of Malaya).

## 40   V. Crinis

Barrientos, S. (2002) 'Mapping codes through the value chain: from researcher to detective', in R. Jenkins, R. Pearson and G. Seyfang (eds), *Corporate Responsibility and Labour Rights: Codes of Conduct in the Global Economy*. London: Earthscan Publishers Ltd, pp. 61–76.

Barrientos, S. and Kabeer, N. (2004) 'Enhancing female employment in global production: policy implications', *Global Social Policy*, 4(153): 153–68.

Bhopal, M. and Todd, P. (2010) 'Multinational corporations and trade union diversity in Malaysia', *Asia Pacific Business Review*, 6 (3–4): 193–213.

Brown, A. and Ayudhya, S. C. N. (2013) 'Labour activism in Thailand', in M. Ford (ed.), *Social Activism in Southeast Asia*, pp. 104–18, New York: Routledge.

Brown, A. and Chatyaweep, S. (2008) 'Women and spaces for labour organizing', in K. Broadbent and M. Ford (eds), *Women and Labour Organising in Asia: Diversity Autonomy and Activism*, pp. 100–14, New York: Routledge.

Crinis, V. (1993) *A Comparative Study of Women Clothing Workers in Malaysia and Australia*, History and Politics Department, Wollongong: University of Wollongong.

Crinis, V. (2003) 'Innovations in trade union approaches in Malaysia's garment industry', *The Economic and Labour Relations Review*, 14(1): 80–9.

Crinis, V. (2008) 'Malaysia: women, labour activism and unions', in K. Broadbent and M. Ford (eds), *Women and Labour Organising in Asia: Diversity, Autonomy and Activism*, pp. 50–65, London: Routledge.

Crinis, V. (2010) 'Sweat or no sweat: foreign workers in the garment industry in Malaysia', *Journal of Contemporary Asia*, 40(4): 589–611.

Cumbers, A., Nativel, C. and Routledge, P. (2008) 'Labour agency and union positionalities in global production networks', *Journal of Economic Geography*, 8(3): 369–87.

DeNeve, G. (2008) 'Global garment chains local labour activism: new challenges to trade unionism in the Tiruppur Garment Cluster South India', in G. De Neve, P. Luetchford, J. Pratt and D. C. Wood (eds), *Hidden Hands in the Market: Ethnographies of Fair Trade, Ethical Consumption and Corporate Social Responsibility*, pp. 213–40, Bingley: Emerald Group Publishing Limited.

Department of Statistics Malaysia (2010) *Report on the Annual Survey of Manufacturing Industries 2008 Summary Findings, Statistical Releases (updated 22 August 2011)*, http://statistics.gov.my/portal/images/stories/files/LatestReleases/findings/Penemuan_Pembuatan_2010_BI.pdf (accessed 19 October 2012).

Elias, J. (2005) 'The gendered political economy of control and resistance on the shop floor of the multinational firm: a case study of Malaysia', *New Political Economy*, 10(2): 204–22.

Elias, J. (2010) 'Gendered political economy and the politics of migrant worker rights: the view from South-East Asia', *Australian Journal of International Affairs*, 64(1): 70–85.

Ford, M. (2009) *Workers and Intellectuals: NGOs, Trade Unions and the Indonesian Labour Movement*. Singapore: National University of Singapore.

Ford, M. (2013a) 'The Global Federations and temporary labour migration in Malaysia', *Journal of Industrial Relations*, 55: 260–76.

Ford, M. (ed.) (2013b) *Social Activism in Southeast Asia*, New York: Routledge.

Galenson, W. (1992) *Labour and Economic Growth in South Asia Countries: South Korea, Malaysia, Taiwan, Thailand and the Philippines*, New York: Prager.

Gamba, C. (1962) *The Origins of Trade Unionism in Malaya: A Study of Labour Unrest*, Singapore: Eastern Universities Press.

Gomez, E. T. (2009) 'The rise and fall of capital: corporate Malaysia in historical perspective', *Journal of Contemporary Asia*, 39(3): 345–81.

Hamid, H. (2010) 'A laborious issue', *New Straits Times*, 5 May, Business Section 1, p. 2.

IndustriALL (2014) 'Sectors', www.industriall-union.org/sectors/garment (accessed 28 August 2013).

International Textile, Garment and Leather Workers' Federation (ITGLWF) (2011) 'First global framework agreement signed by Japanese multinational Mizuno', www.itglwf. org (accessed 23 February 2012).

International Textile, Garment and Leather Workers' Federation (ITGLWF) (2012) 'Union leaders held captive by factory managers in Bangladesh', www.itglwf.org (accessed 23 February 2012).

Jackson, R. (1991) *The Malayan Emergency*, London: Routledge.

Jomo, K. S. (1988) *A Question of Class: Capital, the State, and Uneven Development in Malaya*, New York: Monthly Review Press.

Jomo, K. S. and Todd, P. (1994) *Trade Unionism and the State in Peninsular Malaysia*, Kuala Lumpur: Oxford University Press.

Kabeer, N. (2004) 'Globalisation labour standards and women's rights: dilemma of collective (in)action in an independent world', *Feminist Economics*, 10(1): 3–35.

Ku Ahmad, S. (2003) 'The constant flux, the mobile reserve and the limits of control: Malaysia and the legal dimensions of international migration', in R. Iredale, C. Hawksley and S. Castles (eds), *Migration in the Asia Pacific: Population Settlement and Citizenship Issues*, pp. 141–68, Cheltenham: Edward Elgar.

Loh-Ludher, L. L. (1998) 'Women in industrial sub-contracting in Malaysia: the case of home-based sub-contractors in the garment industry', paper presented at the Neither Costed Nor Valued Conference, University of New England, Armidale.

Miller, D. (2004) 'Preparing for the long haul: negotiating International Framework Agreements in the global textile, garment and footwear sector', *Global Social Policy*, 4(2): 215–38.

Pekwan, T. (2010) 'MTUC: Workers' rights in peril: proposed amendments to three Acts will side the employers, says Rajasekaran', *Malay Mail*, 16 April, www.mmail.com. my/content/33659-mtuc-workers-rights-peril (accessed 16 April 2010).

Rajasekaran, G. S. M. (2010) 'Worst labour law Amendments in 40 years to promote precarious employment', MTUC Press Statement, 15 April 2010, www.facebook.com/ note.php?note_id=10150175842565714 (accessed 20 May 2013).

Rasiah, R. (1993) 'Competition and governance: work in Malaysia's textile and garment industries', *Journal of Contemporary Asia*, 23(1): 3–23.

Rasiah, R. (2009) 'Malaysia's textile and garment firms at the crossroads', *Journal of Contemporary Asia*, 39(4): 530–42.

Rose, R. C., Kumar, N. and Ramasamy, N. (2010) 'Employee's perceptions of trade unions in unionised companies: a survey in Malaysia', *Employment Relations Record*, 10(2): 46–62.

Rowley, C. and Bhopal, M. (2006) 'The ethnic identity in state-labour relations: the case of Malaysia', *Capital and Class*, Spring (88): 87–115.

Todd, P. and Bhopal, M. (2002) 'Trade union dilemmas of diversity in Malaysia', in F. Coglan and S. Ledwith (eds), *Gender, Diversity and Trade Unions*, pp. 73–94, London: Routledge.

Yuen, T. (1999) *Labour Unrest in Malaya, 1934–1941, The Rise of the Workers' Movement*, Kuala Lumpur: University of Malaya.

## 42 V. Crinis

### Newspapers and union newsletters

'Firms urged to pay into fund for Bangladesh factory victims' (2014) *The Express Tribune with the International New York Times.* Monday 24 February. Online at: http://tribune.com.pk/story/675541/firms-urged-to-pay-into-fund-for-bangladesh-factory (accessed 14 March 2014).

*Migration News* (2013) Southeast Asia: ASEAN 2015 October Volume 20(4). Online at: https://migration.ucdavis.edu/mn/more.php?id=3868_0_3_0 (accessed 15 October 2013).

*Migration News* (2014) Southeast Asia January Volume 21(1). Online at: https://migration.ucdavis.edu/mn/more.php?id=3888_0_3_0 (accessed 10 February 2014).

*Migration News* (2014) Southeast Asia April Volume 20(2). Online at: http://migration.ucdavis.edu/mn/more.php?id=3906_0_3_0 (accessed 30 May 2014).

'Minimum wage cheer for workers' (2012) *New Straits Times*, Sunday 1 May. Online at: www.nst.com.my/top-news/minimum-wage-cheer-for-workers-1.79469 (accessed 23 July 2012).

'Minimum wage policy encourages more locals to seek employment: MTUC' (2014) *New Straits Times*, Kuala Lumpur, Wednesday, 25 June. Online at: www.nst.com.my/node/2126 (accessed 1 July 2014).

*Penang Union Newsletter* (1992) 'Kesatuan Pekerja Pekerja Perusahaan dan Pakaian P. Pinang dan S. Perai, 1990 to 1992'.

*Penang Union Newsletter* (1994) 'Kesatuan Pekerja Pekerja Perusahaan dan Pakaian P. Pinang dan S. Perai, 1992 to 1994'.

# 3 Scrutinizing the effectiveness of trade unions in post-socialist Vietnam

*Anne Cox*

In 1986, the Vietnamese Communist government ended its approach of maintaining a closed and centrally planned economy and sought industrialization by allowing private ownership of economic enterprises, encouraging a greater role for market forces and embracing an 'open-door policy' towards foreign investment. Since passing the Law on Foreign Investment in December 1987, there has been a continuous flow of foreign direct investment (FDI) into the country, mostly through the establishment of manufacturing plants by MNCs (Le 1997; Tran 1997). In the space of three decades, foreign investment has become a major and growing factor in the country's economy, particularly in the industrial component and in exports. By June 2011, Vietnam had received commitments of US\$198,889,098,224 for 12,776 projects from 92 countries and territories (MPI 2012) and as of December 2004, foreign-invested firms had created 1,044,851 jobs (GSO 2005: 121). Indirectly FDI has also provided employment through subcontractors and suppliers. Despite its relatively short history of development, Vietnam has been quite successful in attracting FDI compared to its neighbour countries. It ranks third among the investment recipients in the Association of South East Asian Nations (ASEAN) (Mirza and Giroud 2004).

As an integral part of the national economy, the foreign-invested sector has contributed to the development of Vietnam in many ways: attracting foreign capital, improving the balance of international payments, increasing export and access to international markets, accelerating the process of international integration, and deepening cultural exchange etc. Most importantly, foreign-invested firms are the main source of technology and management practices transfer to Vietnam. There is strong evidence that MNCs from developed countries operate more sophisticated human resource management (HRM) policies and practices, including performance-based pay schemes and better training, fair career promotion and skill development (see for example, Vo 2009).

On the other hand, HRM and industrial relations (IR) in labour-intensive sectors and in MNCs originating in developing countries are a lot more complex. According to the Vietnamese General Confederation of Labour (VCGL), from early 1995 to mid-2002, there were 472 strikes, of which 262 incidents happened in foreign-invested companies, accounting for 55.5 per cent of strikes occurring in Vietnam. Labour strikes are highly concentrated in firms invested by Taiwan,

44    *A. Cox*

Korea and Hong Kong, which normally operate in labour-intensive industries – on top of the list are the clothing and footwear industries. Up to 2002, these countries were responsible for 71.43 per cent of strikes. The situation has not changed in recent years, as in 2007 an estimated 350,000 workers of foreign-invested factories were involved in at least 541 strikes across Vietnam (Le 2008). According to VCGL, 336 strikes occurred in Vietnam between January and April 2011, which was a decrease from 762 strikes in 2008 (Majendie *et al.* 2011). Most were in the industrialized provinces or cities such as Ho Chi Minh City, Dong Nai, Binh Duong, Ba Ria Vung Tau, Ha Noi and Hai Duong. Interestingly, all the strikes in the last decade were illegal because in most cases they were organized by the workers themselves, with the unions standing by, and regardless of the fact that they followed the right procedures and processes (Vo 2009). Many are of the opinion (see Vo 2009) that recent labour strikes have been organized by the workers, bypassing the trade unions, due to the general lack of understanding of the Labour Laws and thinking that going on strike is the quickest way to solve labour disputes. In fact, this is only one side of the story. The other reason is the workers' lack of confidence in the official trade unions.

This chapter examines the role of trade unions in the textile and garment industry in Vietnam, focusing on the subsidiaries of MNCs from Taiwan. According to the Vietnamese Ministry of Planning and Investment, in June 2011, Taiwan was the biggest investor in Vietnam with 2180 projects worth US$23,164,997,783 accounting for 11.65 per cent of the total registered capital inflows to the country (MPI 2012). The textile and garment industry was chosen to study because it has emerged as one of the most labour-intensive industries characterized by the highest occurrence of labour conflict (VCGL 2010), and also because it has an essential role in the modernization and industrialization process in Vietnam. In 2010, total export earnings derived from the textile and garment industry reached US$11.17 billion, making Vietnam the fifth largest garment and textile supplier in the world. The sector is also the largest formal employer in Vietnam, providing jobs for more than two million people (ILO and IFC 2011: 6). Furthermore, this sector reflects the fact that most of Taiwanese FDI in Vietnam focuses on light industries, which absorb about 70 per cent of the total accumulated investment capital (Tran 2011: 23).

Going through some key trade unions' organizational issues, especially the expected roles and responsibilities and the constraints they meet in realizing expectations, this chapter shows the transformation of Vietnamese trade unions, intended by the Labour Laws, recent Trade Union Laws and related regulations, has had very limited results. At the present time, trade unions' structure and operations are full of unresolved difficulties. At the workplace level, their formal activities are limited to arranging holidays, organizing social activities with the company's funds, and encouraging workers to fulfil production quotas. However, 'the race to the bottom' within the textile and garment industry has led to violations of labour rights, especially low salaries, benefits and bonuses, and long working hours. Recording a series of labour strikes, including 'wildcat' ones,

I show that workers are not afraid to take aggressive action to protect and improve their rights. I also look at the formation of unofficial labour movements led by unofficial worker representatives, who bypass trade union leaders and have gained significant power to gather thousands of workers in instantaneous strikes, marking a shift in Vietnam from rights-based to interest-based disputes.

The chapter is structured as follows. First, in the literature review I discuss IR in the context of globalization and the nature of the Vietnamese IR system. I then look at the research methodology. The empirical study presented in this chapter discusses trade unions' roles and activities and the elements that constrain or facilitate their mobility at the grass roots level. The chapter ends with discussions and conclusions.

## Literature review

### *Conceptualizing industrial relations*

IR is described as a multi or interdisciplinary field. Institutional-based definitions view IR as the product of the institutions and institutional processes that establish and administer the rules regulating workplace relations. Early approaches to defining IR exhibited a preoccupation with the institutions of job regulation. Dunlop's (1958) conceptualization of IR was bound by what he described as the 'the network of rules' that governs workplaces and the work community. This notion was later developed by Flanders (1965: 10) who described the central foci of IR as the range of instruments that appear in various 'guises' from formal regulations, statutes and employment agreements and contracts, through to accepted informal social conventions, managerial practices, customs and traditions. The term 'rules' was adopted as a generic means of describing the non-exhaustive array of institutionalized relationships that exist in industry (Flanders 1965).

These approaches were duly criticized as being far too restrictive by focusing exclusively on the rules and regulations governing workplace relations. The overemphasis on rules and regulations also led to criticism that these perspectives assumed that the core of IR was maintaining stability, regularity and industrial order. To widen the scope, Hyman's (1975) definition encompassed sources and consequences of conflict, thereby approaching IR as the processes of power and control in workplace relations. His perspective essentially drew on Marxist influences whereby IR is conceptualized as the outcome of the sum of institutions, interactions and processes that are a product of broader social and economic influences. Importantly, Hyman's (1975) theory stressed the dynamic nature of social relationships, and the significance of history.

Aside from developments in the definitions, two ongoing and related debates in the literature concern the impact of globalization on IR, and the question of whether there is a convergence or divergence of national IR systems. While there is little doubt of the significance of IR in the process of globalization, political and economic adjustment and in the transition to a market economy (De Silva n.d.), the implications are heavily contested.

46  *A. Cox*

Those supporting globalization have long held the argument that an open market economy that encourages trade and increased FDI will invariably lead to improvements in employment and income. On the other hand, opponents hold that globalization has and will continue to be responsible for 'the race to the bottom' in developing nations, characterized by diminishing working conditions, employment and earnings (Singh and Zammit 2000).

Cox (1994) describes the 'structural power of capital' as the driving force of globalization, whereby an overdependence on foreign investment and capital leads nation states to be bound by economic policies that create conditions favourable to 'regime shoppers'. In addition to maintaining low wages and long working hours, this leads to tighter controls over labour and union activity.

While the role of unions has rarely been explored in the context of transitional economies, De Silva (n.d.) notes the challenges experienced by countries in transition to a market economy, particularly those seeking to adjust to an IR structure in which pluralism was not previously recognized. Indeed, Zhu in his comparison of IR in Vietnam and China, highlights the lack of distance between management and workers, and the emphasis on the values of harmony and homogeneity (2002: 130).

De Silva (n.d.) suggests that unions in such economies tend to play more of a welfare and supervisory role than a negotiating one. Within these environments, management and unions are more likely to be involved in the implementation of decisions made outside the enterprise than in the process of determining and negotiating the terms and conditions of employment.

On the other hand, in a market economy decisions are largely made within the enterprise. Where decisions are made externally, this is done so with appropriate representation of members' interests and some government involvement. The system is principally based on negotiations between both parties and recognition of outcomes by the state, as long as they are in line with necessary regulations and policies (De Silva n.d.).

The role played by trade unions in post-communist societies therefore raises conceptual challenges for IR theorists. As Zhu and Fahey (2000) argue, if a trade union represents an organization of workers with the capacity to freely and collectively bargain for employees' rights, within these contexts they may not be considered unions at all. At the core, there are fundamental differences between socialist market economies and western democratic systems in the way unions' roles are conceptualized.

De Silva (n.d.) notes that transitional countries are experiencing an array of difficulties surrounding the roles of employer and worker organizations, adopting a tripartite process for IR policy formulation, and developing IR systems that are aligned with their economic policies. He stresses, however, the need for employees and their representatives to be involved in change and in transition, and the willingness of employers to engage them is a critical issue in many Asian contexts.

In this chapter, Lévesque and Murray's (2002) three-power concept will be used to ascertain the formal and informal institutions that impact the mobility and effectiveness of trade unions. The concept's three components are: internal solidarity, which refers to the mechanisms developed in the workplace to ensure democracy and collective cohesion among workers; external solidarity (also termed 'network embeddedness'), which refers to the extent that unions work with their communities, develop horizontal and vertical coordination with other unions, and build alliances among community groups and social movements; and strategic or discursive capacity of unions, or their capacity to identify structure and put forward their own agenda. Indeed, effectiveness and mobility of unions are determined not only by their roles, but also by the relative power and strength they are offered through the institutional environment – aspects I will elucidate in this chapter.

### *The Vietnamese IR system*

Vietnamese workers are represented by the VGCL. It should be noted that the role and nature of trade unions in Vietnam do not conform to the western liberal-democratic model where unions are independent representatives of collective employee interests. In Vietnam, as in other socialist countries, the state is the main employer. In the centrally planned economy, the union does not play the role of protecting or furthering the interests of employees, as workers' interests are assumed to be similar to those of the government. There is no recognition of the possibility that the interests of the three actors – the government, the employers and the workers – might differ.

Economic reform in Vietnam has had an enormous impact on the structure of the Vietnamese economy and consequently on employee working conditions. With rapid changes, and expansion and diversification of the system, the traditional labour legislation proved increasingly inadequate. Recognizing the need to adjust to the changing labour situation, the Vietnamese government passed the new Trade Union Law in 1990, the Trade Union Constitution in 1993, and the Labour Law in 1994. This legislation marks the beginning of the transformation of the IR system in Vietnam.

The Vietnamese Trade Union Law 1990 opens by reiterating, in stereotypical language, that the union is an organization under the leadership of the Communist Party (Article 1.1). However, the substantive details of the law show serious attempts at transforming trade unions by granting them considerable autonomy from the Party and, for the first time, placing them on the opposite side to management. First, there is a clear-cut division between management and labour. The role of the Vietnamese trade unions is no longer limited to assisting management or carrying out managerial functions. They are empowered to 'check on' management (Article 2.2). Second, they have the right to get support from foreign organizations. In particular, they can join international trade union organizations (Article 1.3), accept donations from international sources (Article 16.2.a), and keep these as union assets (Article 17). Third, a Vietnamese union official's salary is to be paid out of union funds (Article 15.3). This means that in the workplace, union cadres are not expected to be on the management payroll and are to be independent of management.

48  *A. Cox*

The Trade Union Constitution in 1993 was geared to help lower levels of the trade union organization to become more autonomous. The local organizations are allowed to establish occupational trade unions (Article 14) thereby reinforcing their ability to voice interests that may be different from those of the state and the localities' governments. Company-based trade unions, therefore, are under the control of two structures. The traditional vertical one represents a geographical or local union structure while the horizontal one is concerned with the occupational structure. All local and occupational trade unions, however, are under the umbrella of the VGCL.

The new Labour Law 1994 represents compromises between the unions and other interests. The government accepted a tripartite structure for IR, consisting of labour, employers and the state. The trade unions' role of protecting workers' labour rights is affirmed. Despite persistent objections from other bureaucracies during the heated debate over the drafts, trade unions are to be set up in enterprises of all ownership types, including foreign-invested firms (Article 153.1). Finally, for the first time since the formation of the Socialist Republic of Vietnam, workers were given the right to strike (Article 173.2). These laws and constitution suggest that the Vietnamese government is willing to relax its hold on the labour unions and that there is a strong legislative base for trade unions to step out of the shadow of the Party and the state and renew their organization and activities to perform the function of workers' representatives in protecting their rights and interests.

There is relatively limited research on the current Vietnamese IR system. The studies that have emerged have favoured a comparative approach, particularly with China as Vietnam's more developed and advanced 'sibling'. For instance, Chan and Norlund's (1998) account focuses on the regulation surrounding union activity in the two countries, suggesting future divergence in labour regimes may eventuate, as evidenced by the relaxation of Vietnamese regulation. In particular, they drew attention to Vietnamese unions' increased autonomy, and the promising future of occupation-based unions, both of which Zhu and Fahey (2000) suggest are yet to be realized. Zhu and Fahey's (2000) comparative study highlights the cultural dimension in workplace relationships, and in particular, the smaller power differential in the relations between Vietnamese employees and their managers to that of the Chinese. Furthermore, they argue that while the trade union movement in both countries 'had its roots in organised political opposition to colonialist oppression' (Zhu and Fahey 2000: 297), their key challenge is how to transform from an administrative role focused on production targets to gaining credibility as labour advocates. They indicate that unions in both China and Vietnam are becoming stronger advocates of workers' rights.

More recently Clarke *et al.* (2007) have examined the development of what they term Vietnam's 'rights-based system' for the regulation of IR in its emerging market economy. Their findings (based on interviews with trade union, employer and government representatives at national, city and district levels, and trade union and employer representatives in five enterprises in Hanoi and Ho Chi Minh City covering the foreign-invested, domestic-private and equitized-state sectors) suggest that trade unions and labour administration have little capacity to ensure the rights of workers are respected by employers. Vietnamese workers were also found not to have actively pursued their interests through the available institutional mechanisms. Clarke *et al.* (2007) note that strikes in the past were a response to various legal violations by employers, which were able to be settled by administrators forcing those employers to accept their legal obligations. However, given the tightening of the labour market, future strikes may focus more on improving wages and conditions beyond existing laws, labour contracts and collective agreements.

Chan (2011a) has explored Vietnam's and China's diverging industrial relations systems through an in-depth study of strikes in Taiwanese-owned factories in both countries. Interestingly, her account of a strike in a footwear company in Vietnam employing 50,000 workers disputes Zhu and Fahey's (2000) claim that unions are becoming stronger advocates of workers' rights. Chan's research revealed that despite a trade union presence since 1996, it was not proactive in protecting the interests of the employees. Rather, the relationship between the union, workers and management was partnership. The spontaneous wildcat strike reflected the frustration of employees at not having their voices heard and had no union involvement (Chan 2011a). Chan, however, says that compared to Chinese workers, Vietnamese workers 'have become emboldened by their experience' and have learnt 'about how to start a wildcat strike' (2011: 34). Interestingly, Chan's (2011) research confirms that of Clarke *et al.* (2007) who argue that strike action in Vietnam is more likely to be interest based with demands that go beyond the minimal legal standards, particularly on matters surrounding pay and wage structures, food and welfare provisions, and dignified treatment. This also appears to be the case in private and state-owned companies in Vietnam. Kerkvliet's (2008) research-based examination of strikes between 1990 and late 2008 shows that over 75 per cent of strikes in private and state-owned companies have centred around wage concerns, followed by a large number of complaints surrounding the inhumane treatment of workers, ranging from extensive working hours to shocking accounts of verbal and physical abuse.

The literature above offers insight into key developments of the Vietnamese IR system over the past decade. These previous studies, however, have focused on the perspective of regulation, regulators, employers, or union or government officials. Consequently, the 'human' element captured through the perspective of shop-floor workers who experience the effects of the institutions and collectively comprise the trade union movement is absent. Another gap is an understanding of the role of trade unions in the context of MNCs in Vietnam. For instance, while foreign-owned companies were included in the population researched by Clarke *et al.* (2007), they emphasized IR regulations, not the role of trade unions, and the interviews were only conducted from an employer and regulator perspective. Further, in Chan's (2011) account, the emphasis is on the events surrounding the strike rather than the role of trade unions within the MNC. Therefore, an understanding of the unions' role in the subsidiaries of MNCs from the perspective of those involved in wildcat strikes, that is, the workers, will give a more complete picture.

## Methodology

The case study is the most appropriate strategy to examine the IR practices of the companies and their relationship with broader company strategies, and to contextualize company practices (Yin 1994; Kelly 1999). Case study research using qualitative methods provides a sophisticated instrument to capture the often subtle, complex and changing ways in which companies operate. Although a quantitative method is very useful in achieving an overview of patterns, it doesn't capture the complexity of the reality and explain the differences in behaviour patterns of the companies.

Interviews were conducted at four Taiwanese companies, focusing on MNCs that have experienced labour strikes in the last five years. Priority was given to firms that have a larger number of employees, where the 'clash' between the management and employees and their representatives is more apparent. The companies are coded as: TW Co1, TW Co2, TW Co3 and TW Co4.

The study took place during late 2005 to early 2010, with two fieldwork trips in Vietnam. Interviews were held with groups of interviewees inside and outside the enterprises. The first group included management, trade union officials and employees at shopfloor level. Conducting interviews at three levels allowed for cross-checking of the information and also helped determine whether the policies described by the management were indeed implemented at the lower level of the organizations. Outside the enterprises, interviews with government officials at national, provincial and local levels were conducted. They provide valuable knowledge of the local environment that foreign-invested firms operate in and help reveal how they come to terms with legal constraints. In total, 39 interviews were carried out, 30 within the four case study companies and nine outside. The average interview took more than one hour. The results of the interviews were strengthened by document analysis and non-participant observation. The combination of data-gathering methods (that is, triangulation) is vital in the case study method for cross-checking data, and thus ensuring reliability (Yin 2003).

*Table 3.1* Interview distribution of the case studies

| Company | Interviews | Board of directors | Human resource manager | Union | Worker |
|---|---|---|---|---|---|
| *Interviews inside companies* | | | | | |
| TW Co1 | 7 | 1 | 1 | 2 | 3 |
| TW Co2 | 7 | 2 | 1 | 1 | 3 |
| TW Co3 | 9 | 1 | 3 | 2 | 3 |
| TW Co4 | 7 | 1 | 2 | 2 | 2 |
| Subtotal | 30 | | | | |
| *Interviews outside companies* | | | | | |
| Subtotal | 9 | | | | |
| Total | 39 | | | | |

## Empirical findings

The Trade Union Law of 1990 indicates that trade unions' roles including providing education to employees regarding labour law and work discipline; organizing social activities; managing the labour force; representing workers in negotiations to resolve labour disputes; representing workers in signing Collective Labour Contracts; and checking on management.

It should be noted that a trade union's mobility is greatly affected by its limited financial resources and the time allocated for leaders and officials. Prior to 1997 companies were required to pay 2 per cent of their payroll to the union's budget (the company unions were allowed to keep 1 per cent and 1 per cent was transferred to the local unions). Since 1997, to improve the investment environment, the government dropped this obligation for foreign-invested enterprises. Their main official financial source is their modest union fees, which are clearly insufficient to pay for the union's activities and finance the salaries of union cadres.

By law, a Vietnamese union official's salary is paid from union funds (Labour Law 1994, Article 15.3), and union finances are sourced from membership fees as well as allocations from state revenue (Labour Law 1994, Article 16.2). This is intended to get the union cadres off the company payroll. In fact, trade union funds have been insufficient to pay the salaries thus making it impossible to maintain full-time company-based union officials. In all the unions investigated, union cadres are also full-time employees who receive a so-called 'supplementary payment' from a higher level of the union (that is, it is a supplement to the salary paid by the companies for their full-time jobs). Some of the union leaders interviewed claimed that they had not received any supplementary payment.

If the firm employs more than 150 persons, the regulation is that companies should allocate six working days for the union president to do union-related work, and if the firm has 80 to 150 workers, three working days (Labour Law 1994, Article 18, Resolution Number 133/HDBT issued on 20 April 1991 by the Minister Council). Managers interviewed acknowledge that the companies are not willing to allow them to have time off for union meetings and activities. In fact, union officers do not formally receive this time off work, they attend to union activities in their own time.

## Organizing social activities

The most recognizable function of a trade union is organizing social activities in the companies and this was their most significant role in the former centrally planned system. In fact, union leaders interviewed said that this is the union's official – and in many cases only – contribution to workers' lives. A cross-check with workers showed that this is the trade union's strongest function and that to the majority of employees the notion of a trade union is linked with 'the organizer of social activities'. This includes sports, recreation, and charity and tourist activities (by themselves and/or in conjunction with locally based or

52    *A. Cox*

occupational unions). Also, unions provide a 'personal touch' by visiting members when sick, attending weddings and funerals of union members and their immediate families, presenting gifts and greetings on birthdays, national holidays, etc. Some unions manage within their budgets, some coordinate with companies. A worker at TW Co1 who identifies trade union with social activities says:

> We do not have a lot of social activities here.... No sport either.... However, the trade union is the one that pays a visit when someone is sick or their family member passes away. They really know what is going on in your personal life, which is nice.

Another worker says:

> The company takes care of us as their 'employees', while the trade union feels more like a 'friend'.

## Resolving labour disputes

In all the companies investigated, the labour–management relationship has deteriorated over the years, with labour disputes unresolved and workers striking, with and without the union leadership. Several strikes at these companies made national headlines during the period 2007–10.

In order to resolve labour disputes, especially in the areas of disciplinary measures and salaries and benefits, the management is required to inform, discuss and agree on the matter with the executive committee of the trade union. However, the nature of the so-called 'discussion' or 'negotiation' between union and management on labour issues is dubious. As TW Co1's trade union chairman says:

> Most of the time, we are not invited to take part in such processes and are simply informed verbally by the management of whatever decisions that they have made.

Furthermore, in the case study companies, there have been several incidents where trade union leaders have sided with the managers and upset employees. This resulted in de facto employee representatives who led 'wildcat strikes', which don't go through the legal procedures and are organized by workers not involving unions.

In 2007, workers at TW Co2 staged a strike demanding better pay and benefits. They complained that besides the low wage of US$44 to US$47.50 per month, the company was also 'harsh and not transparent' in calculating wages. Payments such as social and health insurances, the New Year bonus and maternity leave allowance were normally made late or not at all. Furthermore, many workers protested the factory's policy of searching workers to deter theft. As a TW Co2 factory worker says:

We want to be treated decently. We are poor and need to sell our labour and sweat for a wage but we have as high a self-respect as anyone else! A bodily search is demeaning and makes us appear as either thieves or potential thieves.

The strike at TW Co2 began with 700 workers, however, the numbers rose to 1200 within days. It was only resolved after the provincial trade union stepped in to lead negotiations with the company.

In early 2008, about 2000 workers at TW Co1 went on strike, complaining their wages were not keeping pace with rising consumer prices. In particular, they said the new basic monthly salary from 1 January of VND1,070,000 (approximately US$67) was too low. Recalling the strike, one employee commented that the salary level was 'enough for a single man but not for a family'. Another interviewee added that 'the company made a healthy profit in that year'.

In 2009, TW Co3 workers went on strike demanding the company pay them their year-end bonuses of one month's pay before the start of Tet, the Vietnamese lunar New Year. The company had promised to pay the bonuses before Tet and many of the workers had been counting on them to pay for bus and train tickets to their villages for the holiday. When Tet was approaching and the workers had not received payment, they surrounded the office of the managing director, preventing him from leaving for the holiday. After meeting with local government authorities, soon afterwards the company committed to pay workers a thirteenth month of salary. There have been three wildcat strikes at TW Co3 in recent years, another in 2005 and one in the third quarter of 2009. All three were related to salary payment.

These strikes, which are by no means isolated incidents in the textile and garment industry in Vietnam, confirm the industry's 'race to the bottom', marked by reduced labour rights. In response to this situation, in May 2010 the Vietnam Textile and Apparel Trade Union (representing workers) and the Vietnam Textile and Apparel Association (representing employers) signed a labour pact. The agreement contains 14 conditions on job assurance, minimum salary and overtime pay. It is aimed at reducing the number of strikes both legal and illegal. Under the agreement, if a textile employee works 40 hours per week, the monthly minimum wage will range from VND1.2 million (US$63) to VND1.7 million (US$90). The pact between the trade union and the association also states that employers must consider raising salary grades for their employees every one to two years instead of two to three years regulated by the government.

Writing about 'wildcat strikes', Lee (2006) argues that they involved the majority of an enterprise's workforce and were planned independently, which illustrates that Vietnamese workers have significant ability to coordinate collective action. In 96 per cent of strikes, workers' demands were met (Lee 2006), hence, these 'wildcat strikes' are effective in achieving goals via people power. The 'wildcat strikes' have public support, however, foreign managers are opposed to the government's support, saying it will lead to further stoppages (Lee 2006).

## 54   A. Cox

### Discussions and conclusions

This chapter has argued that the transformation of Vietnamese trade unions, intended by the Labour Law and by Trade Union Laws and related regulations, has had very limited results. The Labour Law 1994 went into effect on 1 January 1995. However, the ideological legacies of socialism and the government's eagerness to maintain labour harmony and to attract foreign capital make for a large gap between the words on paper and the reality of what is implemented.

After the introduction of the Trade Union Constitution in 1993, existing occupational trade unions were to consolidate and strengthen, and new ones were to be established. However, the development and expansion of trade unions in general, and occupational unions in particular, have been constrained by legal and financial difficulties. Any new union needs to be 'approved' by a union at a higher level (Decree 133/HDBT, Article 1.2). Ultimately, the VGCL still has the power to 'decide on the founding or disbanding' of all the confederations and industrial and professional unions (Trade Union Constitution 1993, Article 26). Thus, with the Party behind the VGCL, it is the Party that has the ultimate power of founding and disbanding new unions.

Due to financial limits, in most cases, employees' representatives are chosen from within the companies. Being full-time employees on the company payroll, they are severely constrained in effectively performing their roles representing employees' interests.

At the workplace level, the trade unions' formal activities are limited to arranging holidays, organising social activities with the company's funds, and encouraging workers to fulfil production quotas. These limited activities affect and restrict bargaining rights.

Recent strikes, including 'wildcat strikes' recorded in the case study companies, bring violations of labour laws to attention in the textile and garment industry in Vietnam, while also showing workers taking action to improve their working conditions, instead of claiming their rights in law. The strike movement indicates that workers have begun to perceive that they deserve and could have better working conditions, as well as the power to achieve them. Their once 'silent voice' has become the voice of unofficial union leaders backed by thousands of workers, making them capable of organizing powerful strikes. The findings of our study confirm previous research on strike action in Vietnam (see for example Chan 2011; Kerkvliet 2010), which points to the evolution of a new pattern of strikes and labour disputes, with a shift from rights-based to interest-based disputes. In other words, rather than walking out to claim their rights in law, workers now strike to demand better meals, higher salaries, less overtime – better working conditions than stipulated in law or in labour contracts.

Our findings highlight a number of characteristics of the IR system in Vietnam, some of which are paralleled by its Asian neighbours (see Chan 2011), and others that are arguably unique to the transitory, soft-lined economy of Vietnam. As a centrally planned economy, historically there was no recognition of the difference between government and worker interests (De Silva, n.d.), which is similar to the Chinese context (Chan 2011). Increasing levels of strike activity, particularly by unorganized workers in foreign-owned companies, however, highlight emerging conflict within the system. In fact, the increasing rate of 'wildcat' strikes is one of the more telling findings about this nation in transition.

In particular, the ineffective role played by labour unions in Vietnam has been the key driving force for the increased action taken by unorganized workers. The relative immobility of labour unions is best explored through the lens of Lévesque and Murray's (2002) theory of power resources consisting of three facets: internal solidarity, external solidarity and discursive capacity.

The findings from this study suggest an absence of internal solidarity, with trade unions continuing to play a supportive role to management, similar to their role under the centrally planned economy. They lack democratic structures and have limited financial resources, time and expertise, which renders them powerless. The study supports Chan's (2008) argument that unions do not play a proactive role in supporting the interests of workers. This issue appears as significant in foreign-owned subsidiaries as in some state and private-owned enterprises (Kerkvliet 2008). Moreover, the study found that employees strike in order to get local provincial trade union authorities to negotiate better conditions on their behalf, which is also supported by Chan (2008). While there are still illegal strikes, government authorities are surprisingly tolerant of the breaches (Kerkvliet 2008).

The second aspect of Lévesque and Murray's model is external solidarity which refers to community attachment, relationships with other unions, and alliances with community groups and social movements. A push towards horizontal and vertical integration within the Vietnamese IR system has been facilitated by changes to the regulations. Nonetheless, these findings suggest that this has led to no clear advantage for unions. Rather, the outcome has been reduced effectiveness and more inefficiency due to considerable resource limitations and other institutional factors. Consequently, and as evidenced by Kerkvliet (2008), workers in some companies have initiated wildcat strikes as a means of establishing their own external solidarity by compelling the support of the state and independent labour organizations. While no evidence of seeking external support was encountered in this study, there are signs to support the idea that authorities may be 'attentive' to workers needs once strikes break out in order to stop further disruption and create an impetus for workers to branch out and establish other associations.

Power resources, the third element of Lévesque and Murray's (2002) model, refer to the strategic or discursive capacity of unions to set their own agenda. This study found that, in the Vietnamese context, the lack of separation between union leaders and the companies means they often have the same agenda, and are essentially guided by the company's imperatives. These findings echo the sentiments of the union chairperson interviewed in Chan's (2011) study, which describes the relationship between the union, workers and the company as one of partnership. Chan describes the role of unions as 'working in cooperation' with

56    *A. Cox*

the company and is not 'to struggle on behalf of workers' (2011: 32). Similarly, Kerkvliet (2008) refers to the complacent role played by unions in privately and state-owned enterprises. Rather than support employees' interests these structures effectively reinforce the managerial agenda. At a broader level, the state-socialist regimes' failure to enforce labour reforms, and the abolition of previous requirements to pay 2 per cent of the organizational budget to union fees for foreign-owned companies represent the more debilitating aspects of the institutional environment as far as employees interests are concerned.

The drive for strike action has largely come from workers and has arisen from the ineffectiveness of worker representation (Chan 2011; Kerkvliet 2010; Zhu and Fahey 2000). Indeed, Vietnamese trade unions appear hesitant in their use of strikes, and use them as a last resort. Essentially, this standpoint serves to reinforce the broader political and economic agenda of maintaining Vietnam as an attractive climate for FDI. As a means of luring investors, Vietnam has effectively had to yield to 'the race to the bottom' by reducing labour protection and environmental laws and offering significant tax advantages to promote 'business friendly' conditions (Mantsios 2010; Singh and Zammit 2000; Zhu and Fahey 2000). A similar scenario is true of other Asian nations. For instance, Hewison and Chiu (2009) in their study of the Thai system found state policies restricted labour rights and union participation in decision-making in the IR process. In China, workers cannot expect the support of the state when taking strike action, and often embark on it with an expectation of violent retaliation by both the state and the company (Chan 2011).

Zhu and Fahey's (2000) structural power of capital appears to be an overshadowing force in Vietnam's transitioning economy. They argue that international capital is a key determinant and influencing factor for states' economic decisions. Within this context, Vietnam represents a state that is overly dependent on investment and capital as a means of promoting economic development. The pressure is to create a favourable investment environment for overseas investors. The state's initiatives are hence largely limited by the structural power of capital and the likely outcomes are currently being experienced in Vietnam – restrictions on trade unions, minimal conditions and lack of regulation. Essentially all these factors are aimed at increasing Vietnam's attractiveness for 'regime shoppers'. Consequently, while soft-line, transitional economies such as Vietnam may have experienced reform 'on the books', the progression of these reforms is stunted by the state's political and economic agenda.

Clarke *et al.* (2007) and De Silva (n.d.) show the trade unions' inability to manage working conditions in Vietnam, claiming that an institutional framework that prevents initial action is lacking. There needs to be an effective mechanism to resolve conflict of interest between employers and employees that leads to a compromise embodied in collective agreements. Both De Silva (n.d.) and Clarke *et al.* (2007) see this as the system's weakness. As Clarke *et al.* point out: 'This systemic weakness is a reflection of the weakness of workplace trade unions and their failure to articulate the aspirations of their members' (2007: 565). In Vietnam trade unions either exist through a dependency on management structures or are integrated with management, or don't exist in the case of non-state enterprises. Furthermore, union representatives have limited accountability to members, so represent them on a very basic level, and training and support is not given to them (trade union officials) regarding collective bargaining (Clarke *et al.* 2007). The union framework, therefore, is not equipped to effectively handle disputes and so workers have more positive outcomes through striking.

The concern is that Vietnam is fast becoming a nation where the labour system subordinates workers to capital – an ironic situation when one considers the traditional role of the state was to protect the working class from such agendas. The history of trade unions in Vietnam is tightly linked with the Communist Party regimes fighting against western imperialism and domination (Warner and Zhu 2010). In a regulatory sense, unions and the government share a view of the role of the socialist state as the protector of the working class from 'capitalist exploitation'. This mindset has persisted despite Vietnam's business environment undergoing considerable transformation with more liberal political and economic policies, which have made way for an influx of FDI. In other words, the transformation of the business environment is yet to be matched by a change in fundamental belief systems of union leaders. Continuing state involvement in IR institutions is therefore not recognized as having the potential to prove detrimental to the wellbeing of employees, and thus, there is little motivation to change the current system.

From the company perspective, the prime motivations for continued investment in countries like Vietnam and Thailand are to take advantage of relatively cheap labour and weak IR systems that place the balance of power in the hands of managers. The 'socialist' union structure is considered beneficial to business as it minimizes conflict. Both the formal and informal institutions that regulate employment relations in effect allow the workforce to be controlled with greater ease and hence, there are multiple advantages to be gained from maintaining the status quo (Fahey and Zhu 2000; Warner and Zhu 2010).

## References

Chan, A. (2011) 'Strikes in China's export industries in comparative perspective', *The China Journal*, 65: 28–51.

Chan, A. and Norlund, I. (1998) 'Vietnamese and Chinese labour regimes: on the road to divergence', *The China Journal*, 40: 173–97.

Clarke, S., Lee, C. and Chi, D. (2007) 'From rights to interests: the challenge of industrial relations in Vietnam', *Journal of Industrial Relations*, 49: 545.

Cox, R. W. (1994) 'Global restructuring: making sense of the changing international political economy', in R. Stubbs and G. R. D. Underbill (eds), *Political Economy and the Changing Global Order*, New York: St Martin's Press, pp. 45–59.

De Silva, S. R. (n.d.) 'Elements of a sound industrial relations system', International Labour Organization Publications, Bangkok, www.ilo.org/public/english/dialogue/actemp/downloads/publications/srseleme.pdf (accessed 4 December 2014).

Dunlop, J. T. (1958) *Industrial Relations Systems*, New York: Holt.

58   *A. Cox*

Flanders, A. (1965) *Industrial Relations: What is Wrong with the System?* London: Faber and Faber.

General Statistics Office (GSO) (2005) *Statistical Yearbook 2004*, Hanoi: GSO.

Geppert, M. and Williams, K. (2006) 'Global, national and local practices in multinational corporations: towards a socio-political framework', *International Journal of Human Resource Management*, 17(1): 4969.

Gospel, H. and Palmer, G. (1993) *British Industrial Relations*, London: Routledge.

Hewison, K. and Chiu C. C. H. (2009) 'Hong Kong-invested companies in Thailand: labour relations and practices', *Journal of Contemporary Asia*, 39(1): 1–22.

Hyman, R. (1975) *Industrial Relations: A Marxist Introduction*, Basingstoke: Macmillan.

International Labour Organization (ILO) and International Finance Corporation (IFC), (2011) *Better Work Vietnam: Garment Industry, 2nd Compliance Synthesis Report*, Geneva: ILO.

Kelly, D. (1999) 'Making a good case: the case study', in D. Kelly (ed.), *Researching Industrial Relations*, 2nd edn, Sydney: Federation Press, pp. 119–35.

Kelly, J. and Kelly, C. (1991) ' "Them and us": social psychology and "The New Industrial Relations" ', *British Journal of Industrial Relations*, 29(1): 25–48.

Kelly, J. E. and Nicholson, N. (1980) 'The causation of strikes: review of theoretical approaches and potential contribution of social psychology', *Human Relations*, 33: 853–83.

Kerkvliet, B. (2010) 'Workers' protests in contemporary Vietnam (with some comparisons to those in the pre-1975 South)', *Journal of Vietnamese Studies*, 5(1): 162–204.

Le, D. D. (1997) 'Legal consequences of state-owned enterprise reform', in N. C. Yuen, N. J. Freeman and F. H. Huynh (eds), *State-owned Enterprise Reform in Vietnam. Lessons from Asia*, Singapore: Institute of Southeast Asian Studies, pp. 63–76.

Le, L. S. (2008) 'Labor vs market in Vietnam', *Asia Times Online*, 5 April, www.atimes.com/atimes/Southeast_Asia/JD05Ae02.html, (accessed 11 August 2011).

Lee, C. H. (2006) 'Recent industrial relations developments in China and Viet Nam: the transformation of industrial relations in East Asian transition economies', *Journal of Industrial Relations*, 48(3): 415–29.

Lévesque, C. and Murray, G. (2002) 'Trade union cross-border alliances within MNCs: disentangling union dynamics at the local, national and international levels', *Industrial Relations Journal*, 41(4): 312–32.

Majendie, A., Anstey, C. and Swardson, A. (2011) 'Vietnam cheaper-than-China appeal diminishes as labor strikes', *Hansafx*, 16 June, http://hansafx.net/blog/?p=5969 (accessed 11 August 2011).

Mantsios, G. (2010) 'Vietnam at the crossroads', *New Labor Forum*, 19(1): 32–9.

Ministry of Planning and Investment (MPI) (2012) 'Vietnam's FDI figures, June 23, 2011', http://fia.mpi.gov.vn/News.aspx?ctl=newsdetail&p=2.46&aID=1093 (accessed 28 August 2012).

Mirza, H. and Giroud, A. (2004) 'Regional integration and benefits from foreign direct investment in ASEAN countries: the case of Vietnam', *Asian Development Economic Review*, 21(1): 66–98.

Singh, A. and Zammit, A. (2000) *The Global Labour Standards Controversy: Critical Issues for Developing Countries*. Geneva: South Centre.

Tran, V. H. (ed.) (1997) *Economic Development and Prospects in the ASEAN: Foreign Investment and Growth in Vietnam, Thailand, Indonesia, and Malaysia*, London: Palgrave Macmillan.

Vo, A. N. (2009) *The Transformation of Human Resource Management and Industrial Relations in Vietnam*, Oxford: Chandos.

Warner, M. and Zhu, Y. (2010) 'Labour and management in the People's Republic of China: seeking the "harmonious society"', *Asia Pacific Business Review*, 16(3): 285–98.

Yin, R. K. (1994) *Case Study Research: Design and Method*, 2nd edn, London: Sage.

Yin, R. K. (2003) *Applications of Case Study Research*, London: Sage.

Zhu, Y. (2002) 'Economic reform and human resource management in Vietnam', *Asia Pacific Business Review*, 8(3): 115–35.

Zhu, Y. and Fahey, S. (2000) 'The challenges and opportunities for the trade union movement in the transition era: two socialist market economies – China and Vietnam', *Asia Pacific Business Review*, 6(3): 282–99.

# 4 Before Rana Plaza

## Towards a history of labour organizing in Bangladesh's garment industry

*Dina Siddiqi*

The April 2013 collapse of Rana Plaza, with its attendant death and destruction, is widely seen as a wake-up call for Bangladesh's ready-made garment industry. The title of a report issued by the Center for Business and Human Rights at New York University, *Business as Usual is Not an Option*, captures the general mood of those associated directly or indirectly with the industry, from buyers and intermediate brokers in the global commodity chain to governments, labour advocates and multilateral organizations (Labowitz and Baumann-Pauly 2014).[1] Faced with the worst ever industrial disaster in the country, the government rushed through passage of the Bangladesh Labour (Amendment) Act, 2013 less than three months after the collapse. Hailed as pro-worker by mainstream commentators, the amended labour law – among other things – appeared to remove extant barriers to freedom of association, setting trade unionism 'free', as the country's leading English language newspaper proclaimed proudly (*Daily Star*, 15 July 2013).

Indeed, the number of registered trade unions rose dramatically in the following months. By December 2013, 96 new unions sought registration from the Directorate of Labour (DoL), compared to only two in the previous two years (ILO 2014). Within just over a year, the garment sector had a total of 464 trade unions, up from 132 in 2012 (ILO 2015). With respect to union formation at least, the amended labour law seems to have 'paved the way to improve conditions, workers' rights' (ILO 2014a). At an orientation programme on Freedom of Association for leaders of such unions, an ILO representative declared, 'The formation and registration of new trade unions is the sign of a new era of collective bargaining and freedom of association in Bangladesh which can act as a catalyst for change in other industries' (ILO 2014b). In contrast, left-wing commentators and activists were considerably less sanguine, viewing these new unions with deep suspicion or dismissing them as the equivalent of company shops (Moshrefa Mishu, Garment Workers Unity Forum 2016).

This chapter seeks to complicate the understanding of Rana Plaza as a moment of rupture by situating the new trade unionism within a longer history of labour activism in Bangladesh. The implicitly modernist narrative arc that structures mainstream accounts of the post Rana Plaza period – of individual 'tragedy' in the global South that spurs legal reform and improved oversight through the application of external/Northern pressure – obscures critical ground

*Before Rana Plaza* 61

realities. The persuasive power of this narrative depends upon the active forgetting of the past in which workers have secured meaningful change only after embarking on direct action through often violent street politics.

The ultimate success of the story of legal reforms, of gains obtained through the exercise of newly formed citizenship rights, hinges on the formation of modern labour subjectivity (of individuals armed with knowledge of laws and their rights), waiting to be called into being. In this account, the absence of the modern worker who knows and demands her rights signals the failure of the elite/state/NGOs to produce a culture of liberalism in which such subjectivities seemingly flourish (see Prashad 2015). Recalling a mode of developmentalism rooted in colonial hierarchies, this construction not only displaces structural inequalities and barriers, it erases the agency of Bangladeshi garment workers and their rich history of resistance. The focus on individual consciousness renders invisible the structures of power through which some accounts are privileged while others are dismissed.

Keeping the above in mind, I look to an early moment of labour resistance in order to complicate the view of Rana Plaza as absolute rupture. Through a close reading of a workers' uprising in May 2006 that resulted in significant gains for labour, I suggest that fundamental contradictions and constraints remain untouched by the kind of reforms made after 2013. The situation calls for historicizing as well as the interrogation of the broader political context, including *processes* of union formation, and the level of managerial discretion in determining membership and agenda. After all, unions can have a potentially useful role in containing labour struggles as well as promoting them. It is equally critical to situate the new international recognition of the need for unions to ensure workers rights in shifting ideologies of neoliberal governance.

The chapter is organized into five parts. Section 1 lays out the basic parameters of the apparel export sector, contextualizing its remarkable growth and its significance for the contemporary national economy. The next section sketches the conditions under which trade unions came to operate in colonial Bengal/East Pakistan (later Bangladesh). A brief literature review then examines the major structural constraints to labour organizing in general and the garment sector in particular. Section 4 focuses on the 'uprising' or 'labour unrest' of 2006. The following section offers an assessment of post Rana Plaza unions. Who controls these unions? What kinds of actions are they willing to take and what do they avoid? What kinds of solidarity can they expect from unions and workers in other sectors?

## The Made in Bangladesh label

### *Serendipity by design?*

Any analysis of labour organizing in Bangladesh must keep in mind the conditions of precarity under which the garment industry 'took off', the position of the country within global political-economic structures and so the predicaments

## 62   D. Siddiqi

for labour this particular context produces. Bangladesh's exclusive 'comparative advantage' is its cheap(ened) and relatively unskilled female labour force. As a consequence, the repression of labour can be justified as a valid 'cost' of maintaining the nation's competitive edge, represented as an issue of vital national interest.

The region that is Bangladesh today was renowned earlier as the land of jute, the golden fibre. By the time the garment industry emerged, the demand for Bangladesh's primary export product, jute, was in steep decline. It is a testament to the enduring symbolic significance of the jute economy that some garment workers, in a bid to transcend their stigmatized identities, sought to recast themselves as the Golden Girls of Bengal (see Siddiqi 2009).

Once it took root, the apparel export sector in Bangladesh grew in a spectacular fashion. In 1978, the founder of Desh Garments, acknowledged as the pioneer in the field, signed a five-year agreement with South Korean conglomerate Daewoo. In return for technical and marketing cooperation, Daewoo received 8 per cent commission on all Desh Garment apparel exports. Existing sources do not indicate whether and what kind of knowledge on labour management or industrial relations the South Koreans imparted to the 180 Desh supervisors and managers trained at Daewoo's Pusan garment plant. South Korea's record on this front is not promising. Regardless, within two years, Desh Garments began operations in its Chittagong factory (then the largest in Asia outside South Korea) with 600 workers in six production lines, a capacity of five million pieces a year and $1.3 million in investment (Mahmud 2010: 6).

The industry soon established itself as a central engine of the national economy, in terms of employment, foreign exchange revenue and multiplier effects. In 1984, 385 factories produced for the global market (Shahidur Rahman). Since then, by one estimate, the average growth rate from FY 1983–4 through FY 2009–10 was as high as 20.1 per cent (Yunus and Yamagata 2014). Accordingly, the number of factories registered with the Bangladesh Garment Manufacturers and Employers' Association (BGMEA, established in 1982) went from 3480 in FY 2000–1 to 4296 in FY 2013–14 (BGMEA 2015).[2] Although several Export Processing Zones (EPZs) were established near Dhaka and the port City of Chittagong, currently only 257 of all enterprises are based inside EPZs.[3]

The industry's increasing significance to the national economy can be gauged by the fact that from the mid-1980s until quite recently, total exports and garment exports grew more or less at the same rate (Yunus and Yanagata 2014). During FY 2013–14, RMG exports totalled US$24.5 billion. In the third quarter of 2015, apparel exports accounted for 82 per cent of total export earnings (Bangladesh Bank 2015). At the global level as well, the industry made its mark. By 2010, Bangladesh was already the second largest exporter of garments in the world, behind China (BGMEA). It has continued to hold on to this position despite predictions to the contrary following the 2008 recession and competition from other low wage economies such as Myanmar and Ethiopia.

The garment industry employs an estimated 4.2 million workers today, of whom 60–80 per cent is female.[4] Feminists, as well as owners and policy makers frequently hail garment work as initiating a silent revolution in gender relations, offering a critical site of female empowerment (Azim 2005; Siddiqi 2009). To the rest of the world, Bangladesh's garment sector is known primarily for its feminized labour force, represented either as victimized sweatshop workers in need of rescue or as active subjects emancipated through entry into capitalist modernity (Siddiqi 2014). It is often forgotten, however, that an acute crisis in the countryside – of dispossession, displacement through natural disasters and stagnation in the agricultural sector – provided a seemingly elastic supply of labour. In unanticipated numbers, women and girls flooded into the capital Dhaka and the port city of Chittagong in search of a livelihood. The possibility of escape from poverty and into formal employment also transformed gendered patterns of migration. For the first time, large numbers of women migrated singly.

The phenomenal success of 'garments' is often recounted as the story of heroic individual entrepreneurs risking their financial futures for the sake of the nation (see the BGMEA website). Alternately, it is 'a story of leaks, unintended consequences, and increasing returns' (Easterly quoted in Mahmud 2010: 6). In this paternalist re-telling, it is Daewoo's business expertise, shared with a select group of Desh Garments employees who then 'leaked' this secret knowledge to others that is ultimately responsible for global success. The condescension here is hard to miss. As it happened, converging national and global factors under-wrote the remarkable expansion of the sector in its first two decades.

Along with changes in international trade agreements, the nascent garment industry benefited greatly from a complex interplay of shifting 'local' and global policy prescriptions. By the early 1980s, the socialist policies of Bangladesh's first post-war government had been replaced by the unreserved embrace of open market policies. The militarized regimes of General Zia (1975–81) and General Ershad (1982–90) favoured and enabled this distinct ideological shift.

Around the same time, international financial institutions actively endorsed structural adjustment policies, 'free trade', and export oriented industrialization as pathways to economic development. Southern nations were compelled to liberalize trade policies in order to compete in the new regime of globalization. Bangladesh's extreme dependence on donor funded development pushed the nation toward market liberalization. The 'structural adjustment' upon which International Monetary Fund (IMF) and World Bank loans were conditional ensured that the country's macro-economic policies leaned heavily toward privatization and trade liberalization. With the closing of jute, sugar and other mills, investors in the apparel sector were prime beneficiaries of state support for the export economy.

The resurgence of 'free market' ideologies and neoliberal approaches to development also corresponded to the emergence of the global factory. By the 1980s, rising wages and labour-protective legislation prompted many Northern corporations to relocate manufacturing units out of the United States and Europe to Asia and Central/Latin America. Multinationals in search of ever cheaper labour established post-Fordist, 'flexible' assembly line production across

64   *D. Siddiqi*

national borders. This relentless search for increasing returns effectively *cheapened* labour as Southern economies vied with one another to attract multinational corporations, in what has been called a race to the bottom.

The global factory also brought about major shifts in the international division of labour. A predominantly female, 'third world' migrant labour force characterized the new global assembly line. As such, the emergent proletariat was raced, classed and gendered in ways that reflected older colonial and imperial divisions of consumption and production, as well as of wealth and inequality. Labour precarity – high turnover, job insecurity and casualization – marked work in export factories in Bangladesh as elsewhere. Bangladesh was well-placed to compete in this environment, which relied on a specific presumptive labour subjectivity of 'third world women' – docile, nimble fingered and willing to work for very little. The seemingly elastic supply of young, female rural migrants, and the lowest labour costs in the world made the country an appealing destination. Until December 2013, Bangladeshi workers earned the lowest wages in the world – around BD Tk.3000, which is roughly \$38. The new minimum monthly wage of BD Tk.5,300 (just over \$66) represents a 77 per cent increase. Notably, the government's decision to raise wages came after worker protests shut down around 100 factories in Ashulia, Savar, in November 2013 (Devnath 2013).

Last but not least, the unfolding effects of the 1974 Multi-Fibre Arrangement (MFA) of the General Agreement on Tariffs and Trade (GATT) enhanced Bangladesh's competitiveness as a garment-manufacturing destination at a critical juncture of the industry's formation. The MFA, meant as a temporary measure, imposed quotas on yarn, garments and textile exports from 'developing' countries to 'developed' economies. The idea was to ease the passage into 'free trade' of older industrialized economies by giving them time to adjust to low cost, low wage imports from the global South. Designed as a protectionist measure for Europe and the US, the MFA inadvertently helped 'emerging' economies such as Bangladesh (Bannerjee 2014). Established manufacturing countries such as South Korea found their access to markets in Europe and America blocked. In an effort to bypass MFA rules of origin, they began to outsource the 'Cutting and Making' of garments to nations such as Bangladesh, which were not subject to the same strictures. The quota regime proved to be a boon to Bangladeshi investors and the government, which dispensed licenses liberally to those it wished to patronize. It is no small irony that until the MFA expired in 2004, the spectre of other countries' lost manufacturing opportunities underwrote the Made in Bangladesh label.

## Colonial legacies and capitalist presents

To understand the relative dearth of organized union activity before Rana Plaza, it is essential to contextualize the structural weakness of union activity in the country as a whole. Despite – or perhaps as a result of – their historical role in anti-colonial and nationalist struggles, trade unions in contemporary Bangladesh possess minimal leverage in the public sphere, tend to be highly politicized in their agendas, and are widely perceived as corrupt and self-serving organizations.

First formed under conditions of colonial rule, the appropriation of labour unions into political movements laid the foundations for a peculiar mode of politicization and extreme partisanship in postcolonial Bangladesh. Unions associated with the two main industries in British India, jute and textiles, quickly became part of broader anti-colonial struggles. Given their power to mobilize large groups of workers on the streets, labour unions became 'key organizations on the national political stage' (Rahman and Langford 2012).

A related but different legacy of the anti-colonial struggle, one rarely taken into account in analyses of contemporary labour mobilizations are the particular registers of public protest, 'of breaking the law peacefully', that are deeply embedded, across the political landscape 'as a set of possible languages of political expression and dissent' (Hansen 2008: 3). These possible languages include gheraos, blockades, sit-ins and hunger strikes, all modes of protest invoked by the labour movement in Bangladesh at various moments in recent history.

The 1947 partition, which produced independent India and the two wings of Pakistan (East Pakistan became the independent nation of Bangladesh in 1971), did not interrupt the pattern of political unionism established earlier. Pakistan's first military ruler, General Ayub Khan, introduced factory-level unions to counter what he saw as undesirable communist inroads as well as to extend his regime's hegemony over the working class. The Pakistani state's hostility toward communism and progressives/leftists in the labour movement represented a critical feature of the country's evolving Cold War alliance with the United States. After a formal ban on the Communist Party came into place in 1954, progressive workers and organizers were forced underground. Political and union leaders found themselves under mass arrest during the martial law period. It was during the early stages of the cold war soon after independence that the International Confederation of Free Trade Unions (ICFTU) and the US based AFL-CIO first became active in East Pakistan. The AFL-CIO practiced 'Cold War Trade Union Imperialism', consolidating anti-communist trade union movements, long before its formalized overseas front the Asian American Free Labor Institute (AAFLI) was set up in 1968 (Rahman and Langford 2014: 174). AAFLI was originally targeted at labour in Vietnam, soon expanded its operations to include the Philippines and other Asian and Pacific countries. By the 1990s, it supported unions in approximately 30 countries in Asia, the Pacific and the Middle East, with resident representatives in Bangladesh, Indonesia, South Korea, the Philippines, Thailand and Turkey (Sims 1999: 59).

East Pakistan's labour movement was further divided by the ideological differences between the two opposition parties, the Awami League (AL) and the explicitly left-leaning National Awami Party (NAP) at the forefront of the struggle against West Pakistani economic and cultural hegemony in the 1950s and 1960s. Both NAP and the AL sponsored their own trade union federations. As in the anti-colonial period, union activities became subservient to the immediate needs and strategies of the party and the nationalist struggle. Workers were as involved as students in the mass upsurges of 1968–9, the strikes, blockades and torch processions that ultimately forced the military to call the first parliamentary elections in Pakistan's history.

The Awami League government of newly independent Bangladesh should have been labour friendly. It espoused explicitly socialist values, nationalized key industries and enacted several pro-labour laws. Unfortunately, geo-political and other considerations not entirely within its control soon compelled the new government to dispense with much of its socialist inclinations (Siddiqi 2010). Nationalization effectively politicized labour unions further. The result, among other things, was an increasingly authoritarian bent that eventually rendered the polity into a one party state. All trade unions – regardless of individual ideology – were forcibly incorporated into the ruling party's labour front. The more progressive voices were silenced or forced underground.

A bloody coup in 1975 in which the nation's founder Sheikh Mujib, along with members of his family, was murdered, ushered in 15 years of military rule during which time free market, neoliberal policies geared toward economic growth were consolidated. General Ziaur Rahman initially banned all union activity, but later rescinded the ban with severe restrictions. He also directed each political party to set up its own labour front, effectively diluting the impact of any independent militant unions (Ross 2014: 11). In a bid to secure political legitimacy, General Zia soon established his own political party, the Bangladesh Nationalist Party (BNP), whose labour front was set up in 1979. Sensing the power of organized labour, Zia is said to have bought off labour leaders from the right as well as the pro-Beijing left (Rahman and Langford 2012).

Zia initiated the privatization of state enterprises, a process his military successor, General H. M. Ershad carried forward. The large-scale retrenchment that followed weakened the labour movement greatly. Against the odds, and in response, existing private sector unions formed Sromik Kormochari Oikya Parishad (Workers Employees Unity Council) or SKOP. Despite mounting considerable resistance, SKOP was not able to generate pro-labour policies. Continuing privatization resulted in a steep decline in unionization from which the country has never quite recovered. As unions affiliated with the ruling party spent their energies competing over political patronage and resources, state repression – by the police, army or increasingly by paramilitary forces – of independent labour became the norm.

The reinstatement of parliamentary democracy in 1990 did little to shift the prospects of improved workers' rights since both the AL and BNP, which alternated in power until recently, embrace similar ideologies of free trade, open markets and export oriented development. Currently, the government has an 'Open Door' policy with respect to foreign direct investment (BEPZA). Whatever their other ideological conflicts, both parties concur that economic policy should be geared toward growth, in this case, toward securing the stability and expansion of the garment industry, whatever the implications for workers' rights.

As Rahman and Langford remark, the national political context in which the garment industry took off in Bangladesh in the 1980s was not exactly propitious for labour organizing (2012). In the first place, all struggles were subordinated to the struggle to restore parliamentary democracy. So it was that the lone organization to mobilize garment workers, the Workers' Party, ultimately subordinated worker's interests to the political agenda of bringing down military rule. Second, as noted earlier, this was the phase of globalization when Southern nations were compelled to liberalize trade policies, as conditionality for loans but also to stay competitive under new global conditions. States desperate to retain foreign direct investment actively suppressed, often brutally, worker resistance and protest. Bangladesh was no different.

By this time, progressive, leftist organizations had been marginalized, if not decimated. As for the rest, mandated affiliation with political parties produced intensely clientelist relations. It was not only that party interests always trumped those of workers but the very idea of what constituted workers' interests seemed to have been set aside. In the circumstances, the stereotype of mainstream unions as corrupt, nepotistic and ineffective in promoting and protecting labour rights may not be too far from the truth. According to one study, the majority of Ready Made Garment (RMG) owners in the 1980s perceived unions as undesirable because they [owners] were still 'at the formative phase of their manufacturing businesses', and could not afford to be distracted by 'unreasonable' demands or 'unnecessary interruptions', by labour leaders who 'might try to pursue their own selfish agenda *in the name of workers' participation*' (Khan 2001: 169, italics added). Here we see owners deploying popular negative associations of unions to undermine genuine claims of labour.

## Trade unions in contemporary Bangladesh: a review of the literature

Until recently, scholarship on unions in Bangladesh focused almost exclusively on public sector, male dominated formations. Studies of the apparel sector, in contrast, concentrated overwhelming on female empowerment or lack thereof, or on health and safety issues. However, in the last decade the question of why garment workers 'fail to mobilize' has preoccupied scholars across the political spectrum.

The general impression that unions in the RMG sector are weak or non-existent is not entirely accurate. On the contrary, the bewildering array of garment workers' federations is difficult to keep track of at times. In 1996, S. I. Khan recorded the existence of five registered federations and ten unregistered ones. Of the five registered, one was inactive; of the ten non-registered organizations, one was active full time (Khan 2001: 178). The fluid, often shadowy and somewhat indeterminate nature of federations renders the problem of numbers difficult to resolve definitively. It is possible however to get a sense of scale. A recent newspaper story lists nine 'leading' federations of garment workers, though there is no elaboration of the criteria used for inclusion into the category. According to this list, reproduced below in a bar chart, in the middle of 2014, the number of individual unions was 142. This is in contrast to the ILO figure of 437

68  D. Siddiqi

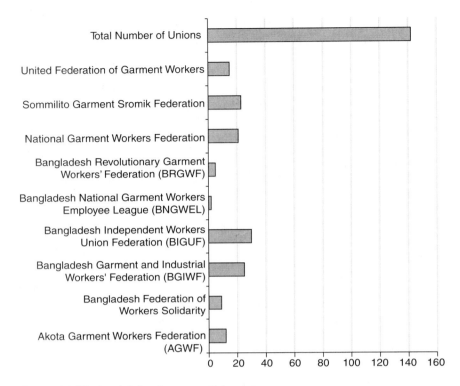

*Figure 4.1* Workers' federations: a partial count.

referred to earlier. In either case, the numbers constitutes a tiny proportion of the labour force of around 4 million working in over 4000 factories.

Curiously, the list above excludes Garment SramikOikkya Forum (Garment Workers Union Federation) and Bangladesh Garment Workers Trade Unity Council (BGWTUC), two small left wing federations that were critical to the 2006 mobilization.

Instead, the editorial to which the list of federations (in graph form) was appended, expressed serious concern regarding recently registered trade unions which, it pointed out, were overwhelmingly affiliated with a single US based NGO, the Solidarity Centre. Acknowledging the need for legitimate unions, the editorial observed that the Centre's accountability was to a foreign organization, 'with motives that do not align with our national interests'. This line of argument is not too far from left progressive critiques of the current spate of internationally sanctioned monitoring and organizing around the garment industry. Questions of accountability and national sovereignty have been paramount in relation to the much-lauded Accord on Fire and Safety (Siddiqi 2015). Yet when such an analysis comes from an avowedly liberal newspaper, owned in part by industrialists with ties to the ruling party, the question of 'national interest', always an opaque category,

*Before Rana Plaza*   69

becomes even more fraught. Whose nation and whose interests are served when the rhetoric of nation appears to be pitted directly against the interests of labour?

As in other fields, the lines between unions and NGOs in garments are frequently blurred in the Bangladeshi context. Several NGOs provide legal support and training on national and international labour rights to workers. They run the gamut, in terms of founding ideologies, funding sources and programmatic approaches. Long-time Bangladeshi NGOs such as INCIDIN Bangladesh and Bangladesh Legal Aid and Services Trust (BLAST), offer programmes for garment workers as part of a broader agenda for the promotions of social justice. NGOs founded exclusively to deal with labour issues, such as The Bangladesh Centre for Worker Solidarity (BCWS) and the Awaj Foundation operate on a somewhat different register. Executive Director Kalpona Akter who set up BCWS in 1991 makes clear that her organization eschews any form of street protest. A 'close partner' of the Washington DC based, AFL CIO affiliated Solidarity Centre, BCWS offers training on labour rights and union formation, in addition to running a day care centre for the children of garment workers (Solidarity Centre 2012). The Awaj Foundation, which, according to its website currently has over 37,000 members and 37 full-time staff, helps settle 'thousands of disputes' regarding wages, overtime, holidays and maternity leave in hundreds of factories. Awaj founder Nazma Akter was originally a member of BIGUF, a federation closely associated with AAFLI in its early days. Kalpana and Nazma, both former garment workers themselves, are perhaps best known outside of Bangladesh. In contrast, the much smaller and radical Garment Sromik Shonghoti (Garment Workers Solidarity), a non-registered organization, does not accept foreign funds but engages in long-term worker mobilization. The Shonghoti coordinator, award winning photographer Taslima Akter has, with the help of colleagues, painstakingly documented the lives of the dead and the missing in Rana Plaza.

Plant level unions are rarely sustainable in the long run without assistance from federations. Individual units tend to fall inactive after an initial period of action either out of fear of harassment and intimidation (or alternately inducements by management to refrain from action).[5] The expulsion or dismissal of unit leaders on charges of 'misconduct', threats of physical violence by hired thugs and lodging false cases are standard retaliatory responses from management (Khan 2001). Most workers cannot afford to fight legal charges or even to pay union dues regularly. Federations ensure some kind of financial sustainability in the circumstances.

It is tempting to attribute the lack of formal labour mobilization to the particular characteristics of the workforce. Most workers are young female migrants from rural areas with little formal education, minimal or no experience of industrial labour and shaped by a 'culturally embedded deference to male authority'. While such features are no doubt disadvantageous in specific situations, they do not seem to have prevented the numerous spontaneous protests and wildcat strikes typical of the industry from its inception. In other words, a culturalist analysis, relying on tropes of deference, industrial inexperience and lack of knowledge provides a partial and ultimately inadequate explanatory framework.

70  *D. Siddiqi*

Explicitly left wing commentators attribute low rates to several factors including, 'fierce owner opposition,' state-sanctioned repression, high labour turnover and lack of industrial experience as first generation workers (see, for instance, Ross 2014: 11). Others look to institutional culture as well as specifically gendered life cycle issues that might dissuade female workers from organizing formally. The garment workers to whom Mahmud spoke reported feeling isolated, with no external support when they raised their voice in protest. They had little incentive to go further. These workers saw themselves as temporarily in the workforce (before marriage or childbirth) therefore lacked what the author calls professional ambition. Mahmud reports that the workers had not absorbed the need for industrial regulations and discipline; at the same time they faced unprofessional conduct from management which had yet to acquire a culture of accountability (Mahmud 2010: 9–10). Mahmud also remarks that conditions of easy entry and exit, combined with informal and personalized recruiting techniques, also discourage collective action, with both employers and workers taking advantage of the possibility for high turnover. Finally, Mahmud argues that poverty and the lack of alternatives compels workers to accept exploitative labour conditions. The analysis, although useful in highlighting key issues, does not offer a sense of how these different factors should be weighted in relation to one another.

Informality is a recurring theme in the literature. Ahmed and Nathan (2014) remark that high rates of turnover (with attrition rates between 5 and 12 per cent) indicate that it is relatively easy for garment workers to move from one workplace to another. The rapid expansion of the industry, the authors suggest, has increasingly opened up more exit options for workers, allowing them to have greater 'voice' than in the past. (This suggestion is echoed to a certain extent by Mahmud 2010). In their words, the ability to switch jobs, 'reduces the pressure to remain quiet about the negative aspects in any job, or, [...] in Hirshmanian terms, the possibility of exit gives more voice' (Ahmed and Nathan 2014: 15).

The relationship between the right to exit, voice and agency may be less straightforward than theorized by Ahmed and Nathan. In the first place, high turnover is not new but has characterized garment work from the outset. Ironically, high turnover is cited as one reason for the non-sustainability of plant level unionization (Khan 2001: 174). Second, as we will see, the right *not to exit* (through unfair dismissals, or lodging of false criminal cases, for instance), rather than ease of exit is generally of more concern to workers. The pressure to remain quiet appears to be related to the relative ease with which dismissed workers can be replaced by others.

An early study by S. I. Khan foregrounds reasons for low levels of unionization that continue to have resonance today (2001). Drawing on data collected in 1996, Khan mapped the ways state and capital – in elaborate collusion with each other – systematically deployed a variety of bureaucratic power as well as, often violent, forms of policing to suppress attempts to organize labour. Rahman and Langford's research, as well as my own experience, bears out the relevance of the issues raised by Khan (Rahman and Langford 2012).

Until the 2013 reforms, unions registration required at least 30 per cent worker representation of an enterprise, approval from relevant state authorities and was subject to cancellation at any time by the Registrar of Unions (with the permission of the Labour Court). Thus the Directorate of Labour, which supervises the process, wields enormous power, exercised as much through inaction and stalling tactics as through direct action. Such power also renders the DoL open to influence from all kinds of external actors.

Khan reports that the DoL routinely refused registration to independent left leaning unions, even if their paperwork was in perfect order, including proof of 30 per cent support at the workplace (Khan 2001: 197). Thus, the culling of radical voices happens at the source. Should such applications slip through, their initiators would confront a host of other obstacles. Close ties between the DoL and factory owners/management enabled the latter to obstruct any effort at union formation. A 'working relation' with the Directorate of Labour, as well as placing 'spies' in the workforce itself, secures an elaborate and efficient network of surveillance. Khan found that DoL employees routinely tipped off owners about pending or newly accepted applications. Individuals responsible for initiating the effort, along with those who signed on in support of unions, were invariably subjected to retaliation by the management. Reprisal took many forms. Most obviously, workers marked as troublemakers would be summarily dismissed, and their names circulated and publicized to enable blacklisting as a whole.

Intimidation and physical torture are other routinized modes of dealing with worker 'unrest' or efforts at unionization. Most factory owners maintain private security forces, which have close ties to the police. Labour leaders demanding back pay or better treatment find themselves threatened with violence or faced actual beatings (Khan 2001). It continues to be common practice (and public knowledge) that factory owners hire local *mastan* or thugs to rough up and intimidate workers they perceive as difficult or outspoken. This often takes place with the active cooperation of the police or paramilitary forces. Labour leaders also find themselves saddled with numerous cases. Suffice it to say, none of these strategies is exclusive either to the garment industry or to Bangladesh.

More striking perhaps are documented cases of owners choosing to close down factories following a successful union drive rather than face the prospect of negotiating with unionized workers (Rahman and Langford 2012: 176). Closing down factories is an expensive proposition. The extraordinary antipathy toward unions deserves further exploration. S. I. Khan notes that the first generation of factory owners maintained a strong grip on management and labour relations by taking 'advantage' of informal labour recruitment practices and work place policies (2001: 168). Practices in question include recruiting workers without appointment letters, and authorizing supervisory staff to hire and fire semi-skilled casual workers. Here I can only speculate but perhaps it was the fear of a more formalized management structure – the potential loss of conditions of control on which low labour costs hinged– that explains the extent to which some factory owners went to avoid unions in their own factories.

72   D. Siddiqi

Discharging workers recruited 'informally', that is without a formal appointment letter, is relatively simple since in the absence of documentary evidence of employment, workers cannot contest arbitrary dismissals.[6] Even if documentation is available, owners were/are able to draw on the language of the law itself to dispense with 'troublesome' workers. My own interviews with workers reinforce Khan's finding that the vague and open-ended category of 'misconduct' under Section 18 of the Employment of Labour (Standing Orders) Act 1965 offers a legal way to dismiss individuals deemed undesirable by management (Siddiqi 2004 and 2015). Last but not least, one of the major reasons for worker protest is the delayed payment of wages, sometimes for months at a time. Workers who are sacked are rarely compensated for back wages and overtime. The near-certainty of not being paid arrears becomes another factor that discourages workers from speaking out, voicing concerns or organizing.

The lack of formal space for the legitimate voicing of grievances is the other side of numerous spontaneous, demonstrations, blockades, sit-ins, marches and destruction of factory property seen in the garment sector as early as the 1980s. The Sparrow apparel strike of the mid-1980s was one of the first sustained actions of this kind (Interview Lovely Yasmin). By the mid-1990s, Khan noted an increasing trend of 'physical assaults, gherao, demonstrations, rallies, work stoppages, and lay-offs' (2001: 171).

## May 2006: reservoirs of discontent spilling over[7]

From late May to the end of June, 2006, Bangladesh's garment industry experienced protests on a scale not seen earlier. In the course of just a few days, workers from around 4000 factories in and around Dhaka city went on a wildcat strike, took to the streets in demonstrations, participated in sit-ins, and blockaded critical highways in support of their demands. The Bangladeshi state responded in full force, sending in police in riot gear armed with tear gas canisters and rubber bullets, and the feared paramilitary force, the Rapid Action Battalion (RAB). The Ashulia–Gazipur area around Dhaka that housed the main EPZs, as well as parts of the capital, turned into combat zones. The protests spread to a workers' neighbourhood where pitched battles with police and private security forces took place. When the movement showed no signs of abating, the government brought in the Army to 'restore order'. Massive, unprecedented and virtually leaderless, the movement quickly became a source of concern and, alternately, of hope.

Events unfolded in an established pattern, with the expression of grievances in one factory spreading to others. In early May, workers at S. F. Sweater Factory in Gazipur began protesting non-payment of wages. Management retaliated by having two workers arrested and firing others. The small, left wing Garment Sromik Oikkyo Forum/Garment Worker's Union Federation (GWUF), which had already been organizing workers at the factory, helped organize a protest on 19 May. Management responded by locking the striking workers in and cutting off power and water supplies. The workers fought their way out, took over the adjacent highway, and were joined by colleagues from other factories. This time, the police used real bullets, killing a worker, and injuring 70 people, including journalists. News of the killing prompted outraged workers from surrounding factories to pour into the streets. The leaders of GWUF announced a dawn to dusk strike in Gazipur for 23 May.

The Bangladesh Garment Workers Trade Unity Council (BGWTUC), another small left wing federation, announced its support for the strike. BGWTUC, had been mobilizing workers at Universal Garments who were owed three months back wages. They had planned a 'grand garment workers rally' on 23 May. The convergence of two unrelated calls to action drew thousands more workers to strike on 22 and 23 May.

At this juncture, the protests moved much beyond the remit of the small federations and issues with which they were originally. What happened next can be seen as the breach of 'reservoirs of discontent' that had been building up over the years. Moshrefa Mishu of GFUW remarked that 'workers had no choice but to go on the street. The violence in Ashulia was an expression of long-simmering resentment/long-suppressed grievances. There was no option but this was a fluid movement incorporating all kinds of people and groups'. Kalpana Akter of BWSC, whose organization formally eschews any kind of 'agitation' reflected similar sentiments. She recalled that 'We couldn't control the workers' rage because their resentment had reached such a point. Let me tell you the story of a simple, ordinary woman, around 29 or 30 years old. She came to the office boiling over with anger'. "I just threw a brickbat in the glass pane of a factory. They kicked me out without paying the 14 days wages I was owed. So today I went and threw a brick at the factory". This was the only way their anger and frustration could be expressed' (Kalpana Akhter, interview).

On the first day of the strike, factory 'security staff' attacked the workers of Universal Knitting Garments. The latter went to neighbouring factories, asking for support. A several thousand-strong procession of workers quickly assembled, as clashes ensued with police armed with real bullets. Unidentified forces set two factories on fire. Five buses were torched and $2 million dollars worth of clothing destroyed. In solidarity, garment workers shut down the industrial areas of the capital Dhaka.

Nine separate protests rallies were held on 23 May. Mass demonstrations demanded an end to repression, release of arrested workers, higher minimum wages, weekly time off, overtime pay for extra work. As clashes with security forces continued, 16 more factories were set on fire and 200 vehicles destroyed. Many owners opted to shut down production temporarily. The government called in the Bangladesh Rifles from their border control duties to help contain the 'unrest'. A reported 3000 armed police, members of the feared paramilitary force RAB and soldiers had been deployed by the end of the day.

The authorities arrested the labour leader Moshrefa Mishu and filed 19 charges against her. Detained for four days, she was threatened with death 'by crossfire' during her time in remand (Moshrefa Mishu, Garment Workers Unity Forum, 2016).

74   *D. Siddiqi*

Despite the violence and associated danger, the protests drew in 'common people', passers by as well those in the immediate locality whose lives were disrupted. The details of an eye witness account are telling of a potentially dangerous class solidarity in the making:

> The day the 'riot' broke out I had been on my way to the office. It is not new, these agitations here in my locality (lot of RMG factories are situated here) ... I have been witnessing this from a year or more ... What struck me most was how this sort of happening readily unified street vendors, rickshawallas in one single angry 'mob', which was throwing stones, crashing cars, setting fire on big Volvo buses. If it's sort of an anarchy, I am for it with some fears inside...'
> (Eye witness testimony 26 May, 2006 in Garment Workers Revolt p. 2)

When it became clear the standoff would be impossible to resolve through the 'routine' application of force, the government finally persuaded the BGMEA members to sit down with the striking workers. It arranged for garment workers to be represented through SKOP, with the government as a third party. The resulting tripartite talks led to a 'historic' Memorandum of Understanding on 12 June 2006, a seeming victory for labour. The BGMEA accepted all union demands which included: issuing appointment letters for all workers; increase in minimum wages; weekly holiday; maternity leave; withdrawal of all cases against workers; the right of trade unions to represent workers. The formation of a Minimum Wage Board was another significant outcome of the agreement. However, the government conceded to BGMEA's demand for the formation of a security force exclusively for the industry.

Complications arose immediately. SKOP had less than neutral credentials in the eyes of many garment workers, who worried SKOP would side with the government and BGMEA. The proliferation of federations – across the ideological spectrum – rendered the question of who could best represent workers interests necessarily fraught. Fault lines were exposed in the debate around why the new minimum wage was eventually settled at only Tk.3000 (US$38), much lower than the subsistence wage of Tk.5000 (US$63) that most workers had demanded. Mutual suspicion and accusations of complicity surfaced immediately. Rahman and Langford contend that 'collaborationist' unions affiliated with BGMEA acted to undercut the workers' initial demand. Long time left wing political workers and labour leaders as well as those affiliated with international labour movements, agree with this assessment (personal communication with two labour leaders who spoke off the record, 2016).

Ultimately, few factories bothered to implement the terms of the agreement, perhaps with the knowledge that the state would remain indifferent at best. This was a reality to which workers were accustomed. It is difficult to cultivate or sustain faith in bureaucratic and legal proceduralism when numerous past agreements have been ignored with impunity. Disenchantment with the system is inevitable. Other more 'violent' waves of demonstrations followed, most notably

*Before Rana Plaza* 75

in 2010. '2010 was even more massive. Because what they learned from 2006 was not about organized movements but a negative lesson. *If we block roads or destroy property, our demands will be heard*' (KalponaAkhter, italics added).

Left wing labour activists see 2006 as a point of no return, one that established a degree of continuity with later protests and that showed the power of collective action (Zonayed Saki, Gono Shanghati Andolon, 2016). In the long run, an intangible but fundamental gain of 2006 lay outside the legal realm. The sheer scale of events secured garment workers public recognition as a constituency with legitimate rights, as a force to be contended with. It also displaced in the public imagination garment owners as the central actors whose interests were to be protected at all costs, 'challenging their previously unquestioned ownership rights' over the fate of the industry (Rahman and Langford 2014).

One rarely noted fallout of 2006 was the consolidation of surveillance of labour activists by state intelligence units in the name of protecting national interest and security. In other words, it is not only hired thugs or the police that labour organizers must fear. During the 2010 protests, three prominent labour leaders, including Moshrefa Mish and Kalpona Akter were detained for a month. In 2012, Kalpona's colleague Aminul Islam 'disappeared'. His tortured and mutilated body was found in a ditch several months later. Four years later, there are no signs of solving the mystery behind his death. It is widely assumed that Aminul was abducted and murdered by the paramilitary RAB. In addition, the government has set up Industrial Police, which has sanction to 'control' workers in the EPZ as and when needed.

## Back to the future? Beyond the 2013 amendments

It should be evident from the foregoing discussion that, until recently, unionization efforts have been met with definitive state and capitalist violence. Much of this violence is openly sanctioned by the state. The 'problem' is not one of a premodern labour subjectivity waiting to come into its own, of workers needing to be educated into their citizenship rights as enshrined in the law. The question is who mobilizes, and under what conditions? The title of a recent Human Rights Watch Report, *Whoever Raises their Head Suffers the Most* aptly evokes the fear of reprisal that discourages labour mobilization (HRW 2015).

In light of the analysis above, how should we read the increase in unions since 2013 and the amendments to the labour law?[8] What are the implications – of control over union actions and agendas – when the process of union formation is top down, not to mention under the gaze of key global players? Under what circumstances would these unions constitute a social force that operates at a level of scale beyond the factory, and would be able to link up with other movements? The answers appear glaringly obvious in some ways.

Key provisions of the 2013 amendments of the labour law leave the discretionary power of the bureaucracy intact. Under the new amendments, the registrar for trade unions can deny workers the permission to unionize if the official is unsatisfied with the petition. 'This provision has angered workers and labour rights activists alike, given the country's infamous history of corruption. The registrar, they worry, may end up catering to powerful businessmen and denying workers their union elections' (Hossain 2013). In addition, as in the past, it is evident that radical left wing unions find it almost impossible to obtain registration. The general impression is that only unions formed with the help of externally funded NGOs (the implication being that they are shorn of any militant agenda, are deemed reasonable/pliant) tend to get approval. According to Dr Shahidur Rahman, a sociologist studying post Rana Plaza union conditions, many leaders of newly approved unions are already disillusioned. They come with high expectations but find that they possess little actual power (Shahidur Rahman BRAC University 2016).

The trope of *dalal*/double agent is a recurring one in labour narratives of unionization, not surprisingly given the account of surveillance, spying and retaliation noted earlier. Most independent labour leaders see the new unions as company shops, working in the interests of capital. Paradoxically, the amendments have actually made it less cumbersome for owners to dismiss workers accused of 'misconduct'; they can do now without payment. If past practice is any indication, this provision will be used even more to target union activists.

Finally, the government reserved the right to prevent any demonstration or strike it deems 'disruptive' to the community or harmful to the 'national interest'. Suffice it to say, what counts as the national interest or as disruption is open to the logic of power. As one commentator observes,

> Since the rise of Bangladesh's garment industry in the late 1970s, every decent-sized demonstration has been declared disruptive. Even the 2006 labour unrest – which, after decades of industrial growth, led to the formulation of the country's minimum wage – was identified by the government as an international conspiracy to destroy the country's garment industry.
>
> (Emran 2013)

The issue of national interest is especially complex because it can be mobilized by those on the right through the language of anti-imperialism. Further, the notion of a conspiracy invalidates labour voice and agency.

The post Rana Plaza period has seen more continuities than ruptures. What then of workers' rights? Perhaps it is time to ask, following Vijay Prashad, if – under prevailing conditions – conventional trade unions are the best form to capture the discontent of workers and to transform their lives? (Prashad 2015: 189).

## Acknowledgements

I would like to thank all those who generously gave of their time to talk to me and to my research assistant about the events of 2006 (listed below). Special thanks to Dr Shahidur Rahman and my former students, Masnoon Khair and Arefin Noman for their assistance.

## Notes

1 Business schools would seem to be counterintuitive sites for the promotion of labour rights. New modes of consumer activism in the north now compel brands to protect and enhance their reputation by claims to manufacture 'sweat free', products, that is, without any apparent exploitation of labour. The resulting pressures brought to bear on manufacturers by primarily northern brands renders intelligible the need for a place like the Center for Business and Human Rights at New York University's Stern School of Business. It is the first of its kind.
2 There is some discrepancy among sources on the actual number of factories at present. Some of this can be attributed to a general lack of documentation of small enterprises, especially if they are subcontractors lower down on the commodity chain. Questions of categorization also produce discrepant figures. As of writing, the exact number is the subject of considerable contention between the BGMEA and the Stern School of Business at New York University. In a recent study, the latter concluded there were over 7000 factories, a figure considerably larger than other estimates. It is beyond the scope of this chapter to examine the issue in detail here. It appears the dispute is primarily around the inclusion of certain subcontractors who may or not be producing for the global market. See *Dhaka Tribune* 'BGMEA slams New York University study on Bangladeshi RMG workers'. 21 December 2015. www.dhakatribune.com/business/2015/dec/21/bgmea-slams-new-york-university-study-bangladesh-rmg-workers.
3 According to the annual report of the Bangladesh Export Processing Zone Authority (BEPZA), there were 104 garment enterprises, 72 garments accessories enterprises, 40 knitting and other textile products enterprises and 41 textile product enterprises in FY 2012–2013. See http://epzbangladesh.org.bd/files/reports/file_1448276002.pdf.
4 There are differences in the estimate of how many women are employed in the industry. The conventional figure of '90% women' does not capture the heterogeneity of the industry. Knitwear, for instance, which accounts for over 40 per cent of apparel export, is produced primarily by male workers.
5 Section 195 of the Bangladesh Labor Act, 2006 (amended 2013) outlaws numerous 'unfair labor practices'. For example, no employer shall

> dismiss, discharge, remove from employment, or threaten to dismiss, discharge, or remove from employment a worker, or injure or threaten to injure him in respect of his employment by reason that the worker is or proposes to become, or seeks to persuade any other person to become, a member or officer of a trade union.

6 Prashad, V. (2015). 'Workers' yarns'. *HIMAL Southasian*. Special Issue on the Bangladesh Paradox. 28(3): 180–9. http://himalmag.com/workers-yarns-vijay-prashad-review-song-of-the-shirt-seabrook/.
7 The phrase is Vijay Prashad's (2015: 183).
8 On a related note, Sanchita Bannerjee's comparative research makes an important intervention by delinking the abstract concept of 'improved labor conditions' and 'worker empowerment'. She argues that one should not assume that better labour conditions automatically translate into an empowered workforce. She also concludes that change and improvements stemming from top-down programmes, though they may be initially effective in improving basic standards, do not help in furthering coalitions with labour groups and institutionalizing their role in policy making (Bannerjee 2014).

## Bibliography

Ahmed, N. and Nathan, D. (2014) *Improving Wages and Working Conditions in the Bangladeshi Garment Sector: The Role of Horizontal and Vertical Relations*. Working Paper 40 Dhaka: DFID/BIDS.

78   *D. Siddiqi*

Azim, F. (2015) 'Feminist struggles in Bangladesh', *Feminist Review*. 80: 195–7.

Bangladesh Bank (2015) *Quarterly Review on RMG April-June 2015*. Dhaka: Bangladesh Bank Research Division. www.bb.org.bd/pub/quaterly/rmg/apr-jun2015.pdf

Bannerjee, S. S. (2014) *Made in Bangladesh, Cambodia, Sri Lanka: The Labor Behind the Global Garment and Textile Industries*. Amherst, NY: Cambria Press.

Berik, G. and Van Der Meulen Rodgers, Y. (2010). 'Options for enforcing labour standards: lessons from Bangladesh and Cambodia', *Journal of International Development* 22: 56–85.

Brooks, E. C. *Unraveling the Garment Industry: Transnational Organizing and Women's Work*. Minneapolis: University of Minnesota Press, 2007.

Devnath, A. (2013) 'Bangladesh labor protest on wages shut 100 factories'. Bloomberg News, 12 November 2013. www.bloomberg.com/news/articles/2013-11-12/bangladesh-labor-protests-on-wages-shut-100-garment-factories.

Al-Faruque, A. (2009) *Current Status and Evolution of Industrial Relations System in Bangladesh*. Ithaca: Cornell University ILR School.

Hansen, T. B. (2008) 'The political theology of violence in contemporary India', *South Asia Multidisciplinary Academic Journal (SAMAJ)* [online]. 2: 1–12.

Hasan, J. (2008) *Labor Rights in the Ready Made Garments Industry in Bangladesh: Perspective*. Dhaka: Odhikar.

Hossain, E. (2013) 'Bangladesh's labor reform puts profits before workers', *Huffington Post*.7July.www.huffingtonpost.com/2013/07/25/bangladesh-labor-reform_n_3653850.html.

Human Rights Watch (2015) *Whoever Raises their Heads Suffers the Most: Workers' Rights in Bangladesh's Garment Factories*. 22 April. www.hrw.org/report/2015/04/22/whoever-raises-their-head-suffers-most/workers-rights-bangladeshs-garment.

International Labour Organization (2014a) *Union Registrations Rise Sharply in Bangladesh Garment Sector: New Labour Laws Pave Way to Improve Conditions, Workers' Rights*. Press Release. 10 February. www.ilo.org/dhaka/Informationresources/Publicinformation/Pressreleases/WCMS_236042/lang-en/index.htm.

International Labour Organization (2014b) *Officials of Over 140 Newly Registered RMG Sector Trade Unions Receive Orientation on Freedom of Association*. Press Release. 22 April. www.ilo.org/dhaka/Informationresources/Publicinformation/Pressreleases/WCMS_241344/lang-en/index.htm.

International Labour Organization (2015) *Trade Union Registration Boosts after Rana Plaza Tragedy* (reprint of story in *Dhaka Tribune*, 31 August 2015). http://apirnet.ilo.org/news/trade-union-registration-boosts-after-rana-plaza-tragedy.

Khan, S. I. (2001) 'Gender issues and the ready-made garment industry of Bangladesh: the Trade Union context', S. Rehman and N. Khundker (eds.) *Globalization and Gender: Changing Patterns of Women's Employment in Bangladesh*. pp. 167–218. Dhaka: University Press Limited.

Labowitz, S. and Baumann-Pauly, D. (2014) *Business as Usual is Not an Option: Supply Chains and Sourcing After Rana Plaza*. Center for Business and Human Rights. NYU. Leonard N. Stern School of Business.

Mahmud, S. (2010) 'Why garment workers fail to mobilize', in L. Thomson and C. Tapscott (eds), *Citizenship, Mobilization and Social Movements in the South: The Challenges of Inclusive Government*. New York: Zed Press.

Mridha, R. U. (2013) 'Trade Unionism to be set free', *Daily Star*. 15 July 2013. http://archive.thedailystar.net/beta2/news/trade-unionism-to-be-set-free/ (accessed 10 February 2016).

Prashad, V. (2015). 'Workers' yarns'. *HIMAL Southasian*. Special Issue on the Bangladesh Paradox. 28(3): 180–9.

Rahman, S. (2014) *The Broken Promises of Globalization: The Case of the Bangladesh Garment Industry*. New York: Lexington Books.

Rahman, Z. and Langford, T. (2012) 'Why labour unions have failed Bangladesh's garment workers', in S. Mosoetsa and M. Williams (eds), *Labour in the Global South: Challenges and Alternatives for Workers*. pp. 87–106. Geneva: ILO.

Rahman, Z. and Langford, T. (2014) 'International solidarity or renewed Trade Union imperialism? The AFL-CIO and garment workers in Bangladesh', *Working USA: The Journal of Labor and Society*. 17: 169–86.

Ross, L. (2014) 'Defying the stereotype: women textile workers in Bangladesh', *Marxist Left Review* 8, Winter 2014. (Page numbers not available).

Siddiqi, D. M. (2009) 'Do Bangladesh sweatshop workers need saving? Sisterhood in the post-sweatshop era', *Feminist Review* 91: 154–74.

Siddiqi, D. M. (2014) 'Solidarity, sexuality and saving Muslim Women in neoliberal times', *Women's Studies Quarterly* 42: 292–306.

Siddiqi, D. M. (2015) 'Starving for justice: Bangladeshi garment workers in a 'post-Rana Plaza' world', *International Labor and Working Class History*. 87: 165–73.

Sims, B. (1999) *Workers of the World Undermined: American Labor's Role in US Foreign Policy*. Boston: Southend Press.

Yunus, M. and Yamagata, T. (2014) 'Bangladesh: market force supercedes control', in T. Fukunishi and T. Yamagata (eds) *The Garment Industry in Low-Income Countries: An Entry Point of Industrialization*. IDE-JETRO Series: Springer.

# Interviews

My research assistant Arefin Noman carried out interviews with the following individuals:

Amirul Huq Amin, Convenor National Garment Workers Federation.

Kalpona Akter Executive Director, Bangladesh Center for Worker Solidarity.

Nazma Akter, Awaj Foundation.

Moshrefa Mishu Convenor, Garment Workers Unity Forum.

Sirajul Islam Rony, Bangladesh National Garment Workers (BNGWEL) Employees League.

Zonayed Saki, Convenor, Gono Shonghoti Andolon (People's Solidarity Movement).

Lovely Yasmin, Joint Convenor, Bangladesh Labor Rights Forum and President, RMG Workers Federation.

The author conducted an interview with Dr Shahidur Rahman, Associate Professor, Economics and Social Sciences Department, BRAC University on 19 January 2016.

# 5 Migrant workers in the clothing industry

## Networking in Christian spaces

*Vicki Crinis and Angie Ngọc Trần*

As noted in the introduction to this volume, global commodity chain analysis has a tendency to ignore what is actually happening on the ground in countries where clothing is assembled. There are excellent analyses of globalization and the clothing industry (Bonocich and Applebaum 2003; Bruce and Daly 2004; Hale and Willis 2005; Bair 2005; Chan 2011), and of the global commodity chains that clothing production generates (Gereffi 1994; Gereffi and Memedovic 2003). However, the latter has focused on evaluating industrial upgrading and assumes that the workers' situation will improve during the process. In recent times, less attention has been directed to the labour conditions of workers, especially of the growing army of temporary migrant workers recruited to work in export-oriented factories across Asia.[1] These workers do not enjoy the rights of citizens and often encounter new forms of contract-based engagement in which recruitment firms mediate the relationship between workers and factory managers (see Barrientos 2013). In this new context, it is very difficult for traditional union-based labour activism to flourish (Knutsen *et al.* 2013). However, new forms of resistance are emerging via migrant networks, NGOs, churches and self-help groups. The experiences of migrant workers in Malaysia shed new light on these emerging organizational forms and their multi-scalar links.

The research that informs this chapter was conducted between 2008 and 2010 in Johor and Batu Pahat and then in Penang, Kuala Lumpur and Batu Pahat between 2009 and 2013.[2] In these industrial towns immigrant workers live close to factories in hostel-type accommodation. Group interviews were organized within the various hostels and at other sites in Malaysia. From these groups, a convenience sample of 13 female and three male Vietnamese workers and seven male and one female Nepalese workers who worked in clothing factories in Malaysia were interviewed in order to compare and contrast their experiences. We selected workers on the basis of their availability and willingness to participate in the interviews. Vietnamese was the primary ethnicity selected because one of the authors is Vietnamese American and speaks fluent Vietnamese. The Nepalese men work alongside the Vietnamese women in the clothing production lines. Indonesians, Chinese and Cambodians also commonly work in the Malaysian clothing factories. Some of the workers we interviewed participated in Christian fellowships. As well as participant observation in hostels and church

*Migrant workers in the clothing industry* 81

agencies, interviews with clothing textile trade unionists, NGOs and church advocates were conducted to complement workers' accounts.

The chapter is structured as follows. The first section provides an outline of Malaysia's state-managed migration policies and the resulting exploitative circuits of labour migration. The second section briefly outlines the history of labour migration in Malaysia to show the connections between migration, the state, NGOs and civil society. Its historical account of labour migration traces the boundaries of inclusion and exclusion that have been created by the state and capital and shows how these processes are gendered and racialized. The third section examines the roles of NGOs and Christian associations in supporting migrant workers. It explains how the NGO movement has been instrumental in making the government accountable for its ad hoc migration policies, while church groups have taken up welfare service provision and creating worker support networks. In the final section we assess these interventions as nascent forms of worker organization. We observe that the new attachments are based on ties to ethnicity and are created when workers congregate at locations outside the workplace, such as in a particular hostel or shopping centre or other ethnic space.[3] These spaces serve the needs of migrant workers and provide the basis of resistance to exploitation.

## Background

Malaysia is able to operate as a supply site for high-end sportswear production because it has a supply of flexible and temporary migrant labourers who do not qualify for the rights of citizens (Crinis 2012). These migrant workers provide a highly flexible workforce, the new equivalent of the 1970s offshore proletariat (Sassen 2000). In 2012, of the more than 3.1 million authorized and unauthorized migrant workers in Malaysia, 700,000 were employed in the manufacturing industries including clothing, textiles, foodstuffs and electronics (*Migration News* 2012: 1). Most of these workers were from Indonesia, Cambodia, Vietnam, Nepal and Burma and most were women. Flows of workers into Malaysia are the outcome of government-to-government MOUs with sending nations, and the popularity of particular ethnic groups among Malaysian employers. Malaysia has become a popular destination because recruitment costs are low compared to other higher wage paying countries (Crinis 2010).

Malaysian migration policies are predicated on the idea that unskilled migrant workers are temporary residents, and that their presence in Malaysia should not endanger the nation's established ethnic composition, which in the past has been a source of political tension (Crinis 2005). State migration policies are complex because they address economic, political and security issues simultaneously. The Malaysian government endeavours to ensure that migrant workers are recruited and repatriated without cost to the state, in terms of welfare or services, and without migrants perceiving any right to settle in Malaysia.

Clothing manufacturing in Malaysia profits from the poor working conditions endured by thousands of migrant workers. Their exploitation has been sanctioned by receiving and sending governments as well as by employers. The means by which this political structure is maintained is a system where workers are employed by specialized labour-importing firms and then contracted to manufacturing plants. This arrangement – which in many ways resembles the activities of labour hire firms in advanced economies (Peck and Theodore 2001) – places migrant clothing workers in a vulnerable and precarious position. It renders them both compliant and disposable. First, workers and their families invest in the system by signing up for placement, so there is a strong incentive to stay the course of a usually three-year contract. Second, once in Malaysia, workers' legal status, living arrangements and working conditions are set out in their employment contract and their wellbeing and security are controlled by their employment/migration agent, the police and the Immigration Department. The managers of manufacturing plants in the clothing industry pay a levy to the government and a fee to the intermediary firm to place a migrant worker; the high recruitment costs mean that these workers are considered an investment. Once recruited, factories are therefore keen to retain the services of suitably compliant recruits. Often they attempt to prevent workers from leaving by holding their passports, withholding wages or restricting their mobility. If the employer is not happy with any worker, he/she is under no obligation to extend or continue the contract. If a worker's contract is terminated, their work permit becomes invalid, so workers are unable to seek alternative employment and must return home at their own expense. In addition to these general rules, a number of immigration laws in Malaysia apply only to women. Female migrant permit holders are not allowed to become pregnant or to deliver a child while employed in Malaysia. If a female worker is pregnant she must return to her country of origin. This policy is often contested on the grounds that it breaches human rights protocols.[4]

The constant threat of termination secures worker compliance. Because workers have to consider the possibility of returning home prematurely, they become a malleable workforce, rarely motived to cause trouble or to participate in collective action (Arnold and Hewison 2005). In addition to difficult, exploitative and confusing employer restrictions, migrant workers in Malaysia face language barriers and exclusion from the general population. Fear also raises workers' anxiety levels, inducing them to work long hours (if available), but this work ethic sets the migrants further apart from their Malaysian counterparts. Workers accept these conditions in order to pay debts and return home with some money. Many feel the urge to run away and have to struggle to remain in Malaysia.

## Migrant workers in Malaysia

Like workers elsewhere, migrant workers in Malaysia face challenges regarding their working arrangements: wages, overtime, bonuses, health and safety issues and unfair dismissal rights (Tran 2004). But migrant workers' problems begin with poorly organized and corrupt profit-seeking recruiters. A number of workers we interviewed were duped by a recruitment agency that had made inflated promises about clothing industry salaries in Malaysia. As one Nepalese worker explained:

> When there is overtime, the salary is good. But there is only sometimes overtime work. When there is overtime work, they give us RM3 (US79 cents) per hour. They had told us that we can save 30,000 to 40,000 Rupee (US$295 to US$393) every month after food. If it was like that, we told ourselves in the village at home that we should go and we came to Malaysia. But what we were told there and what is happening here is indeed very different.
>
> (Bahadur)

Some workers had difficulty understanding wage calculations but many accept the unfair conditions because they do not have the language skills to communicate with management:

> When I just arrived I saw the contract is not fair. The management is not proper so sometime we get high, sometime we get low wage. Even when the operation is the same process, wages are not equal.
>
> (Chi)

All Vietnamese and Nepalese workers we interviewed had borrowed money to travel to Malaysia and were keen to work overtime because the flat rate of ordinary work hours did not pay them enough to cover debts and savings:

> It is not easy because prices have gone up. It is very difficult to pay for the living expenses here as well as send money home. We get paid at the end of the month but if need arises we can get advance in between.
>
> (Narayan)

Once workers are in Malaysia there is little option but to try to complete the contracted work:

> But if we have doubt about this, who is going to listen to us? Even if things are like this, now that we have come to this country, whatever it is like here, we will complete the three years and if things work out well, we will stay one more year. If not, we will go home.
>
> (Vijaya)

However, if management is happy with factory output the workers are rewarded:

> If we complete three years' contract, boss will purchase ticket for us to return to Vietnam. At the end of the year the company gave us RM500 (US$131) for the bonus, beside, they gave us bonus for the Vietnamese New Year as well. If any one of us extends the employment contract, they gave

us another RM200 (US$52). But for those who do not fulfil the duty or take a day off without notice for a few days continuously, the company will cut off their bonuses.

(Phuong)

Once in Malaysia migrants calculate the ability to repay their costs based on the expectation of working overtime, so many feel cheated if there is no overtime. In some instances workers break the contract and leave because there is no overtime in their factory or because their daily work target is set too high. Rising and falling production targets – a perennial feature of the seasonality of clothing manufacture – makes the situation worse for migrant workers when their work hours are allowed to expand and contract with demand. Workers deemed unproductive may have their contracts cancelled after the first three-month trial period, after which they must return to their country of origin.

This places considerable pressure on workers to conform to company discipline. For some workers, this is too much to bear. We interviewed one worker who had run away from her employer. Rita had been working for a clothing factory in Ipoh, in Perak. During the recruitment process in Nepal she was told that the company would pay for accommodation, living expenses and health benefits. But once in Malaysia and working at the clothing factory, she discovered that the factory deducted the levy from her monthly wage as well as all living and health expenses. After working for 12 months she left the company because she did not earn enough to pay her debts and, as the daily piece-rate was set so high, she had little opportunity to earn higher wages. Rita is now an 'illegal' working in a factory in Kuala Lumpur, which she will do until either the debt is paid off or she is arrested and repatriated. She must be careful not to be arrested under the Ops 6p *Bersepada*, the State Immigration Department illegals round-up operation. Since Ops started, 300 undocumented Nepalese have been arrested and repatriated as well as a large number of workers from other countries (*New Straits Times*, 9 February 2014: 4). Rita is now in a worse situation than when she left Nepal. When we asked workers how they cope and to whom they turn for help, most agreed they would ask their friends. Workers help each other and many share resources.

Some migrant workers – those who meet the employers' expectations – are offered contracts for extra years and in some cases they are promoted to supervisory roles. But even then it is not easy to live in Malaysia, because migrant workers face violence from both Malaysians and other ethnicities:

If we return from work late, we have to walk in groups. If we walk on our own, they mug us, beat us and rob us. Sometimes they also kill. We have to be especially careful on pay days. We are even scared that they come to our room to steal the money.

(Narayan)

Female workers are especially frightened living in Malaysia, given the number of robbery and rapes involving migrant workers. In a recent incident a Vietnamese woman was abducted and raped by three men impersonating policemen after they robbed 26 foreign workers at their hostels (*New Straits Times*, 18 August 2013).

### Resistance and struggles

When migrant workers encounter unfair conditions, their main avenues of response are direct action on the factory floor or they seek help from their embassy. In factories, workers of different ethnicities sometimes join 'sit-in' strikes, hoping to raise the wages to a decent level. But they do not unite with other workers in other clothing factories. According to one Nepalese worker:

> Sometimes when the rate, per piece is very low we stopped work for 1 to 3 hours. Sometimes we talk to the supervisor. But then the company will sort the matter out with the supervisor and that is where it ends. They put up the rate a little bit and that is where it ends.
>
> (Vijaya)

Worker resistance is tolerated to a degree but workers identified as troublemakers increase their likelihood of being deported if involved in large-scale strikes. Workers (mostly Vietnamese) in the Esquel Malaysia clothing factory went on a three-day strike in 2008 to demand higher wages (*Infoshop News* 2008). According to NGO reports, the factory's 2000 workers, mostly recruited from Vietnam, had received less pay than they had been promised. Also according to NGO reports, the employer's response to the strike was rapid, with 300 Vietnamese workers repatriated without compensation. The Vietnamese government has since introduced regulations to discipline migrant workers who break contracts or become 'troublesome' in the host country.

Like Vietnamese workers, a group of Nepalese factory workers staged riots after their employer ignored one of their colleagues having difficulty breathing (*New Straits Times*, 2 January 2014). Between 100 and 200 workers gathered in front of the employer's house, demanding immediate action to help a worker whose condition was worsening at the workers' hostel. The Nepalese workers became more agitated after realizing that their friend had died and were blaming it on the employer. The employer called the police and three of the workers, believed to be their leaders, were arrested.

Despite language barriers, wildcat outbursts against unfair treatment sometimes involve more than one ethnic group. In another incident, 500 foreign workers in Johor Bahru staged a protest over the death of a colleague (Shadige 2010: 42). The employer had refused to send the sick worker to hospital and he died. The death was perceived as an injustice and offended notions of morality across all ethnicities. The seven-hour protest, which took place at the workers' residential hostel rather than in the workplace, involved workers from Nepal, India, Myanmar and Bangladesh.

But this is exceptional. In general, migrant factory workers do not unite with workers from different ethnicities. Ethnic groups have resisted and marched on their embassies to protest labour exploitation, but they have rarely joined forces with other ethnic groups. In 2008, 779 Bangladeshi workers boarded buses and left their four textile factories in Batu Pahat to meet their High Commissioner in the Bangladesh Embassy in Kuala Lumpur to complain that their wages were lower than promised by the outsourcing company (*Khaleej Times*, 9 October 2006). They were unsuccessful and the leaders were arrested by immigration personnel and sent to a detention centre for deportation. Indonesians and Vietnamese men have rioted in the streets against random drug testing and state brutality.

But Indonesian, Vietnamese and Malaysian workers have also engaged in violence against each other, resulting in riots and gang violence. A newspaper reported more than 200 textile workers clashing outside their hostel, leading to a number injured as well as arrests and deportation (Sennyah 2011: 1). After scuffles between Indonesian and Vietnamese workers in the textile industry the Human Resource Minister asked clothing and textile managers to segregate foreign workers into separate dormitories to prevent further ethnic tensions (Firdaus 2002: 1). In the 1990s problems involving Indonesian and Bangladeshi workers in the textile industry led to an increase in the numbers of production workers from other countries in the region. This inter-worker conflict perhaps expresses the extent of migrant worker disempowerment. When these uprisings occur, they are suppressed by a violent state apparatus and the leaders are arrested and repatriated. The Malaysian government has continued to prevent large public gatherings which they believe may lead to public disorder, racial clashes and street violence, and compromise the country's 'stable workforce' credentials with investors.[5] Migrant workers are not welcome to protest in public spaces. In 2013 about 100 Nepalese workers were arrested after the police heard they intended to hold a protest to demand wage increases. Teams of police established roadblocks and arrested the workers as they marched down the street. According to the police, 'we had to stop them before they gathered as they could have started a riot' (*New Straits Times*, 7 March 2013). As in previous instances, strike leaders and rioters were repatriated to their home countries.

Unlike the clothing and textile industry's solidarity of the past, which was focused on worker unity and common class interests, ethnicities are the main source of unity and conflict among these workers. Because these ties are not industry based they act to divide and splinter workers, stifling the possibility of a regional or national labour movement emerging (Murali 2002: 5). In this context, traditional union-based forms of worker organization are difficult to develop. There is only one textile factory and no clothing factories registered with the union in Penang and Selangor, and a few clothing factories registered with the union in Johor. In this situation both NGOs and Christian social movement advocates have developed strategies to empower migrant workers and help them to build their own worker support networks. These new intermediaries are moving increasingly from their initial concern with human rights advocacy to labour rights.

## Labour migrants and community advocacy

Migrant workers who are cheated by employers or fearful of neighbourhood violence clearly express their need for help. Workers feel less vulnerable if they have access to a migrant community agency or other civil society support association. This support mainly comes from NGOs and Christian church groups. The two operate in different ways to support migrant workers, but both have moved gradually from a pastoral role to advocacy and labour movement politics.

In Malaysia, labour NGOs first developed in response to poverty on rural rubber-production estates. With the entry of young Malay women into the industrial workforce in the late 1970s, and the increasing numbers of overseas migrant workers subjected to abuse in factories and violence from state officials, their role expanded. The Women's Aid Organization (WAO) was established in 1982 to advocate against domestic violence in the rural estate sector. The feminist labour NGO Sahabat Wanita (Friends of Women), a national organization of women, was established in 1984. Sahabat Wanita started as a small locally born feminist organization directed by educated women to organize young Malay women in the labour-intensive industries, particularly in the electronic industry in the Sungai Way Free Trade Zone (FTZ). A third group, Tenaganita (Women's Force) is the most well-known migrant labour NGO in Malaysia. Sahabat Wanita usually refers migrant workers to Tenaganita. The NGOs were the first to highlight corruption in the (Bangladeshi) migrant worker recruitment process. The government had to respond by diversifying its intake of foreigners to include workers from Cambodia, China, Myanmar, Nepal and Vietnam (Murali 2002: 5).

In 1990, Tenaganita started to advocate for migrant workers through global human rights advocates and at the national level. On the global level it worked with international human rights groups such as International Migrant Workers Alliance (IMA), which consists of both international NGOs and migrant workers. It also formed coalitions with regional NGOs such as the Coordination of Action Research on Aids and Mobility Research (CARAM), Amnesty International and Human Rights Watch. It sponsors programmes to improve conditions for migrant workers and to advocate for business accountability and responsibility. It is involved in CSR and other stakeholder initiatives in the Malaysian clothing industry. Via this framework, the rights of migrant workers are linked to processes of globalization (Crinis 2008). At the national level, Tenaganita works with local professional groups such as the Bar Council, labour unions and Christian civil society groups and has had significant success bringing migrant worker abuses to the forefront of public debate (Tenaganita 2008). The organization gained international recognition after its director and co-founder Irene Fernandez was arrested for publishing a report on the abuse of migrant workers in Malaysia.[6] After comments in the overseas press exposing the abusive treatment of Bangladeshi workers at the hands of recruitment agents and employers, Fernandez was blamed for making Malaysia look bad in the eyes of the international community and for attempting to destroy diplomatic relations between Malaysia and Bangladesh. Around the same time, Fernandez's

## 88   V. Crinis and A. Ngọc Trần

statement in the *Jakarta Post* accusing the vigilante group RELA (a government-sponsored group) of using their power to abuse migrant workers, led to another lawsuit. Yet Fernandez's arrest points to the extreme measures that the Malaysian government is willing to use to silence debate around migrant workers.[7] Fernandez's persistent criticisms make it difficult for the government to ignore the situation.[8] Since the report was published, the government has been forced to engage in issues concerning migrant workers. It has since signed but not ratified the International Convention on the Protection of the Rights of all Migrant Workers and Members of their Families.

Meanwhile, and over a longer period, Tenaganita has also been active locally. During fieldwork in 2009, an NGO spokesperson was interviewed and was asked how the organization assisted migrants:

> We work closely with other local non-government organizations to identify those who need our assistance. We help arbitrate between the workers and their employers, we help argue their cases in court, and we counsel those who are in need of advice. In the future we have plans to invite experts and guest speakers to impart to them useful skills, such as financial management skills, because most of them are still poor when their work contract expires.
> (Penang Tenaganita spokesperson, pers. comm., 2009)[9]

The organization's role was exemplified during an interview with an NGO officer, when a young worker was brought into the office suffering injuries sustained at the hands of his employer. The NGO officer photographed his injuries, sent the worker to a doctor for treatment and rang a lawyer to file a complaint in the labour court. Professional networks outside the NGOs act with them to help migrants in distress.

Fernandez, Tenaganita's leader, holds the government responsible for the mismanagement of migrant labour programmes. According to Fernandez the line between documented and undocumented migrants is blurring due to lax management of the outsourcing of the recruitment process. The recruitment companies outsource workers to clothing factories. The clothing company takes no responsibility for wage discrimination and workplace accidents because the outsourcing company is the employer not the clothing factory. NGOs and human rights lawyers in Malaysia view the recruitment and outsourcing of migrant workers as a form of labour trafficking.

Since 2007, Fernandez has worked to bring the local and the international scales of action together. She has exposed the exploitation of migrants under the government's labour outsourcing recruitment programmes. She has argued that migrant workers are the victims of a harsh immigration and outsourcing system that borders on corruption. Trafficking is rife within Malaysia and other destination countries of migrant workers (Tenaganita 2008). The organization's focus on trafficking and labour smuggling is now linked to international civil society movements such as the Vietnamese American Boatpeople (Boat People SOS 2009) and the Coalition to Abolish Modern-day Slavery in Asia (CAMSA)

(CAMSA 2009). Boatpeople SOS started after the end of the Vietnamese War to help the large numbers of Vietnamese fleeing Vietnam in 'leaky boats' and SOS is well organized in defending the rights of migrant workers abroad, while CAMSA is a part of the global anti-trafficking movement (CAMSA spokesperson, pers. comm., 2009). So far, the organization has helped over 3000 workers from Vietnam and other countries in about 40 cases of labour exploitation or trafficking. CAMSA operates in three locations – Malaysia, Thailand and Taiwan – and has connections and communication with advocacy organizations in both source and destination countries throughout the Asia-Pacific region (Daniel Lo, CAMSA, pers. comm., 2013). NGOs have played a leading role in speaking up for and protecting the interests of migrant workers in national and global fora, especially by linking with international human rights groups who are committed to stopping the injustices committed by states in relation to refugees, border crossings and migrant slave labour. NGOs, where possible, perform the work of trade unions. Although they are unable to organize large numbers of workers, they act with unions and work with other social movement organizations to support migrant workers.

Christian advocacy groups, on the other hand, have taken a more localized, pastoral approach to the care of migrant workers. Migrant workers in Malaysia have become the 'objects of benevolence and the recipients of goodwill' (Cheah 2006: 257) of the Christian churches operating within the Muslim Malaysian state. Unlike Tenaganita, however, these religious organizations escape the state's wrath because they do not challenge or threaten it. Pastoral care involves helping and caring for others in their church or wider community. It involves listening to, supporting, encouraging and befriending migrant workers and helping them negotiate health, social and moral issues, 'church people treat us well. They love us like family member. If not, nobody care about us' (Phan). This involves engaging with workers in their leisure time, 'If it is a long holiday, my company will organize for us to a sightseeing. If it is a short holiday I go shopping and also save time to study the Bible' (Xuan).

Religious pastoral care relieves the Malaysian government of responsibility for the welfare of migrants in distress. Most workers we encountered reported that church groups had made their stay in Malaysia more bearable and, in many cases, even enjoyable.

The three Christian churches that provide pastoral care to migrants in Malaysia are the Methodist, Presbyterian and Catholic churches. The two Protestant churches offer similar pastoral care and religious service to migrant workers, but the Catholic Church stood out because its migrant worker ministries addressed labour problems directly. The differences between the churches depend on their ability to coordinate and fund social networks. The Wesley Methodist Church and the Presbyterian Church in Batu Pahat, Kuala Lumpur and Penang (Protestant churches) have Nepalese or Vietnamese ministers. The Nepalese pastors in Kuala Lumpur and Batu Pahat have a background similar to the Nepalese factory workers they serve, with limited English and Malaysian language skills. The Kuala Lumpur pastor had become involved in Asian Outreach Nepal and worked

90   *V. Crinis and A. Ngọc Trần*

his way to a position whereby he was recruited to go to Malaysia to assist migrant workers. In Malaysia he started work in a factory but after making himself known to the ministers in Kuala Lumpur, he was given space in the Wesley Methodist Church to minister to the needs of the Nepalese workforce. Since starting the Nepali Sangati, the pastor sees an average of 60 to 80 Nepalese workers each week. His lively evangelistic services start around midday and are followed by light snacks in a cafeteria courtyard. This time allows for fostering closer relationships among the Nepalese worker group. The Nepalese pastor in Batu Pahat, who did not speak English, offered similar services. The two Nepalese pastors were in close communication with each other despite working in different churches (Methodist versus Presbyterian) and in different states. The Vietnamese Ministry nurtured parishioners among the migrant workers, but it also had connections with local and international civil society groups. The following account by the Vietnamese American pastor of the Presbyterian Migrant Ministry in Batu Pahat describes this work:

> The Malaysian government allowed Vietnamese to work in factories about six years ago. About 100,000 came in the first year. We had about 6000 Vietnamese working here in Batu Pahat. The church started reaching out to meet their needs about four to five years ago, as the church is located very near to the industrial estate in Batu Pahat. We teach the workers English and Mandarin because they need language skills to communicate with the management and also other workers. We also provide for those who are sick and those in financial difficulty and we hope to welcome them into our church. We also share with them the gospel of salvation as that is the best gift we can give to them. They respond very well to the gospel and many believe in Jesus Christ as their Lord and Saviour.
>
> (Lau Joshua, pers. comm., 2009)

He also stressed the evangelical tone of his ministry, 'Those believers who returned to Vietnam in turn share the gospel of eternal life to their parents, family and relatives. As a result, many also believe in Jesus Christ'.

Workers attended church services and other social activities on their day off, on Sundays when they relaxed and enjoyed their time away from the factory. At church, friends listened to each other and discussed their daily life situations and compared wages and employers. On one particular Sunday observed in Batu Pahat, socializing with other workers appeared to be the most important reason for workers attending the fellowship. These young workers started their Sunday with a 10 am bible study at a local Christian church; male and female Vietnamese workers were divided into study groups and adjourned to cool areas under large trees to read and discuss sections of the bible. When bible study ended, workers were transferred by minibuses to a suburban home belonging to the Vietnamese American Ministry and sublet as a hostel to a group of Vietnamese women. A group of young male and female workers prepared food while the others chatted to each other and talked on their mobile phones. Vietnamese food was served and workers chatted through the meal. Afterwards a nominated group cleaned up while others relaxed; some played musical instruments, some talked on the phone and others fell asleep for a few hours. Later in the afternoon another nominated group prepared food for dinner. Following dinner the workers gathered for prayers (which were rather noisy due to the unleashing of emotions during prayer time). After evening prayers some workers weeded the garden while others waited outside for the minibuses to deliver them home. On other Sundays, the researcher attended Nepalese services conducted in both the Presbyterian and Methodist churches in Batu Pahat and Kuala Lumpur respectively. In Batu Pahat, Nepalese workers were attending a church service in the church hall around the same time as the Vietnamese bible study was held. But there was no interaction between the Nepalese and Vietnamese groups – this observation was a constant throughout the research.

The Catholic Church has built support networks for migrant workers across the Asia Pacific. Like the Protestant churches, the Catholic Church employs religious workers from the migrant worker sending countries. It educates the parishioners about the problems of migrant workers in Malaysia and involves the local population in volunteer programmes and ethnic ministries. In Malaysia it commenced working with Filipino domestic workers in the 1990s and developed connections to Filipino NGOs. The church established the National Office of Human Development (NOHD) in Kuala Lumpur, and the Catholic Human Resource Development in Penang, which supports and assists migrant workers to deal with the harsh realities of labour migration. The Migrant Workers and Refugees Support Centres in Penang and Kuala Lumpur are funded by the Catholic Church Archdiocesan Office for Human Development (Josephine Tey, Coordinator – Migrants and Refugees, pers. comm., 2005). The welfare of migrant workers and refugees held in the 13 detention centres across Malaysia is of particular importance. Ministry personnel together with Malaysian volunteers with medical experience visit detention facilities to administer medical attention to the numbers of inmates who fall ill during the time spent in detention (Catholic Church spokesperson, Penang, pers. comm., 2007). Under the law, many 'illegals' spend time in the detention centres while waiting for deportation. According to the government it takes time for the embassies to issue detainees with travel documents to facilitate the return journey to the sending country.

The NOHD has also extended its services to incorporate assistance to Vietnamese, Burmese, Nepalese and Indian workers (Catholic Church spokespersons, Penang 2006 and Kuala Lumpur 2009). These grassroots ministries offer employment-related information and liaise with unions to assist workers (Christine Yubong, Migrants and Refugees Ministry, pers. comm., 2010). They operate welfare shelters for abused workers, advocate, and provide support and legal aid to workers who need help. They arrange locations for the different ethnicities to socialize and in these locations workers have formed migrant councils, organized activities and opened restaurants, such as the one situated at the Bukit Nanas Community Centre (set up by the NOHD) (Ng *et al.* 2007: 194). These centres provide a sense of community in an otherwise desolate environment.

## From human rights to labour rights

Some scholars see church organizations as agents of politicization, as paving the way for a more political contest between workers and the state. In Korea, for example, scholars argue that these groups have created a space for a migrant worker resistance movement (Moon 2000; Grey 2007). In the Malaysian migrant worker case, the mix of ethnicities among workers combined with a repressive state that routinely uses violence against workers makes the situation more complex.

Christian advocacy services have provided an avenue for campaigning against an unfair labour and immigration system by encouraging workers to help each other. The personal stories of Tan, a young Vietnamese Catholic volunteer; Su, a detention-centre inmate; and Dong, a Vietnamese worker who is a friend of Su reveal how these networks operate. Tan speaks Vietnamese and English and translates for troubled workers through the Catholic Church. Previously he worked in a restaurant, but switched to part-time employment to allow more time for this voluntary work. He said, 'Right now I just want to help Vietnamese workers deal with working in Malaysia' (Tan, pers. comm., Kuala Lumpur 2009). Su had sought Tan's help in obtaining a new passport. He had been held in the detention centre for nine months and was not well. His parents had organized payment for a plane ticket home but he could not get to the Vietnamese Embassy to arrange a new passport. Dong, his friend, visited the Embassy six times but without a satisfactory outcome. Feeling powerless, Dong contacted Tan and quickly the problem was resolved. Su was released and returned home.

Christian advocacy has empowered workers to organize their own migrant worker organization. Nepalese workers have started a foreign worker association called Gefont, which operates under the auspices of the MTUC and Nepalese trade union council (also called Gefont) in Nepal but also has connections with the Nepalese Ministry at the Methodist Church. This association is operated by the workers for the workers and employs a coordinated community response to help their situation in Malaysia. Such shifts reflect the way workers are using the different organizations and church associations for their own self-interest. This nascent worker association is also involved in pastoral care. For example, the leader of the Nepalese Workers' Association Gefont speaks Nepalese and some English. He operates a 24-hour SMS hotline for troubled workers, 'We help workers, not just Nepalese, we help Burmese, Indians, Bangladesh and others with salary complaints, accidents and any other problems they may have working in Malaysia' (Janek, pers. comm., Kuala Lumpur 2009).

The leader of the association has experience working in Malaysia. After working for seven years, he returned home for 12 months and his employer telephoned to ask him to return to work in the factory. He agreed to work for another three years. At present he works in a factory, lives in a hostel with nine other workers and sends a remittance to his wife to care for their child, his ageing parents and large extended family in Nepal. He intends to make his time in Malaysia worthwhile by helping to organize workers through the Nepalese

Workers' Association and provide help through the crisis hotline. He related a number of examples where migrants needed assistance in times of crisis. For example, recently Rita phoned the hotline wanting help to retrieve her lost passport. The factory had confiscated the passport as soon as she arrived in Malaysia and since she had left the factory she had no passport. Without it she would have trouble returning to Nepal. Feeling powerless, she contacted the hotline and the problem was resolved. The factory management returned her passport but refused to pay the back pay owing.

We agree with Ford (2009) that grass-roots NGO and migrant organizations are a new form of labour networking and should be considered a part of the labour movement. By making these alliances explicit, we can be more aware of the ways workers are building safety nets to address labour abuse and exploitation. Christian outreach associations also provide migrants with services, encouraging them to develop a sense of commitment to each other, and in times of distress to care and look out for each other. The Christian organizations have not led to worker unions as such, but they have provided networks that migrants can use to reach other workers from the same ethnicity, and workers are forming their own associations. Like Korea, migrant workers in Malaysia have moved from an objective position within the human rights movement to a subjective position within a workers' rights-based movement. But the movement continues to be divided along the lines of ethnicity and it is questionable whether these ethnic divisions can be removed to create a strong migrant worker union movement in the near future.

The roles of the churches must be understood in the context of the place of religion and discipline in Malay society. This was questioned by Ong (1987) in a comprehensive study of young Malay women in the electronic industries. Ong argues that although Malay women resisted capitalist discipline, capitalists and state apparatus were able to deploy Muslim religious and Asian values to stifle resistance. The notion of 'Asian values' that was invoked to explain the compliance of factory workers across Asia in the 1980s has now been replaced with a more sober view of repressive regulation. The contemporary workforce of temporary migrant workers is supported by Christian organizations that operate following Christian values. However, little is known about the relationship among workers and Church organizations. The question is, do Christian civil society organizations offer migrant workers protective and supportive networks that may lead to migrant labour resistance, or does the pastoral care offered by religious organizations assist in shaping workers into a more docile labour force? Our objective here is to pay close attention to forms of workers' agency.

Further research is needed to illuminate the connections between Christian churches and migrant worker organizations. Does the Protestant ethos have special significance because workers interpret Christian values in such a way that they will put up with suffering and exploitation in the workforce? Do workers discipline themselves in the hope that their situation will change and, if not, will they be rewarded for putting up with hardship? Does the Catholic Church provide a space more open to organization and resistance than say the

94 *V. Crinis and A. Ngọc Trần*

Protestant churches? We need to conduct separate interviews with foreign workers and their employers who are Chinese non-Muslim Malaysians and members of the same churches in order to understand whether these religious alliances help to diffuse worker resistance in the clothing industry or whether they are avenues for resistance. In part it appears that resistance patterns are evolving because in earlier times wild-cat riots were directed at the police and immigration officials, while the later protests were pleas to their embassies to stop the corrupt recruitment process that migrants believed led to their situation in Malaysia. The later protests have been organized around specific notions of labour rights and minimum wage legislation.

## Notes

1 We would like to express our gratitude to Sally Weller for her generous assistance reviewing, commenting and editing the chapter.
2 The research this chapter is based on was assisted by the generous support of the Australian Research Council (ARC). The chapter is part of an ARC collaborative study of the clothing industry and its workers in the Asia Pacific. Part of this chapter was presented as a conference paper at the Vietnamese Update in Canberra, Australia, in 2008.
3 Migrants, for example, meet in Komtar in Penang, a mostly migrant shopping centre too old and run down to attract the local population. These spaces house different ethnic restaurants and other migrant facilities.
4 In addition to the breaches, the Malaysian government continues to lead efforts to create an impasse to negotiate a legally binding instrument for the protection and promotion of the rights of migrant workers under the ASEAN Committee on Migrant Workers.
5 Malaysia is ranked number 12 out of 185 on the World Bank's ranking of best economies for investors doing business. For protecting investors, Malaysia is ranked fourth.
6 Fernandez was arrested in March 1996 after she passed a copy of a Tenaganita report to the *New Straits Times* (Wickramasakara 2004). Irene Fernandez was charged in 1996 under Section 8A(2) of the Printing Presses and Publications Act (1984) (PPPA) for maliciously publishing false news (Gurowitz 2000).
7 In support of Irene Fernandez, Malaysian NGOs comprising women, consumer and environmental groups, human rights and civil society organizations and trade unions came together to launch a campaign to support Fernandez. Sadly Irene Fernandez passed away in 2014.
8 The WAO was falsely accused of trying to convert migrants to Christianity and Tenaganita of publishing false statements about migrant worker abuse (Ng *et al.* 2007).
9 Despite the sending government's attempts to use labour-exporting policies to ease the poverty in the sending country, it is obvious that this type of work does not lift workers out of poverty.

## References

Arnold, D. and Hewison, K. (2005) 'Exploitation in global supply chains: Burmese migrant workers in Mae Sot Thailand', *Journal of Contemporary Asia*, 35(3): 319–40.
Bair, J. (2005) 'Global capitalism and commodity chains: looking back, going forward', *Competition and Change*, 9(2): 15–180.
Barrientos, S. (2013) 'Labour chains: analysing the role of labour contractors in global commodity chains', *The Journal of Development Studies*, 49(8): 1057–71.

Boat People SOS (2009) www.bpsos.org (accessed 8 October 2009).

Bonocich, E. and Applebaum, R. P. (2003) 'Offshore production', in D. E. Bender and R. A. Greenwald (eds), *Sweatshop USA*, pp. 163–88, New York: Routledge.

Bruce, M. and Daly, L. (2004) 'Lean or agile: a solution for supply chain management in the textiles and clothing industry', *International Journal of Operations and Production Management*, 24(2): 151–70.

Chan, A. (2011) *Walmart in China*, Ithica, NY: Cornell University Press.

Cheah, P. (2006) *Inhuman Conditions: On Cosmpolitanism and Human Rights*. London: Harvard University Press.

Coalition to Abolish Modern-day Slavery in Asia (CAMSA) (2009) www.camsa-coalition.org/index.php?option=com_content&view=article&id=3&Itemid=6 (accessed 20 October 2009).

Crinis, V. (2005) 'The devil you know: Malaysian perceptions of foreign workers', *Review of Indonesian and Malaysian Affairs (RIMA)*, 39(2): 91–113.

Crinis, V. (2008) 'Malaysia: women, labour activism and unions', in K. Broadbent and M. Ford (eds), *Women and Labour Organising in Asia: Diversity, Autonomy and Activism*, pp. 50–65, London: Routledge.

Crinis, V. (2010) 'Sweat or no sweat: foreign workers in the garment industry in Malaysia', *Journal of Contemporary Asia*, 40(4): 589–611.

Crinis, V. (2012) 'Global commodity chains in crisis: the garment industry in Malaysia', *International Journal of Institutions and Economies*, 4(3): 61–82.

Firdaus, A. (2002) 'Ruling on Indo workers stays: Malaysia to maintain sectoral deployment of foreign labour', *New Straits Times*, 8 February, p. 1.

Ford, M. (2009) *Workers and Intellectuals: NGOs, Trade Unions and the Indonesian Labour Movement*, Singapore: National University of Singapore Press.

Gereffi, G. (1994) 'Capitalism, development and global commodity chains', in L. Sklair (ed.), *Capital and Development*, pp. 211–31, London: Routledge.

Gereffi, G. and Memedovic, O. (2003) *The Global Apparel Value Chain: What Prospects for Upgrading by Developing Countries?*, Vienna: United Nations Industrial Organization.

Grey, K. (2007) 'From human to workers' rights: the emergence of a migrant workers' union movement in Korea', *Global Society*, 21(2): 297–315.

Gurowitz, A. (2000) 'Migrant rights and activism in Malaysia: opportunities and constraints', *The Journal of Asian Studies*, 59(4): 863–88.

Hale, A. and Willis, J. (eds) (2005) *Threads of Labour: Women Working Worldwide*, Oxford: Blackwell.

Knutsen, H. M., Bergene, A. C. and Endresen, S. B. (2012) 'Re-engaging with agency in labour geography', in H. M. Knutsen, A. C. Bergene and S. B. Endresen (eds), *Missing Links in Labour Geography*, pp. 2–15, Farnham, Surrey: Ashgate.

*Migration News* (2012) Southeast Asia, July, Volume 19 Number 3, https://migration. ucdavis.edu/mn/more.php?id=3776_0_3_0 (accessed 12 August 2012).

Moon, K. (2000) 'Strangers in the midst of globalization: migrant workers and Korean nationalism', in S. Kim (ed.), *Korea's Globalization*, pp. 147–69, Cambridge: Cambridge University Press.

Murali, R. (2002) 'Indonesian workers go on rampage', *New Straits Times*, 18 January, p. 5.

Ng, C., Mohamad, M. and Tan, B. H. (2007) *Feminism and the Women's Movement in Malaysia*, Abingdon, Oxon: Routledge.

Ong, A. (1987) *Spirits of Resistance and Capitalist Discipline, Factory Women in Malaysia*, Albany, NY: State University of New York Press.

## 96    V. Crinis and A. Ngọc Trần

Peck, J. and Theordore, N. (2001) 'Contingent Chicago: restructuring the spaces of contemporary labour', *International Journal of Urban and Regional Research*, 25(3): 271–496.

Sassen, S. (2000) 'Women's burden: counter-geographies of globalization and the feminization of survival', *Journal of International Affairs*, 53(2): 503–24.

Sennyah, P. (2011) 'Workers clash over a woman', *New Straits Times*, 9 June, p. 1.

Shadige, J. (2010) '500 riot over death of worker, *New Straits Times*, 16 August, p. 42.

Tenaganita (2008) *The Revolving Door Modern Day Slavery Refugees: Stop Trafficking in Persons*, Kuala Lumpur: Tenaganita SDN BHD.

Tran, A. N. (2004) 'What's women's work: male negotiations and gender reproduction in the Vietnamese garment industry', in I. Drummond and H. Rydstrom (eds), *Gender Practices in Contemporary Vietnam*, pp. 210–30, Singapore: Singapore University Press.

VietnamNet Bridge (2012) 'Vietnamese who make their living in Malaysia', http://english.vietnamnet.vn/fms/society/51962/vietnamese-women-who-make-their-living-in-malaysia.html (accessed 10 November 2013).

Wickramasakara, P. (2002) 'Asian labour migration: Issues and challenges in an era of globalization', *International Migration Papers* No. 57e, Geneva: International Labour Office.

### Newspaper articles

'100 Nepali workers stopped from holding protest over minimum wage', *New Straits Times*, 7 March 2013, p. 5.

'800 Bangladesh workers protest in Malaysia', *Khaleej Times*, 9 October 2006, www.malaysia-today.net/blog2006/newsncom.php?itemid=8968 (accessed 20 October 2009).

'3700 illegals, 30 employers held in Ops 6p raids', *New Straits Times*, 9 February 2014, p. 4.

Infoshop (2008) 'News campaign wins justice for Vietnamese guest workers in Malaysia', http://news.infoshop.org/article.php?story=20080606120412812 (accessed 20 October 2009).

'Minimum wage cheer for workers', *New Straits Times*, 1 May 2012, www2.nst.com.my/top-news/minimum-wage-cheer-for-workers-1.79469 (accessed 23 July 2012).

'Nepalese workers try to stage riots in Pokok Sena', *New Straits Times*, 2 January 2014, www2.nst.com.my/latest/nepalese-workers-try-to-stage-riots-in-pokok-sena-1.460537 (accessed 18 March 2014).

'NGOs, Rela lodged police report against Irene Fernandez', *New Straits Times*, 16 May 2012, p. 6.

'Three rape Vietnamese worker after robberies', *New Straits Times*, 18 August 2013, www.nst.com.my/nation/general/three-rape-vietnamese-worker-after-robberies-1.339624#ixzz2yLm5iYy6 (accessed 18 March 2014).

# 6 China's migrant workers and the global financial crisis

*Kate Hannan*

In 2009 I was interviewing Chinese migrant workers at a Guangzhou railway station where they usually break their journey from various rural locations before travelling to or from cities such as Dongguan and Shenzhen further south. These cities are the centre of low-end labour-intensive manufacture in the Pearl River Delta. When I was interviewing a worker others nearby would often gather around and listen and would be keen to add their own comment. I was talking to a young woman who was explaining that her wages had dropped to almost half as the 2008 global financial crisis affected orders for the factory employing her. She was 'going home'. She said her wages were too low to compensate for living in a ten-bed dormitory while being obliged to tolerate superiors who were 'high and mighty' and 'nasty to workers'. She added that worker contracts were not offered at her factory and in any case the contracts were 'not worth anything'. Two other young women listening to this exchange pointed out that factory management goes around contract conditions. They were keen to point out that they had heard that when workers in their factory had been dismissed, they were receiving only around 80 per cent of their due wages. These two young women had also chosen 'to go back home for now'.

After China was accepted as a member of the WTO in November 2001 and the MFA lapsed in December 2004, there was unprecedented global demand for China's low-cost textiles and clothing. China soon became the world's largest exporter of textiles and garments. By 2010, in spite of the negative effect of the 2008 GFC, the country was exporting 30.7 per cent of the world market's textiles and almost 36.9 per cent of the global market's garments. In the first three quarters of 2011, China was enjoying 29 per cent year-on-year rise in textile output value (*Xinhua*, 29 October 2011). However, contrary to immediate appearances, China's ongoing role as the 'workshop of the world' for low-cost goods, including textiles and clothing, was under threat. China's low-priced product manufacturers were soon to face twin but contradictory demands. They had to maintain their price advantage in order to attract export contracts and protect global market share. At the same time, there was a chronic shortage of the rural workers they employ. China's rural-to-urban migrant workers were increasingly unwilling to accept the wages and working conditions on offer.

98    *K. Hannan*

Over time migrant worker dissatisfaction translated into strike action and export manufacturers found they must pay higher wages.

By the end of 2011 China's migrant workforce was estimated to number over 250 million, with well over 150 million working outside their home province (*China Daily*, 23 June 2010a; *Xinhua*, 22 August 2012). A more recent government estimate of migrant numbers is 274 million by the end of 2014 with 168 million working outside their home province (*Xinhua*, 28 February 2015).

In this chapter I have used two primary research sources. The first is the rich vein of articles in China's print media, particularly in the government-sanctioned *China Daily* and *Xinhua*. The other is interviews conducted with migrant workers. I approached the workers in neutral territory, away from their places of employment. Books, chapters and journal articles also provided me with valuable insights together with comment by human rights groups, particularly China Labor Watch.

## Migrant workers in short supply

From as early as March 2004 it had become clear that the MFA, which for 30 years had apportioned textile, clothing and footwear markets in developed countries, would lapse and would not be replaced by a similar WTO-sponsored agreement. It was then recognized that there would be a substantial increase in investment in low-cost manufacture and particularly in textile and clothing production in China. This investment would exploit the low wages paid to China's migrant workers and would benefit from the basic literacy skills of these workers in concert with the production flexibility afforded by long hours of usually unpaid overtime. However, as China's volume of low-cost goods for export increased, the shortage of workers willing to be employed became increasingly evident.

In 2009, as the contracts lost to the GFC were reinstated, Chinese media noted that 'about 45 per cent of the enterprises in the Pearl River Delta and 34 per cent in the Yangtze River Delta' were looking for workers (*China Daily*, 16 April 2009). By 2010–11 media sources noted that 67 per cent of producers in the Yangtze River Delta were short of workers, with a similar situation in the Pearl River Delta. Today (in 2015), it is estimated that the low-end manufacturing centre of Dongguan alone is short of 100,000 migrant workers (*Xinhua*, 8 May 2015). The deltas have been 'the preferred location for low-cost export manufacturers' (*Xinhua*, 25 March 2010).

The growing shortage of migrant workers was attributed to a number of causes. By 2006–7 a popular view among China's academic commentators was that labour shortages were short-lived anomalies. However, there was another equally popular view that was diametrically opposed: that labour shortages were a result of an inevitable structural Lewisian turning point (Rapley 2002: 14–15, 30). Economists at both China's Academy of Social Sciences and at the Institute of Population and Labor Economics argued that 'most developing countries experience a common process of dualistic [two-step] economic development'

(*China Daily*, 9 March 2007). In this process 'the surplus rural labor force provides cheap labor for industrialization and the wage level increases slowly' (*China Daily*, 9 March 2007). As this process continues, it is expected that the seemingly endless supply of rural labour is absorbed. The Academy and Institute economists stressed that as China reached 'its second stage of development [and rural labor became scarce], it must face a situation where wages are rising'. They advised that measures were needed to cope with these rising labour costs. In addition it was expected that 'the supply of rural labor cannot [and will not] meet the urban need' (*China Daily*, 18 June 2007b). This conclusion was a factor in the central government's policy choice to downgrade labour-intensive manufacture in favour of capital-intensive 'high-tech' production.

While the Lewisian argument continued to be popular, the 'short-term anomaly' argument tended to lose ground. In a collection written by respected Western and Chinese scholars in 2010, the Lewisian turning point is invoked to address the 'considerable controversy over labor shortages and rising wages for unskilled workers' (Oi *et al.* 2010: 27). Cai Fang, Director of the Institute of Population and Labor Economics of the Chinese Academy of Social Sciences (one of three authors of the chapter cited directly above), then offered similar comment in a *China Daily* editorial. He declared that 'the rising cost of labor in China is an inevitable result of supply and demand and not the growing awareness of workers in sweatshops'. He stressed that 'the [Lewisian] turning point in the supply of labor is the primary cause for labor clashes' and argued that low-end industries must be 'transformed'. They must 'improve labor efficiency, so that the rising cost of labor does not result in the loss of China's [overall] comparative advantage in the global economy' (*China Daily*, 30 November 2010).

An argument that does use the short-term anomaly thesis (rather than the Lewisian turning point) posited that migrant workers were in short supply because they had come to expect more than they were offered. As a result, a significant number of migrant workers decided that low-end urban-based employment was not worthwhile. This dissatisfied workers thesis attributes choice and agency to China's migrant workers and is the thesis I prefer. It is supported by a call for 'decent work' that has been increasingly evident since the latter 1990s when a second generation of rural-to-urban migrant workers have been employed in urban-based labour-intensive production. These workers are better educated than their parents. This has improved their efficiency and it has raised their expectations. They have made it very clear that they are unwilling to follow their parents in undertaking dirty, exhausting and backbreaking work. They want more (Hannan 2008; *Xinhua*, 13 January 2011).

Between 2004 and October/November 2008, the shortage of migrant workers was cited as the reason for a slow but steady increase in wages. At the same time, China's central government was supporting migrant workers by once again demanding that manufacturers pay their wages in full and on time. Wage payment has been a persistent problem. Wages are often delayed months and even as much as a year. The Central Government was also pushing for improved working conditions. However, Beijing had at the same time adopted taxation initiatives aimed at encouraging investors to move from labour-intensive low-profit margin export manufacture to capital-intensive, high-tech production. These measures included a significant step-by-step reduction in the export taxation rebate offered to textile and clothing manufacturers, which further squeezed their narrow profit margins and reduced the capacity of manufacturers to pay wages in full and on time and to increase workers' wages. These export rebates were reinstated at the height of the 2008 GFC, but were reduced again in the last half of 2010 (*Xinhua*, 15 July 2010). Today (in 2015) the emphasis is on increasing the administrative efficiency of the export rebate process to ensure that companies receive full and prompt reimbursement of funds due (*China Daily*, 18 September 2015).

In the period immediately before the global financial crisis when Beijing was reducing export rebates, measures were also adopted that were aimed at closing small (and in many cases medium-sized) enterprises deemed to be particularly low tech, inefficient, energy hungry and polluting, and by early 2008 the new Labour Contract Law was making the business environment even more difficult. Manufacturers were complaining that 'the new labor law should be amended to protect business interests' (*China Daily*, 15 April 2008). The smaller manufacturers were hardest hit. They could not be expected to – and proved to be unable to – absorb increased production costs, particularly labour costs. A '30 to 50 per cent jump in [manufacturing] costs in the last twelve months [prior to January 2008]' was cited (*China Daily*, 15 April 2008). This clearly represented a substantial increase. Researchers at China's National Development and Reform Commission subsequently noted that during the first half of 2008 many previously profitable small manufacturing enterprises collapsed (*China Daily*, 28 September 2009). The stress felt by China's low-end low-profit manufacturers – especially during the first three quarters of 2008 – left this sector particularly vulnerable to the impending effect of the GFC.

## The 2008 global financial crisis (GFC)

In the first week of November 2008, on my way to undertake a short period of research, my train passed through Dongguan station. Dongguan and its sister city Shenzhen in southern Guangdong Province are, as I note above, important centres within the Pearl River Delta export manufacturing hub. By the time of the global financial crisis Shenzhen's annual growth had been 25.8 per cent for the almost 30 years of its existence as a centre for foreign investment and labour-intensive, low-cost manufacture for export (*China Daily*, 7 September 2010, 9 September 2010). Dongguan had been established for less time, but had had similar annual rates of growth (*China Daily*, 25 November 2009).

As my train slowed and stopped at Dongguan station, many migrant workers were standing in line on platforms ready to board trains to Guangzhou from where they would go on to their rural homes. This would have been only the tip of the iceberg as most workers travel between Dongguan and the Guangzhou rail hubs by bus because it is cheaper and the buses run more often. These workers had either lost or left their jobs. The factories where they worked had closed or the management had decided to downsize the company's workforce, or they reduced wages and conditions from an already low base and workers decided to leave. Almost all migrant workers who continued in employment had their hours and wages substantially reduced.

On the same day as I saw the migrant workers queuing for passage out of Dongguan, Chinese newspapers announced that orders for toys, furniture, textiles and garments had dropped 20 per cent, while electronics and footwear sales had dropped 15 per cent. The anticipated fall in demand for 2009 was greater: 30 per cent for shoes, and 35 per cent for textiles and garments, toys and electronics (*China Daily*, 4 November 2008). Export manufacturing enterprises in the Yangtze and Pearl River Deltas had spent the previous four to five years complaining that they were chronically short of migrant workers, and then there was an about-face. Overnight, a large number of migrant workers left Guangdong Province due to the GFC (*Xinhua*, 8 January 2009).

Hubei provincial sources reported that 300,000 of the province's seven million migrant workers returned home in just two months – October and November 2008. The Jiangxi provincial administration reported that 300,000 of the province's 6.8 million migrant workers had returned by mid-November 2008 and administrators from the Hunan provincial government were estimating that 2.8 million migrant workers would return to their province in 2009 (*China Daily*, 9 January 2009). In the manufacturing hub of Guangdong, the Deputy Governor noted that by the end of 2008, 600,000 migrant workers had left his province and he predicted that by the beginning of 2009 as many as 'one in every three migrant workers employed in Guangdong might have left' (*Xinhua*, 8 January 2009).

China's residential registration system (the *hukou* system) has long provided a basis for classifying migrant workers as rural residents. The rural status of these workers has been used to justify their low wages and has legitimized their low social status. Migrants are 'illegal' workers rather than permanent urban citizens. It is also on the basis of their rural *hukou* that migrant workers have been denied urban-based medical services, education and housing. The residential registration system has made a significant contribution to China's persistent and ever-growing rural–urban inequality. The Chinese government's estimation is that in 2011 the Gini coefficient, 'an index reflecting the rich–poor gap', 'stood at 0.3949' and would narrow in China, as in other developing countries. This was an improvement on the 2005 figure of 0.47 (the warning level set by the United Nations (UN) is 0.4), but Chinese scholars did not believe the government's figure for 2011. Chinese media sources reported that based on the large income gap between residents of urban and rural areas 'scholars believe the index is currently between 0.45 and 0.50' (*Xinhua*, 21 August 2012). The government's more recent 2014 Gini-coefficient measure was 0.460 (*China Daily*, 27 January 2015).

In addition to the disadvantage associated with the residential registration system noted above, in the context of the downturn in export orders and manufacture brought about by the 2008 GFC, the *hukou* system meant that

## 102 K. Hannan

unemployed migrant workers were effectively exported to their rural homes scattered across the country and this fragmentation of the migrant worker cohort proved to be highly effective in averting the organized social unrest the government had feared (*Xinhua*, 13 April 2009).

## Low wages persisted after the 2008 crisis

The GFC meant that China's rural-to-urban migrant workers, particularly those employed in low-end labour-intensive manufacture, went from receiving relatively low pay to even less pay.

In April/May 2009 and then in July/August I went to railway stations in Shanghai and Guangzhou and interviewed migrant workers who were either travelling to the Yangtze and Pearl River Deltas to find work or were returning home to the countryside. In the case of the latter group, I wanted to know why they were returning to their rural homes. Some had lost their jobs, but many had decided they could no longer afford to live and work in the city. A typical example of this situation is evident in my interview with a young woman passing through Shanghai on her way to Wenzhou where she had been working weaving fabric for five years. She had been working 15 hours per day for seven days per week. By the second half of 2009 she was working nine hours per day for six days per week and was earning only 1000 yuan per month. Her wage was half what it had been and she had to pay for factory-based accommodation and food from this sum. Like most migrant workers she was not working under a contract. She wondered how long it would be before she decided to return home because her present situation was not worthwhile. Another young woman waiting nearby said that she had also worked in the Greater Shanghai area for around five years and that she had previously been earning 3000 yuan per month. When I spoke to her she was earning less than half that amount. She said 'the situation is not good' and that she was going home. Others, such as a young couple who worked in a clothing factory in Suzhou for around five years and worked without a contract, said they were alright at the moment. However, they were worried about their employment security and wondered whether their wages would be maintained. Their concerns were well founded.

The situation was similar among the migrant workers outside the railway station used as a transit point in Guangzhou. I interviewed a couple who had worked in a shoe factory in Dongguan. They were going home because the amount they were now earning did not cover their expenses. The factory where they worked manufactured for export and had lost orders. They also pointed out that management had become more vigilant over matters such as production quality (driven by their buyers' leverage in a tightened market), and that this was happening at a time when the factory was experiencing a relatively rapid turnover in its workforce. It was losing experienced workers who were unwilling to work for the lower wages and the couple wondered how quality would be improved as expertise was lost.

The migrant workers I interviewed were knowledgeable. They recognized many of the issues that the GFC had visited on them and their employers. They

## China's migrant workers    103

pointed out that while a factory may not directly dismiss workers, factory managers expected workers to leave when it was obvious that there were insufficient orders to maintain the workforce. Factory managers would often broadcast information about loss of orders as a way of 'encouraging' workers to leave. These workers also noted that as wages plummeted factory managers were flouting provincial government basic wage rate regulations and a number of factories were charging extra for hostel accommodation and were stepping up their use of already well-established practices such as 'trying out' workers without payment and then employing them for long periods at very low wages before formally employing them. Later (in 2012), the Foxconn corporation added a new approach to this type of ploy when one of its manufacturing centres promoted arrangements with vocational training colleges and universities that required students to serve an 'internship' with the company as a prerequisite for successfully completing courses and degrees. They paid the students a basic salary of only 1550 yuan per month. By 2012 this was a very low wage (*China Daily*, 7 September 2012).

Older workers (in their late 30s and 40s) were more likely to be dismissed from their jobs than their younger colleagues. Most migrant workers are aged 16 to 30. The average migrant worker had finished middle school (*China Daily*, 23 June 2010a). The older workers said they would not be returning to the city to find work. Unlike their younger colleagues who left their family homes and went to the city to work as soon as they finished their education, many 'middle-aged' migrant workers had some farming or other village-related skills. The younger workers I interviewed all said they would return to urban areas to look for work.

I also interviewed migrant workers at a Guangzhou bus station. One, who had been working in Dongguan, said that her company (a well-known international brand of clothing and women's accessories) had coped with reduced overseas orders by shutting down for seven days each month. She had been working six days per week for around ten hours per day. She said that her wages were relatively 'good', the company provided her accommodation and she had a contract. She was very proud of the company, saying that it was a cut above the average, which gave her status. However, a number of studies undertaken by academics and human and worker rights groups make it clear that manufacturers filling brand-name contracts have been cited for poor treatment of migrant workers. Well-publicized examples include footwear giant Reebok and the Foxconn complex which manufactures products for Dell and Apple and other well-known brands.

Another couple I interviewed was on their way to Shenzhen. The man had worked in a shoe factory and was bringing his new wife to find work, he hoped, at the same factory. Like others I interviewed at the Guangzhou bus station, they expected to earn between 1300 and 1500 yuan each per month. However, my research was showing that 1000 yuan a month was usual at that time (in mid-2009), 1200 was quite good, and a low salary could be as little as 760, but was probably more likely to be around 900 yuan per month.

The effect of the global economic downturn on China's rural-to-urban migrant workers was not surprising. What was surprising was that less than a

104   *K. Hannan*

year after the GFC, China's export manufacturers, particularly low-end manufacturers, were finding that demand for their products was recovering well. They began to complain again that they could not attract sufficient migrant workers. Headings in the Chinese newspapers included 'Labor shortage hinders Guangdong factories', 'More factories experience a labor crunch', and 'Textile firms grapple with labor woes' (*China Daily*, 25 August 2009, 14 September 2009, 29 October 2009). They reported blackboards with 'Help Wanted' signs offering work to those 'who can sew belt loops' and 'who can stitch pockets' as well as for a fabric stretcher, a pants hemmer and a zipper stitcher (*China Daily*, 14 September 2009). As workers I interviewed a few months earlier had pointed out, there was clearly a shortage of skills in China's low-end manufacturing sector and worker turnover had increased at the same time as buyer leverage ratcheted upward. Companies had more readily raised wages for skilled workers, but the shortage persisted and some manufacturers resorted to somewhat underhand methods not only to access workers, but also to retain skilled workers. Human rights and labour watch groups reported significant fines levied on workers who resigned. As spokes-persons for non-government organizations were noting, when employing highly skilled workers (cutters, dyers or sewers for example), companies may require them to work for at least two years in order to avoid a substantial fine when resigning (*China Labor Watch*, 30 November 2011: 10).

By the end of 2009 factory administrators in the Pearl River Delta were complaining that 'for every 10 people we look for, we can only find two or three, while in Zhejiang in the eastern Yangtze River Delta a shortage of as many as 250,000 migrant workers was reported' (*China Daily*, 14 December 2009). Guangdong Province was estimated to be 900,000 migrant workers short. In January 2010 it was said that in the export manufacturing centre of Dongguan 'the job requirement rate in the city [had] hit nearly 1:2 last month, which means one worker is offered two jobs'. Factory managers were complaining that 'wages had come way down, and now they're starting to inch up again because a lot of the labor had migrated away'. There were warnings that 'the demand for workers is putting upward pressure on wages' and so has the 'potential to eat into the already wafer-thin factory margins' (*China Daily*, 14 December 2009). For low-end manufacturers, worse was to come. Relatively large wage increases for migrant workers were adopted when first, the shortage of migrant workers became even more entrenched and the timely filling of export orders became difficult, and second, a rolling series of strikes in May, June and July 2010 disrupted production and openly flagged migrant worker dissatisfaction and frustration.

A number of media discussions published between the last months of 2009 and May 2010, when migrant worker strikes began, insisted that the shortage of migrant workers was because they were unwilling to return to the cities when the global financial situation continued to be fragile. Commentators said that migrant workers did not want to risk the economic cost of returning. After all, 'spending the cash for a job search in a faraway province can be a big

_China's migrant workers_ 105

investment' and 'many don't want to risk it now if the prospects aren't solid' (_China Daily_, 14 September 2009). The same sources added that 'many workers are savvy enough to understand business trends and are cautious about whom they work for because they might get axed again'. They also pointed to the increase in jobs in inland China (_China Daily_, 14 September 2009). Many new job opportunities in central and western areas had resulted from the government's large stimulus package prompted by the 2008 GFC. The package included worker training programmes, as well as assistance and loans to open small businesses. At the same time, a significant number of export manufacturing companies were encouraged by Beijing to relocate to inland cities. Relocation usefully offset rising production costs, including and particularly wage costs.

When I asked workers why they were not returning to work in low-end labour-intensive export manufacturing jobs, they were keen to point out that wages had been lowered in response to the GFC and not raised again, and this explained their reluctance. One interviewee, who had been working in a series of clothing factories, stated that he 'would be willing to work for the average wage of 2000 yuan a month', however, he 'doubted that any of the factories would pay him that much for long' (_China Daily_, 14 September 2009). Similar worker interviews in September 2010 reinforced this point. This research showed that while manufacturers maintained they could only afford to pay their workers 1500 yuan per month, 'most of the young workers asked for 1800 or more' (_China Daily_, 25 March 2010). Some, like the interviewee cited above, were asking for 2000 yuan per month.

## Strikes and wage increases

The rolling wave of strikes taking place in China's export manufacturing sector in May, June and July 2010 did not begin, as we might expect, in the low-end low-profit manufacturing enterprises. The strikes began in May 2010 with a 'wildcat work stoppage' at Honda Auto Parts in Foshan in Guangdong Province. Four days later a strike started at the Foshan Fengfu Auto Parts Co. (which produces exhaust and muffler parts for the Honda assembly line), and there was a third associated strike when Honda Lock (Guangdong) Co. workers left their jobs (_China Daily_, 3 June 2010a; see also Yang 2014: 21–42). The Honda strikes closed down four assembly and engine plants and adversely affected production in other plants.

At the beginning of June workers at Hyundai's parts factory staged a two-day strike. A Toyota supplier also went on strike in June and workers at the No. 2 plant of Toyota Gosei (Tianjin) Co., situated in an economic development area that houses a further 30 Toyota suppliers, refused to work (_China Daily_, 23 June 2010c). During May and June strikes also affected sporting goods and textile and garment factories and the Japanese-owned Brother sewing-machine plant. In the latter case it was noted that the 'expanding industrial unrest [is] pitting manufacturers against increasingly assertive workers'. The workers made banners demanding increased wages and improved working conditions. One banner tied

106    *K. Hannan*

to a factory gate read 'We want a pay raise' and 'We want fair treatment' (*China Daily*, 2 July 2010).

In the face of the growing number of work stoppages and strikes China's trade union administrators (together with their local government comrades) were accused by workers, central government officials, and by the Chinese media of 'keeping one eye closed' in their approach to solving migrant workers' problems (*China Daily*, 19 June 2010). In an article in *China Daily*, the Australian academic Professor Anita Chan noted that the migrant workers have a stereotypical image of the official trade unions as 'useless'. She made this comment when discussing the worker problems at the giant Foxconn site in Shenzhen. She added the damning observation that

> at Foxconn [where worker frustration had even taken the form of suicides], the union did not even come forward to make a statement while at Honda, the union blatantly sided with the local government, which in turn was on the side of the employer.
>
> (*China Daily*, 18 June 2010)

Human rights groups made similar points. They suggested that trade unions are usually better described as 'company unions' rather than unions representing workers' interests. They recognized that even allowing for the 'hard-nosed competition realities at marketplace', China's workplace unions are not seeking to bridge the gap between the employers' interests in maximizing profit and migrant workers' need to earn at least 'a living wage' (Yu 2008). The result of this ineffective representation of workers' interests by unions was that less than 5 per cent of workers 'would resort to labor unions for assistance when in trouble'. In more recent years workers have been increasingly turning to what have been aptly described as 'grassroots migrant labour NGOs'. Many of these NGOs are situated in the Pearl River Delta where there have been on-going and an unprecedented number of labour disputes. These non-government organizations are recognized to have grown-up in the face of 'the defective labor union system' coupled with a 'vast demand' for assistance from migrant workers (Jingwei He and Genghua Huang 2014: 474–6).

Migrant workers involved in the 2010 strikes returned to work after gaining a substantial increase in their wages (*China Daily*, 3 June 2010b, 2 July 2010).

While strikes were rolling across China's automobile, electronic, sporting goods, textile and clothing and low-cost goods export manufacturing sectors, press attention was focused on the dramatic situation unfolding at the Taiwanese-owned Foxconn manufacturing centre. The complex is said to be the world's largest manufacturer of electronics. It employs a young Chinese migrant workforce to produce for well-known brands including Dell, Apple, Hewlett Packard, Sony and Nokia. Many of the then (in 2010) 430,000 workers at Foxconn's Shenzhen site were officially between 18 and 24 years old, but forging credentials is so common that they could easily have been younger. They were accommodated in hostels located in a closed industrial compound. At this time

Foxconn workers' wages were relatively low and overtime was encouraged. Then, the suicide deaths of 10 young workers (with a reported 18 employee suicides attempted) exposed the extent of management problems in China's low-end labour-intensive industries (*China Daily*, 25 June 2010, 24 April 2014). However, the problem of distressed workers was not addressed by changing the controlling management style, but by raising wages. At the beginning of June, wages were increased by 30 per cent (a few days earlier a 20 per cent increase had been suggested). Foxconn management argued that it would improve their workers' lifestyle because it would 'help employees increase incomes while reducing overtime, and [they] would have enough time for leisure activities' (*Xinhua*, 3 June 2010b). The company's workers were estimated to be averaging 28 hours per month in overtime, with their dormitory accommodation inside the factory and overwhelming dependence on their company making them easily accessible whenever management required.

By 2011, Foxconn had opened a large manufacturing complex in the western Chinese manufacturing hub of Chongqing where the price of land, utilities and migrant worker wages was lower. The company then announced it would add 300,000 robots to its assembly line. This was only the beginning, because over a period of three years, Foxconn intended to 'replace some of its workers with one million robots ... to cut rising labor expenses and improve efficiency' (*Xinhua*, 21 November 2011). The robots would undertake 'routine' jobs. Now (in 2015), a migrant worker doing a ten-hour shift for six days per week may earn as much as 4000 to 5000 yuan per month, but this wage level combined with the on-going 'struggle with labor shortages' and the central government's promotion of a high tech approach to production has further promoted replacement of migrant workers with robots. The Guangdong provincial government recently announced it will spend 943 billion yuan 'to replace human laborers...' (*China Daily*, 24 April 2014; *Xinhua*, 27 March 2015).

In February 2012 Foxconn announced that it had raised the base wage for new assembly-line workers from 1550 to 1800 yuan per month and that it would rise to 2200 yuan after six months of training. Interestingly, company sources explained that 'we are increasing the base pay to ensure that our workers' earnings will not drop much when their overtime hours are reduced' (which was expected with the slow US recovery and continuing European economic problems). Foxconn sources added that, 'though the pay rises will definitely increase our costs, they will help save on recruitment expenses and lower the defect rate of our products' (*China Daily*, 23 February 2012). It is worth noting that in spite of the wage increase the problems at Foxconn continued. In September 2012 it was reported that as many as 40 people were injured in clashes at the plant.

While the slow post GFC recovery of the US and European economies was affecting Chinese manufacturing orders, at Foxconn, contrary to earlier expectations, long overtime hours were resulting from the need to meet orders generated by the promotion of Apple's latest iPhone. Pressure to meet production deadlines together with 'strict quality control standards' insisted on by Apple 'despite design defects' was again creating a pressure-cooker situation. Quality control inspectors came into conflict with line workers and management chose to ignore the mounting tension. Human rights groups were soon reporting that the workers just had too much pressure (*China Labor Watch*, 5 September 2012) and the Chinese media were again reporting that Foxconn's young workers were treated badly. The media was also keen to draw attention to 'the uneasiness of a new generation of migrant workers' who feel isolated and 'unable to realize their dreams' (*China Daily*, 25 September 2012).

With persistent migrant worker shortages combined with strike action, both the high-profit automotive manufacturers (where the strikes began and who employ local urban residents and migrant workers) and low-priced goods/low-profit producers (usually employing only migrant workers) found they had to increase wages and improve their management style. China's booming automotive sector and much of the high-tech electronic sector could afford to pay higher wages, although they were apparently maximizing their profits by deferring wage increases. However, much smaller factories in the automotive and electronic assembly sector, which carry out subcontract work for larger manufacturers, were often operating with the same wafer-thin profit margins found in other areas of China's low-end export manufacturing sector. The managers of these enterprises made it clear that 'the increase in labor costs ... is seriously eating into company profits'. A substantial number of subcontracting producers and low-priced goods manufacturers predicted they would 'have to shut down production' (*China Daily*, 11 March 2010).

Labour-intensive low-profit-margin manufacturers had once been proclaimed the 'pillars' of China's export sector, but by 2010, many found their production processes were 'unsustainable' and that the Chinese government had decided they were expendable.

I returned to China to conduct interviews in November 2010 and noted that the rising cost of living was weighing particularly heavily on migrant workers. Subcontracting factories often paid around 1000 yuan per month and larger factories paid from 1500 to 2500 yuan depending on the worker's skill. Several interviewees based in Shanghai and surrounding areas said it was difficult to live on 1000 yuan, basing their assessment on 600 yuan for food and 400 yuan for rent, which was usually a room they reasonably regarded as inadequate. Workers coming into Shanghai and the surrounding Yangtze River Delta were expecting to earn more than those already employed. In 2010, incoming workers were expecting to earn between 2000 and 2500 yuan per month. While Foxconn agreed to pay this amount in February 2012, low-end textile and clothing manufacturers and subcontracting factories routinely paid considerably less.

In November 2010, I also conducted interviews with migrant workers in Guangzhou. A couple who had both worked in a clothing factory and now had their five-month-old baby with them knew they would each earn 2000 yuan per month. The man said that wages had risen around 200 yuan in recent months. He added that he thought the shortage of workers was responsible for this increase, but other workers I interviewed pointed out that often factories without enough workers continued to pay relatively low wages.

I also interviewed a young couple who were working in a jewellery export company. They said their company was always short of workers because it paid low wages, paying 1500 yuan per month with accommodation provided. A young woman I interviewed in Shanghai added that the conditions in jewellery factories were often unacceptable due to the air quality. Like others in her situation, she was concerned that her health would be damaged when grinding was involved in the production process and there was inadequate ventilation. The same is often said about paint factories or plants where toys and other goods are finished using paints and enamels.

I also interviewed three migrant workers in Guangzhou. The group consisted of a young husband and wife, and the wife's older sister. They were all working for garment manufacturers. The couple was earning around 1500 yuan per month each, and their sister/sister-in-law was earning 2000 yuan. I asked about the discrepancy in wages and the young man told me that people born in the 1990s (the second generation of migrant workers) were not prepared to work long hours and so he and his wife were earning less. He also said his wages were too low but that he didn't think he should have to work excessive hours in order to earn an adequate income. (The factory must have been paying wages at an hourly or piece-work rate or paying overtime, though the latter is much less likely to be the case.) The couple worked for the same company and they were living outside the factory, which was expensive. The factory was relatively small, but did supply accommodation and food, however, they described the factory accommodation as 'awful' and as newly-weds they wanted to live together, which under the usual factory hostel system was not permitted. The man described the food as 'no better than pig food', and so the couple was forced to buy their own food. His wife's sister worked in a nearby clothing factory. She was working longer hours and so was earning a higher salary, and she was saving money by living in the accommodation provided. This was also a relatively small factory. Both clothing factories employing these three workers were in the city of Guangzhou. All three respondents noted that worker turnover was a problem in their workplaces. They also said that a shortage of workers was an ongoing problem and that while the wages they were receiving were lower than they thought fair, they accepted that they were paid an average rate. They then said that being treated badly by management was the primary reason workers changed jobs and that access to higher wage rates was probably the second reason.

As well as the rising cost of urban living, management issues were commented on much more this time than in earlier interviews. Also, a larger number of workers had moved on to the service sector. However, some found the employment conditions were far from ideal and in some cases they were very bad indeed. Two girls I interviewed in Shanghai had been employed in a small café/restaurant. They worked around 11 hours per day for seven days a week and were earning 1300 yuan per month. They were fed up and were returning home. First they said that too much work was expected for too little pay, but further conversation led to an outpouring of grievances over how they had been treated by the café owners. They were expected to sleep on the premises and they felt

## 110 K. Hannan

controlled. They were 'pushed around' and treated rudely. They said they would not return to the city for work, though I don't think even they believed their 'never again' statement. Another young woman I interviewed found work in a supermarket and she was paid by the hour. Her working conditions were far better than those experienced by the young women café workers. Self-employment also stood out in these interviews. Buying clothing and selling it at home in the countryside was seen as a way of accumulating funds and making contacts that would eventually lead to establishing a small clothing outlet. Another young woman I interviewed had a small shop where she was selling cigarettes and cool drinks. Sales was another employment avenue taken up by several of the migrant workers I interviewed in Guangzhou in 2010. One young woman was offered 1800 yuan per month by her company, but only if she reached her sales target. Very few could reach the target and if you fell short you received less – 1600 to 1700 yuan per month. There was no accommodation or food provided.

### After the global financial crisis

In 2010–11 it was estimated that 67 per cent of firms in parts of the Yangtze River Delta were short of workers, the situation was no less severe in the Pearl River Delta (*China Daily*, 21 October 2011a) and matters were about to become more difficult for manufacturers. As in 2010, by October 2011 there was a rolling wave of strikes and again employees complained about low wages, penalties, autocratic management and unattractive working conditions. A strike at the Citizen watch plant was widely reported in the Chinese media. Workers complained that the company had unjustifiably deducted payments from their wages. A few weeks later, 3000 workers at a factory from the Japanese Hitachi group joined the strikes. These workers were keen to ensure that their existing benefits would be protected when the factory was sold to US interests. By the end of the year a number of export manufacturers, including the South Korean-owned LG plant, had experienced strikes. The LG strike was resolved when migrant workers had their yearly bonus raised from an amount equivalent to one month's wage to two months' wages (*China Daily*, 29 December 2011). A December 2011 survey showed that the average migrant worker wage had risen to around 2150 yuan per month, with at least one source estimating that even this amount was a substantial 1700 yuan below migrant workers' expectations (*China Daily*, 9 December 2011b). Figures published in August 2012 estimate that the average monthly wage for migrant workers under 35 years of age was 2513 yuan in 2011, 'which hardly covered expenses', but which nevertheless represented 'a 29.4 percent increase from 2009' (*China Daily*, 8 August 2012).

At the end of December 2011, the management of a Japanese company said that a significant earthquake that had shaken Japan was the reason they were reducing workers' bonuses from twice the base salary to 1.5 times. The migrant workers pointed out that 'inflation has increased the cost of living everywhere in China' and, in any case, the orders received by the company in 2011 were very close to the same number received in the previous year. And, the workers had another substantial grievance – they were enduring 12-hour working days and around 50 hours overtime each month (*China Labor Watch*, 28 December 2011).

As I have noted, wages increased and working conditions improved in large, usually overseas invested companies employing local urban residents and migrant workers, and smaller, often Chinese owned enterprises employing migrant workers, were obliged to pay similar wages. In just one small city (Zengcheng) in the Pearl River Delta there were more than 3000 denim jean producers and by mid-2011 the pressure of migrant workers demanding wage increases was being described as 'a challenge' (*Xinhua*, 18 June 2011). As happened elsewhere, the workers were not only dissatisfied with their wages, they complained about management style and attitude. They also said they resented the feeling of being 'outsiders' in the urban areas where they worked and lived. Strikes and demonstrations followed publicity about an incident where a pregnant migrant market vendor was mistreated by local authorities (*Xinhua*, 18 June 2011).

While the low-cost low-profit manufacturers were stating their intention to move up the value chain as the Chinese government decreed, they first had to access sufficient workers and meet migrant worker demands. A jeans manufacturing company established 22 years previously and manufacturing export brand names including Polo, Lee and Guess found its 'profit margins are getting thinner' (*China Daily*, 12 August 2011). In 2011 the company employed around 3000 workers. At the same time, the manager of a much smaller company employing only 60 workers in a factory rented for only three years said, I now 'make only 1 yuan for every pair of jeans I ship out' (*China Daily*, 12 August 2011). The small company was one of an estimated 2000 street-side workshops in a relatively small geographic area. They were subcontracting to larger factories. They sorted, altered and labelled jeans. The acute vulnerability of the small companies was obvious (*China Daily*, 12 September 2011).

By November 2011 the growth in exports had slowed to 22.1 per cent from 28.73 per cent the month before, and a large number of Chinese sources were reporting that 'slow global growth [was] dampening overseas demand and slowing exports' (*China Daily*, 11 December 2011). The government advice given in this context was that companies, like the jeans manufacturers cited above, must concentrate on producing more for China's domestic market and, wherever possible, they must focus on trade with emerging markets. Media sources were keen to point out that 'investing in other countries in Asia, transferring the labor-intensive industries there and exporting the goods produced there will become the new pattern…' (*China Daily*, 13 December 2011). Other central government advice given to textile and clothing manufacturers was that they should attempt to establish their own brands for both the domestic and export markets. Meanwhile, the central government continued to insist that an ever-widening technology and productivity gap must be closed. Clearly, larger manufacturers had far more capacity to adopt the government's preferred measures than smaller enterprises (*China Daily*, 22 August 2011).

In 2011 government sources were ridiculing 'the old-fashioned machines' that continue to be used in textile factories. Images such as the following were used: machines 'churning out reams and reams of cheap cloth to supply garment manufacturers' and 'workers [who must] toil in the heat and noise inside the grim workshop that conjures up images of Dickensian conditions'. Machines 'whirl and grind' while the country is 'falling behind'. Chinese workers were depicted as 'sweating in workshops without air-conditioning, using the sort of machines that disappeared from Japanese factories about 20 years ago' (*China Daily*, 22 August 2011).

A spokesperson for the well-established and well-known textile manufacturer Silk Road underscored the problems and benefits for manufacturers who were faced with higher migrant wages and improved working conditions at the same time as the government was pushing them to increase labour productivity by purchasing new higher-tech machinery. They were repeatedly urged to 'move to the upper end of the industry chain'. Silk Road was waiting for new machinery to arrive. The old, noisy non-computerized machines were purchased for 5000 yuan in the 1990s and would be sold for 3000 yuan. The new machines cost 500,000 yuan each. It was expected that 'with the new machines, the productivity of each worker would be increased 20-fold annually ... [and] the products will also be improved and employees would work in a more comfortable environment...' (*China Daily*, 22 August 2011). However, workers reported that they had not received the full monetary benefit promised to them by productivity increases predicated on either multi-skilling and/or the use of updated machinery. There were reports that line supervisors had been obliged to record workers' productivity inaccurately or face discipline measures over breaching factory-imposed wage ceilings. As a migrant worker employed as a stitcher said

> I was trained as a multi-skilled worker and required to take two work assignments. My line supervisor told me I would be paid by production output, so my piece-rate wage could reach 1000 RMB yuan. But finally, I found my piece-rate wage was merely 700 RMB yuan.

In this case the supervisor's wage ceiling did not allow for the wage to rise to more than 800 yuan (Yu 2008: 517, 522).

Chronic labour shortages and increased wages for China's migrant workers made low-end low-profit export manufacture unsustainable, for example, in 2011 it was estimated that 'wage rates in China's key manufacturing heartland of Guangdong had increased by 158 per cent over the past 10 years' (*China Daily*, 21 October 2011b). This increase was exacerbated by what some estimated to be a 30 per cent rise in the cost of raw materials for production during 2011 alone. It was again said that 'the traditional means of turning a profit through low labor costs had come to an end in China's coastal regions...' (*Xinhua*, 23 December 2011).

Academic and media commentators who had imbibed the Lewisian explanation of their country's migrant labour market argued that migrant worker shortages are 'normal shortages'. They said that while the shortage of workers in the low-end labour-intensive export manufacturing sector located on the east coast eased in the face of reduced export orders, 'the eastern areas [particularly the

Yangtze and Pearl River Deltas] development model was now a thing of the past'. These commentators argued that the repeated practice of battling for migrant workers only to drive them away when export orders decline would soon be overtaken by new arrangements. They insisted that a chronic shortage of migrant workers interspersed with periods of worker oversupply during periods of economic contraction in importing countries indicated a lack of maturity in China's labour market (*China Daily*, 30 November 2010).

## Conclusion

While China's 2001 membership of the WTO followed by the end of the MFA in December 2004 promoted a substantial increase in the manufacture of low-cost goods for the global market, particularly textile and clothing manufactured for export, the basis of China's global competitiveness has been low migrant worker wages. These wages have risen and Chinese factories that have 'devalued their employees' salaries in order to provide multinational companies with cheap products to be sold in the West' (China Labor Watch 2011: 22) are now obliged to change course.

For most of the last decade and beyond (from at least 2004) export manufacturers in the Yangtze and Pearl River Deltas have been chronically short of migrant workers, but it is an open question whether or not these shortages are the result of a 'natural' development as those subscribing to the Lewisian 'turning point' thesis argue. They insist that worker shortages will inevitably occur as development takes place. They present the phenomenon as 'an unavoidable growing pain for employers of all emerging economies' (*China Daily*, 30 November 2010). What cannot be disputed is that in China 'labor shortages and rising labor costs' are a feature of the labour-intensive manufacture for export sector (*China Daily*, 30 November 2010).

The central government's solution to the persistent migrant worker shortage and worker demands for increased wages and improved working conditions rests on a programme for 'realizing healthy and rapid economic growth through technical innovation and industrial upgrading'. This approach is combined with the promotion of domestic consumption. Industrial upgrading from labour-intensive low-profit production methods to more capital-intensive high-tech production processes was promoted even as the 2008 GFC slowed China's manufactured exports (*China Daily*, 4 November 2008). Indeed, the global economic downturn was seen by some Chinese commentators as a useful means of promoting a policy they aptly described as 'emptying the cage for new birds' (Hannan 2008). It was expected that a significant number of low-end export manufacturers would be pushed out of business and this would leave room for more desirable high-tech industries to be established. However, in late 2008 and early 2009, with the length and extent of the effects of the financial crisis still unknown, more cautious Chinese planners and media commentators argued that concern must centre on avoiding social unrest predicated on job losses and the significant reduction in migrant wages (Hannan 2008).

By 2010, in the context of returning export orders, Chinese policymakers and administrators were again actively promoting their argument that the country's manufacturers must 'move up the value chain'. There was no opposing argument this time. China's policymakers and commentators agreed that 'the rising cost of labor could spur consolidation and innovation among embattled Chinese manufacturers'. They buttressed their argument by stressing that 'the heyday of manufacturing T-shirts, toys, etc.... is gone' (*China Daily*, 8 June 2010a: 8). In the wake of migrant worker strikes in May and June 2010 and again in the latter months of 2011, articles in the Chinese press went further. They presented the view that the low-end, low-cost, labour-intensive model of export manufacture is a flawed 'eastern areas' development model. It is a 'model' that has failed to increase the productivity of migrant workers. While the workers' level of education rose, labour-intensive production processes continued and authoritarian management practices persisted. Wages are expected to rise with increased productivity based on upgrading the nation's manufacturing industries, and particularly with investment directed into service and high-tech industries. The increase in workers' wages associated with more high-tech capital-intensive higher-skilled production has been presented as the key to long-term dampening of social unrest while assisting the much promoted need for increased domestic consumption (*China Daily*, 30 November 2010, 18 February 2011, 28 September 2012, 6 March 2013). The Lewis Turning Point is now presented as China's 'new normal' with the high-tech approach to manufacture coupled with increased domestic consumption deemed to be central to the 're-balancing' of the Chinese economy (*China Daily*, 5 March 2015; Yu Bin and Wu Zhenyu, 2015: 1).

The 2008 GFC reduced orders for China's low-end manufactured products and provided some relief for manufacturers faced with an overall shortage of migrant workers, but the underlying problem of low wages and low profit margins predicated on global market share that depended on a relatively low and highly competitive product price had not been resolved. Low-cost labour-intensive production of goods for export has made a central and substantial contribution to China's healthy foreign exchange reserve of US$3 trillion by 2010 (*China Daily*, 13 December 2011) and an estimated US$3.84 trillion by the end of 2014 and US$3.6 trillion at the end of August 2015 – the latter after four monthly drops in value in a row (*China Daily*, 26 February 2015; *Xinhua*, 17 September 2015), but it is now deemed to be an unsustainable development approach out-of-step with China's continued modernization.

## References

Dittmer, L. and Yu, G. T. (eds) (2010) *China, the Developing World, and the New Global Dynamic*, Boulder, CO and London: Lynne Rienner.

Fulong, W., Jiang, X. and Gar-On Yeh, A. (2007) *Urban Development in Post-Reform China*, London: Routledge.

Guoguang, W. and Lansdowne, H. (eds) (2009) *Socialist China, Capitalist China*, London: Routledge.

China's migrant workers 115

Hannan, K. (2008) 'China: migrant workers want "decent" work', *Copenhagen Journal of Asian Studies*, 26(2), pp. 60–81.

Harney, A. (2008) *The China Price*, New York: Penguin.

Jingwei, H. and Genghua Huang, H. (2014) 'Fighting for migrant labor rights in the world's factory: legitimacy, resource constraints and strategies of grassroots migrant labor NGOs in South China', *Journal of Contemporary China*, 24(93), pp. 471–92.

Lee, C. K. (2007) *Against the Law*, Berkeley: University of California Press.

Lee, C. K. (ed.) (2007) *Working in China*, London: Routledge.

McLaren, A. E. (2004) *Chinese Women – Living and Working*, London: Routledge Curzon.

Midler, P. (2009) *Poorly Made in China*, NJ: Wiley.

Murphy, R. (ed.) (2009) *Labour Migration and Social Development in Contemporary China*, London: Routledge.

Naughton, B. (2007) *The Chinese Economy*, Cambridge, MA: MIT Press.

Oi, J. C., Rozelle, S. and Xueguang, Z. (eds) (2010) *Growing Pains*, Walter H. Shorenstein Asia-Pacific Research Centre, Freeman Spogli Institute for International Studies: Stanford University.

Pun, N. (2005) *Made in China*, Durham, NC: Duke University Press.

Rapley, J. (2002) *Understanding Development*, Second Edition, Boulder, CO and London: Lynne Rienner.

Shenggen, F., Rai, K. and Xiaobo, Z. (eds) (2009) *Regional Inequality in China*, London: Routledge.

Yang, O. R. (2014) 'Political process and widespread protests in China: the 2010 labor protest', *Journal of Contemporary China*, 24(91), pp. 21–42.

Yeoh, E. K-K. (ed.) (2009) *Towards Pax Sinica?*, Kuala Lumpur, Malaysia: Institute of China Studies, University of Malaya.

You-tien, H. and Lee, C. K. (eds) (2010) *Reclaiming Chinese Society*, London: Routledge.

Yu, B. and Wu, Z. (2015) 'Transitional changes and rebalancing relating to China's economic performance', *Development Research Center of the State Council of the People's Republic of China Research Report*, 123, p. 1.

Yu Xiaomin (2008) 'Impacts of corporate code of conduct on labor standards: a case study of Reebok's athletic footwear supplier factory in China', *Journal of Business Ethics*, 81, pp. 513–29 (reproduced by China Labor Watch).

## Chinese media sources

'10 injured in fight at Foxconn plant', *Xinhua*, 24 September 2012.

'20% of workers not to return to S China's Dongguan', *Xinhua*, 9 February 2010.

'40 injured after Foxconn plant clashes', *China Daily*, 25 September 2012.

'600,000 migrant workers leave Guangdong amid financial crisis', *Xinhua*, 8 January 2009.

'As old industry bites the dust, new sectors begin to bloom', *China Daily*, 10 November 2008.

'Big wheels get ready for the fast lane despite labor bumps', *China Daily*, 23 June 2010b.

'China buys and sells more textiles', *Xinhua*, 24 May 2011.

'China dismisses worries about capital outflow', *Xinhua*, 17 September 2015.

'China focus: growth in farmer-turned-laborers slows', *Xinhua*, 28 February 2015.

'China has 245 mln migrant population', *Xinhua*, 18 November 2014.

116    K. Hannan

'China sets plan for reducing unemployment in 2 years', *Xinhua*, 13 April 2009.
'China stabilizing foreign trade through taxation', *China Daily*, 18 September 2015.
'China to quicken urbanization to restructure economy', *China Daily*, 8 August 2010.
'China's "miracle" Shenzhen marks 30 years', *China Daily*, 9 September 2010.
'China's economic and social development in 2014', *Xinhua*, 26 February 2015.
'China's Guangdong Province invests billions in robot factories', *Xinhua*, 27 March 2015.
'China's textile industrial output up 29% in Q1-Q3', *Xinhua*, 29 October 2011.
'Chinese exports drop as EU debt crisis heightens', *China Daily*, 11 December 2011.
'Chinese manufacturers learn to love labor lost', *Xinhua*, 25 March 2010.
'Country roads take migrant workers home', *China Daily*, 28 September 2009.
'Economic hubs face tough times', *China Daily*, 9 January 2009.
'Experts call for narrowing of wealth gap', *China Daily*, 20 May 2010.
'Export slump eases as demand revives', *China Daily*, 12 December 2009.
'Facing problems of toying with industry', *China Daily*, 4 November 2008.
'FDI focus continues to shift', *China Daily*, 16 December 2011.
'Foxconn 4 years on', *China Daily*, 24 April 2014.
'Foxconn adds robots, pledges no layoffs', *Xinhua*, 21 November 2011.
'Foxconn announces another pay hike', *China Daily*, 8 June 2010b.
'Foxconn hikes workers' pay rises by nearly 70% after serial suicides', *Xinhua*, 7 June 2010.
'Foxconn promises 66% salary hike before Oct.', *China Daily*, 7 June 2010.
'Foxconn raises base wages, reduces overtime hours', *China Daily*, 23 February 2012.
'Foxconn raises workers' pay by 30% after suicides', *Xinhua*, 3 June 2010b.
'Government pledges job support to labor-intensive sector', *China Daily*, 28 October 2008.
'Growing pains of labor market', *China Daily*, 30 November 2010.
'Growth of rural income to slow', *China Daily*, 16 April 2009.
'Higher labor costs coming', *China Daily*, 18 June 2007b.
'Holiday labor shortages', *China Daily*, 14 December 2009.
'Honda hobbled by strike at parts plant', *China Daily*, 31 May 2010.
'How to deal with the future labor shortage?', *China Daily*, 9 March 2007.
'Hundreds strike at Japanese-owned plant in S China', *Xinhua*, 8 December 2011.
'Income inequality a battle for China, US and the world', *China Daily USA*, 27 January 2015.
'Jiangsu to suffer most from scrap of tax rebate', *Xinhua*, 15 July 2010.
'Jobless blues', *China Daily*, 29 December 2008.
'Journey to the west', *China Daily*, 21 October 2011a.
'Labor shortage eases in East China', *Xinhua*, 23 December 2011.
'Labor shortage hinders Guangdong factories', *China Daily*, 25 August 2009.
'Labor unrest and role of unions', *China Daily*, 18 June 2010.
'Low wages come in the way of finding a mate', *China Daily*, 12 September 2011.
'Manufacturing goes up the value chain', *China Daily*, 21 October 2011b.
'Many rebounding companies having tough time finding workers', *Xinhua*, 24 January 2010.
'Measures urged to cope with rising labor costs', *China Daily*, 18 June 2007a.
'Migrant worker shortage seen as good sign', *China Daily*, 18 February 2011.
'Migrant workers bear brunt of crisis', *China Daily*, 21 November 2008.
'Migrants cash in on labor shortage', *China Daily*, 11 March 2010.
'More factories experience a labor crunch', *China Daily*, 14 September 2009.

'Moving on from the low-cost era', *China Daily*, 15 April 2008.
'Moving up the value chain', *China Daily*, 8 June 2010a.
'Nation may face labor shortage', *China Daily*, 12 May 2007.
'Nation weaning itself off export model faces range of challenges', *China Daily*, 28 September 2012.
'New day dawns for labor rights in Pearl River Delta', *China Daily*, 16 May 2014.
'New day dawns for labor rights', *China Daily*, 23 May 2014.
'New generation of migrant workers face old problems, Shanxi survey finds', *Xinhua*, 13 January 2011.
'New strike halts Toyoto production', *China Daily*, 23 June 2010c.
'Out with the old, in with the new', *China Daily*, 22 August 2011.
'President hails Shenzhen SEZ a world "miracle"', *China Daily*, 7 September 2010.
'Recent shutoffs won't start trend: minister', *China Daily*, 19 June 2010.
'Regional worker shortage should be addressed by industrial upgrading', *Xinhua*, 3 March 2010.
'Rural exodus to cities continues', *China Daily*, 8 August 2012.
'Seven opportunities of China's economy under the "new normal"', *China Daily*, 5 March 2015.
'Shifting labor, rising incomes, spur demand', *China Daily*, 6 March 2013.
'Strike action ushers in new era of work relations says expert', *China Daily*, 3 June 2010a.
'Strike hits citizen watch plant in South China', *Xinhua*, 24 October 2011.
'Strike hits electronics plant', *China Daily*, 2 July 2010.
'Strike signals end to cheap labor', *China Daily*, 4 June 2010.
'Students made to work at Foxconn as interns', *China Daily*, 7 September 2012.
'Suicides at Foxconn reveal woes', *China Daily*, 25 June 2010.
'Survey: small businesses struggle to survive along Pearl River Delta', *China Daily*, 11 October 2011.
'Sustainable and quality growth "to be achieved"', *China Daily*, 14 November 2013.
'Textile factories grapple with labor woes', *China Daily*, 29 October 2009.
'The new drivers of Asia's economy', *China Daily*, 13 December 2011.
'Top ten news events commemorating WTO entry', *Xinhua*, 9 December 2011a.
'Two million people leave Dongguan during economic crisis', *China Daily*, 25 November 2009.
'Undercover at Foxconn shows workers "numbed"', *China Daily*, 2 June 2010.
'Unrest signals time to improve welfare of migrant workers', *Xinhua*, 18 June 2011.
'Wealth gap in rural China nears warning level', *Xinhua*, 22 August 2012.
'Wearing thin', *China Daily*, 12 August 2011.
'Weighing wages on the scales of progress', *China Daily* Hong Kong edition, 24 June 2010.
'Wen urges innovation amid economic slowdown', *Xinhua*, 1 April 2009.
'Workers strike at LG display's Nanjing plant', *China Daily*, 29 December 2011.
'Xinhua insight: robot factories China's answer to labor shortage', *Xinhua*, 8 May 2015.
'Young migrant workers have "high expectations"', *China Daily*, 23 June 2010a.
'Yuan's upturn unravels textile manufacturers', *China Daily*, 17 September 2010.
'Zhejiang keeps closer eye on smaller private businesses', *China Daily*, 9 December 2011b.

## 118   *K. Hannan*

### China Labor Watch online

'3000 to 4000 workers strike at Foxconn's China factory' (2012) 5 September online at www.chinalaborwatch.org/news/new-433.html (accessed 14 July 2014).

'8000 Workers protest cancellation of annual bonuses as strikes continue across China' (2012) *China Labor Watch*, 16 January www.chinalaborwatch.org/news/new-407.html (accessed 14 July 2014).

'China sets plan for reducing unemployment in 2 years' (2009) www.chinaview.cn 13 April online at http://en.nsd.edu.cn/article.asp?articleid=6440 (accessed on 14 July 2014).

'Investigation of two clothing and apparel factories in China: excessive overtime, student workers, and exploitative wage systems' (2001) report by *China Labor Watch*, 30 November, pp. 1–33 online at http://digitalcommons.ilr.cornell.edu/cgi/viewcontent.cg i?article=2167&context=globaldocs or http://chinalaborwatch.org/pro/proshow-174. html (accessed 10 June 2012 and 14 July 2014).

'Labor violations, bogus standards in Wal-Mart's Chinese supply chain' (2009) *China Labor Watch*, 29 July online at http://chinalaborwatch.org/pro/proshow-123.html (accessed 14 July 2014).

'Urgent appeal for help: Mattel supplier factory female workers committed suicide' (2011) *China Labor Watch*, 3 June online at http://chinalaborwatch.org/news/new-345. html (accessed 14 July 2014).

'Workers on strike at auto parts factory in Guangzhou over bonus reduction' (2011) *China Labor Watch*, 28 December online at www.chinalaborwatch.org/news/new-408. html (accessed 14 July 2014).

### Interviews with migrant workers

I held interviews with migrant workers at the Shanghai Main Railway Station and at Guangzhou's central station (rather than the larger east railway station) and at a nearby domestic bus station. The first group of interviews were conducted between 27 April and 6 May 2009. The railway station interviews were conducted over several days and at different times of the day. The bus station interviews were more concentrated. They were conducted on one day (6 May) in the morning and again in the afternoon. I repeated this process with a second group of interviews conducted at the end of June 2009. I returned to China at the end of July and the beginning of August 2009 and again interviewed migrant workers at the Shanghai Main Railway Station and at the Guangzhou central train station and the near-by bus station used by migrant workers to book tickets and board buses taking them south to the export manufacturing centres in Dongguan and Shenzhen. I repeated the process in November 2010. I conducted interviews in Shanghai on 18 and 19 November and in Guangzhou on 24 and 25 November.

# 7 Workers in the Indian export garment industry

## Surviving neoliberal reforms

*Ruchira Ganguly-Scrase*

This chapter examines the concerns of workers about labour rights in the Indian export garment industry in the post-MFA era. First, I outline the historical and contemporary factors that have affected the industry itself and the labour processes therein. These factors are both contingent on domestic matters and more recently on global factors, such as neoliberal trade policies, global commodity chains and MNC practices. The neoliberal policy agenda tends to focus on the economic imperatives of the Indian export garment sector, which both inhibit and benefit India's export potential. The human aspect of labour rights is either ignored or is targeted as a potential threat to the maximization of profit. Second, using data from intensive fieldwork, and interviews with workers and exporters, the chapter provides the foundation necessary for understanding the predicament faced by Indian export garment workers today. It situates their experiences within the economic, social and political specificities of localities that form part of the Indian export garment sector and, in turn, are part of the wider global commodity structures. I pay particular attention to the ways in which India's post-independence, dualist development agendas with their historical particularities have shaped the experiences of garment workers.

This chapter shows that the existence of small-scale cottage industry together with large-scale industrial production helps to explain the contemporary conditions of workers in the export garment industry. Though the textile and garment industries constitute one of India's largest sectors of production and export earners, there is a high concentration of cheap and flexible labour. Yet, exporters and industrialists claim that productivity is lower in India because of 'inflexibility' and they bemoan the strict labour laws. They argue that compared with their competitors in other Asian countries, they are disadvantaged because not only is labour inefficient, but also the Indian garment industry is subject to undue restrictions on hiring and firing. Although India does have robust labour protection laws, since joining the WTO, these are slowly being eroded (Kolben 2006) because of constant industry pressure to become more 'flexible'. However, my findings question these assertions, given that most garment workers are in the informal economy and are therefore unprotected by labour laws and legislation.

## Features of the Indian garment sector

India's textile and garment industry is its second-largest industry after agriculture, and is one of the most important sectors in terms of foreign exchange, foreign and domestic output, and employment. The textile and apparel sector accounts for 18 per cent of employment in the industrial sector, 20 per cent of industrial production, 9 per cent of excise duties collections and more than 30 per cent of the country's total exports. The value of textile exports increased from INR15,038.07 million (US$227593663.660) in 1992–3 to INR82,879.14 million (US$12543380027.030) in 2006–7 and has continued to increase (Hirway 2008; WTO 2015). In 2009, India held 3.9 per cent of the global garment sector (Osakwe 2009), with ready-made garments and cotton fabrics making up the highest proportion of the sector's foreign earnings (Hashim 2004: 2; see also Vijayabaskar 2002: 6).

Some of the central locations for the export garment industry in India are in New Delhi, Kolkata (formerly Calcutta), Chennai, Mumbai, Bangalore, Cochin, Jaipur, Tiruppur, Ludhiana and Hyderabad. The largest concentrations of manufacturing are in New Delhi, Mumbai, Tiruppur and Kolkata. The latter has more safety and industrial clothing (CEC 2004: 16), along with small export houses catering to fashion labels. It is thought that one of the significant advantages India has in an increasingly competitive global market is a high concentration of cheap and flexible labour (CCC and CEC 2006: 3; De Neve 2008: 215; Doshi 2006: 4; Hashim 2004; Hirway 2008).

Although it may appear that textiles and garments might be one of India's most promising export industries, Das in a commentary in the *Economic and Political Weekly* (*EPW*) argues that there continues to be 'a lack of substantial growth in exports of labour intensive, relatively low technology manufactures' (Das 2004: 2192). Similarly, Hirway's (2008) comparative accounts of the organized and unorganized sectors of the garment industry note that most workers are concentrated in the latter, marked by low productivity. In contrast, the capital-intensive organized sector employs fewer workers with high output. There appears to be growth in medium-to-high technology products such as pharmaceuticals, software and automobiles, which are manufactured by a highly skilled, professional minority. Therefore, in India there is 'the phenomenon of fairly high rates of growth with very minimal increases in employment' (Das 2004: 2192; see also ILO 2005: 9).

India and China, in particular, have been considered among the main beneficiaries of the post-MFA era (Hashim 2004; ILO 2005; Verma 2002). Productivity levels, availability of raw materials, quality and cost of output including labour, economies of scale and design are all imperative to competitiveness (Doshi 2006: 5). Yet, compared with China, for example, India is lagging behind, with the threat of price-cutting emerging as a burgeoning reality. Inevitably, a quick fix in a labour surplus economy such as India's would be to cut costs by decreasing wages and raising output expectations (Das 2007: 93). De Neve (2008: 221–2) contends that the introduction of payment by garment piece rather than fixed wages has increased demand and hours for workers.

## Labour rights in the Indian garment export industry: review of literature

For export-producing nations, structural changes forged in the post-MFA era have intensified exploitative wages and working standards in global factories as manufacturers enter an open international market (CCC and CEC 2006: 3). Within the Indian export garment industry, the post-MFA regime is marked by a growing informal sector (De Neve 2009; Mezzadri 2010; Pande 2007). The opportunity to circumvent labour regulations provides a major incentive for business owners to perform the bulk of operations within the unorganized sector (Hirway 2008). Even in the formalized sector, stringent labour laws can be bypassed, as de facto flexibility is acquired through leveraging contract and casual labour (Nathan and Kalpana 2007: 11).

The textile and garment sector in India makes a crucial contribution to the national economy, accounting for almost 13 per cent of total exports (Ministry of Textiles 2010) and employing an estimated 35 million workers (UNCTAD and GOI Report 2011: 29). India's mass of cheap and flexible labour is considered one of its most significant advantages in a highly competitive and labour-intensive global industry (CCC and CEC 2006: 3; De Neve 2008: 215; Doshi 2006: 4; Hashim 2004; Hirway 2008). According to Ghosh (as quoted in CEC 2004: 9), 'the reduction of protectionism and increased market access to developed countries was supposed to lead to an increase in employment in the developing world, but this did not happen'. On the contrary, in 2008–9, the global economic slowdown led to decreased employment in the sector, which caused various export promotion councils and trade bodies to appeal for government support (Ministry of Textiles 2009). Towards the end of the MFA period, India was projected to capture 6 per cent of the global garment market by 2010 (Chatterjee 2004: 5; Singh 2007: 230), yet in 2009, its market share was less than 4 per cent (Osakwe 2009).

Sluggish growth has been considered a result of primitive technology which has adversely 'affected the productivity of capital as well as labour in the garment sector' (Hashim 2004: 8), resulting in India's exports being 'only 35 per cent of US levels – compared with the 55 per cent achieved by Chinese exporters' (Padhi *et al.* 2004: 9). Yet caution must be exercised not to interpret the rate of labour productivity as an essential 'innate' characteristic of Indian labour. It should be noted that low literacy levels and work-related skills are an outcome of the Indian government allocating more funding to the expansion of higher education than to mass primary education for 'nearly a half century' (Weiner 1996: 3007). This historical legacy has entailed substantial subsidies for education and training at the tertiary level (that is, for doctors and engineers), and lack of public investment in quality high school education and industrial training (Nathan and Kalpana 2007: 12). Indeed, V. N. Rajasekharan Pillai of the Indira Gandhi National Open University estimates that the number of skilled labourers in the Indian apparel industry is below 5 per cent (Fibre2Fashion 2009). In 2006, the Indian government estimated a shortage of half a million trained workers in the apparel industry (cited in Khan 2009: 65). Thus, in order to meet international demand, 'in terms of both volume and quality, the need for larger investment in both machinery and skill formation has been felt across the industry' (Das 2007: 92). Prior to the abolition of the MFA, quality assurance and skilled labour were less of a problem. Garment manufacturers were as concerned with productivity levels as they were with the variety of concessions on offer to SMEs (Kashyap 1988).

Along with the 'absence of a technically trained workforce and lack of formally educated management' (Rao 2010: 53), low productivity in the Indian garment industry has been attributed to pre-existing infrastructural constraints, such as power and water shortages, and inadequate irrigation, road connectivity and port facilities (CEC 2004: 10; Das 2007: 77–8; Doshi 2006: 5; Khan 2009: 66–7). It has also been attributed to the legacy of SME reservations (CEC 2004; Chatterjee 2004: 5; Das 2007; Hashim 2004; Hirway 2008; Khan 2009; Ramaswamy and Gereffi 2000; Vijayabaskar 2002). The reservations, together with the existence of small-scale enterprises (SSEs), are in part an outcome of post-independence India's dual development strategies. The policy of reservations derives from the Industries (Development and Regulation) Act 1951. It was a central development strategy of planned industrialization intended to foster the dispersal of industrial activity, provide increased employment opportunities and broaden entrepreneurship. It meant that 'reservations' were placed on items that were exclusively targeted for the small-scale sector. With high tariff and trade barriers the domestic market for these items would grow. Therefore it is a term widely used in the Indian literature to refer to protectionist policies and government subsidies to provide large-scale regional local employment.

## India's post-independence development trajectory

Broadly speaking, in postcolonial India, the state pursued two development trajectories. The strategy was characterized by inward-looking, state-regulated policies that were largely protectionist and focused on import-substituting industrialization. The dual development agenda comprised large-scale manufacturing and agricultural modernization together with the promotion of SSEs (Jha 2001). This approach dominated until the late 1980s and then, in 1991, a dramatic reorientation of policies aimed to foster economic development by shifting resources in favour of the global market (Chandrasekhar and Ghosh 2004).

The result of these two trajectories is currently visible in India's economic structure. On the one hand, emphasis is placed on large-scale, capital-intensive industries that rely on high levels of technology and productivity in the private and government-owned sectors, while on the other, there is a focus on small-scale units in the SME sector (Das 2004).

## Dualism in the garment sector

The different strands of the dualist agenda come together in the garment industry. Being a 'buyer-driven commodity chain' (Ramaswamy and Gereffi 2000:

192) means that the large retailers and trading companies control the production networks of the exporting garment industry. Since 'market power has shifted from manufacturers to retailers' (Ramaswamy and Gereffi 2000: 196), the Indian garment industry is heavily affected by demand uncertainty, price fluctuations and retailers' order-fulfilment practices.

As outlined earlier, the garment industry in India consists of a considerable workforce, although much of it is characterized by fairly autonomous, small-scale units in poor rural areas, typically feeding into semi-urban industrial centres. The range and dispersal of activities, along with the low technical requirements, means the industry employs a relatively large proportion of informal sector workers, who carry out their work either at home, the typical cottage industry, or at SMEs (Bhavani 2002). As Ghosh (2005) notes, the dependence of the garment industry on subcontracting casual and informal workers was a result of various factors, including 'the seasonal nature of export demand, the tight deadlines faced by producers and the competitive pressures from other developing country exporters'. Also, non-farm rural industrialization did not manage to provide employment to a large cross-section of the rural population (Mukherjee and Zhang 2005), which spurred people to take up casual employment opportunities in the garment industry.

It can be argued that SMEs have placed a stranglehold on capital and employment growth due to their inability to implement economies of scale 'whether in production or in marketing' (Das 2004: 2192). According to Kesab Das (2007: 74), despite interventions, SMEs have scarcely improved quality or exportability in terms of product and process innovations, diversification and wider market access. This has not only restricted India's comparative advantage, but has also undercut domestic trade as overseas competitors offer cheaper garments to local consumers (Das 2004: 2192; Hirway 2008). This problem is compounded by SME owners who resist up-scaling operations in order to capitalize on 'inefficiency incentives' offered to them as small businesses (Das 2004: 2193; Kashyap 1988) – such as preferential credit and investment subsidies (Ramaswamy and Gereffi 2000: 202) – and due to fear of workers organizing in larger units (Das 2004; Hirway 2008).

## SMEs: help or hindrance?

While acknowledging the restraints caused by poor productivity, obsolete technology and fragmentation, Tewari argues that former SME reservations protected skill diversification, encouraged efficiency and allowed exporters to secure long-term trading relationships with high-value, small and moderately sized European importers, while sheltering producers from the early 'Walmart-ization' of the industry, that is, powerful global retailers stipulating low prices and high volume (2006: 2335). Tewari's (2008) evaluation of the post-MFA Indian garment industry points to its spectacular success in the global market. She argues that India defies all generalized patterns of growth. However, her analysis and recommendations neither address employment issues for the vast majority

124    *R. Ganguly-Scrase*

within the textile and garment sector, nor recognize that the fragmented production structure of small-scale industry has been conducive to the violation of core labour laws. Indeed, her accounts make no mention of labour rights. These are critical omissions in the context of a globalizing industry marked by the informalization, contractualization and casualization of labour which beget job instability, lower wages, lack of social security benefits, labour law evasion, repression of trade unionism and increased exploitation of women and migrant workers (CCC and CEC 2006; Das 2007; Fair Wear Foundation 2003; Hirway 2008; Manicandan *et al.* 2006; Nathan and Kalpana 2007; Sluiter 2009). Nevertheless, much of the literature based on neoliberal discourse has ignored on-the-ground realities and focused instead on India's economic prosperity, appealing for the relaxation of labour laws in order to match the 'unpredictable demand, seasonality and labour intensiveness' of the market (Ghosh quoted in CEC 2004: 2; see also Khan 2009: 78–9), to attract foreign investment and to boost overall competitiveness (Doshi 2006: 6; Hashim 2004: 46; Khan 2009: 67). India's global competitiveness cannot rest entirely on domestic factors, however, as government intervention is limited in its ability to influence an international trade dictated by 'unpredictable demand and short-lived products', with consumption patterns in the apparel industry relying more on taste than objective consumer needs, and long-range forecasts hard to predict due to seasonal fluctuations (CEC 2004: 4).

Some writers have considered these stark realities and complexities, despite not directly addressing the question of the wellbeing of workers; in their accounts they emphasize the importance of better worker education and training, technical upgrades and infrastructural improvements (Hirway 2008), and advocate the elimination of an SME monopoly to make way for more broad-based growth (Das 2004: 2193). This would create a demand for a more skilled workforce and thus provide an impetus for the Indian government to improve literacy levels. In terms of producer-centred solutions for managing seasonality, Nathan and Kalpana (2007: 11) propose the amalgamation of smaller units into large-scale firms that would cater for a diverse range of products. This would sustain higher rates of employment throughout the year – a significant goal as permanent employees are protected by legislation and company codes of conduct which, when enforced effectively, promote worker solidarity, social security benefits, improved occupational health and safety and job security.

Despite the rhetoric surrounding private regulation, Hale and Shaw (2001: 525) raise important concerns that codes of conduct implemented by corporations have not yet made a 'serious beginning', while Franck (2008) argues that presently not even the ILO is capable of thwarting breaches of its own core standards. These fears are reflected in a study conducted in New Delhi, which found both permanent and non-permanent workers deprived of social security benefits despite the presence of codes (Manicandan *et al.* 2006: 21).

Contrary to most economic literature, van der Meulen Rodgers and Berik create a motive for corporate compliance through exploring the overall positive impact it would have – with government support – on competitiveness in terms

*Indian export garment industry* 125

of exports and foreign investment, and on 'society at large' (2006: 82). According to Barrientos and Smith (2007: 724), compliance can be achieved by bolstering consumer demand and NGO activism, while Hale and Shaw emphasize that for sustainable improvements in labour conditions, regulation must be 'based on workers' own awareness and organizational ability' (2001: 525).

In this context, a Cividep report (2009: 26) underlines the importance of allowing trade union activities on factory premises, the quashing of which, according to Nina Ascoly, former International Secretariat of the Clean Clothes Campaign (CCC), is 'chronic' in the industry (Sluiter 2009: 186). While freedom of association is a fundamental labour right and a 'crucial facilitator and guarantor of related labour rights' (De Neve 2008: 214), traditional trade unions have been routinely shown to neglect informal workers, who are not covered by labour laws and are difficult to locate in small-scale units (Sluiter 2009). They rarely incorporate the needs of women workers (Chakravarty 2007; Franck 2008), and in some cases even engage in corrupt practices (CEC 2004: 24). Against the backdrop of declined trade union membership, as discussed by De Neve (2008) in his study on the garment cluster in Tirrupur, it is crucial that trade unions find new and innovative ways of organizing and mobilizing workers.

De Neve (2008: 218) further argues that worker organization born on the 'shop floor' may no longer cope with the intricate web of agents involved in global commodity chains. From this perspective, workers will attain rights when they become involved in political processes and organizations that move beyond the workplace to include global and national networks of activists, particularly cooperation between trade unions and NGOs (Hale and Willis 2005: 9). For example, a CEC study (2004: 19) recommends the formation of an 'All India Board for Workers' specific to the garment sector which would allow collective negotiation of workers' rights at the 'macro level', while reinforcing the value of government implementation of social security. Crucially, failed collaborative efforts indicate that improvements in global factories will only be achieved when there is a solid 'understanding (by both international activists and in academic scholarship on activism) of the wider political economy of labour at the sites of struggle' (De Neve 2008: 235).

## Methodology

The research findings reported in this chapter are qualitative in nature and are based on my long-term intensive fieldwork among marginalized communities in West Bengal and more recently in New Delhi. My claims primarily rest on ethnographic research carried out among various subsections within the textile, clothing and footwear (TCF) industries, spanning more than a decade from the early 1990s to 2010 (Ganguly-Scrase 1995, 2013). The strength of this ethnographic research lies in the richness of the feedback from day-to-day participation in communities, observations and responses of informants and interviewees, together with my observations in the field. It provides insight into what people

126　*R. Ganguly-Scrase*

*do* rather than what they claim to do. Fieldwork in ethnography emphasizes the irreducibility of human experience and rests on 'thick description' (Geertz 1973) rather than simple truth claims (Hammersley 1998). Over the past six years, additional informal unstructured interviews were conducted in New Delhi and Kolkata. Two field assistants transcribed and collated interviews and some observations.

The development trajectory presented earlier contextualizes the situation of workers in the present study. It is also important to note, when considering the experiences of those in Kolkata, that the Partition of India in the process of postcolonial nation making dramatically transformed the lives of workers there. Textile production in both West Bengal and East Pakistan (now Bangladesh) was dealt a severe blow during independence as several Kolkata-based Muslim *ostagar*s (master craftsmen in tailoring) of the *dorji samaj* (tailoring community) departed for the newly formed East Pakistan, while Dhaka, its capital, was left without the necessary industrial base, since most mills were concentrated in Kolkata.

In Kolkata and its surrounding areas, I interacted with male and female workers, and interviewed *ostagars* and exporters, activists, and garment traders and middlemen – the latter based in Murshidabad–Bongaon, border areas of the state. Altogether, 15 key informants were drawn from the different groups. The attitude of many participants (except workers and activists) was suspicion and mistrust. Pseudonyms have been used in this study to protect their identities.

In the Garden Reach–Metiabruz belt on the western fringe of Kolkata, adjacent to the docks, we met traditional *ostagars*, who have become suppliers to the export market in the globalized world. While they were eager to discuss the trade others, such as larger factory owners, were reluctant. The trade is enveloped in an uncanny atmosphere of secrecy (for reasons noted below) and the factories are fortress-like structures. The laundry or fade-wash centre owners explained that they did routine washing at a laundry with valid trade licences, while carrying out the fade business clandestinely.

Working men and women were more willing to share their experiences; they expressed their helplessness with their irregular wages and working conditions. My contacts in the border districts of Murshidabad and North 24 Parganas (while undertaking ethnographic fieldwork on undocumented cross-border migration) and more recent contacts in the docks area,[1] facilitated access to garment traders and middlemen. Some were engaged in smuggling and more than one candidly confessed that they take this great risk because of the lack of an alternative livelihood. Activists from the environmental and trade union movements also provided insights into the illegal practices prevalent in the export-oriented garment manufacturing business.

In New Delhi, in-depth interviews were carried out with male and female formal and informal sector workers. To identify formal sector workers, a number of companies were contacted for first-hand information about countries they export to. From there, target companies were selected for interviews with workers based on convenience sampling, that is, companies located close to each other. Workers would usually live in the same neighbourhoods and a respondent would refer other workers for interviewing; participants were also gathered through personal contacts. Workers were interviewed during their lunch breaks and after work at their homes. The response rate was 1:5, that is, to interview ten workers, about 50 workers were approached. Respondents were revisited several times over the course of five years of the study. While some workers had changed companies or gone back to their homes, most had remained where they were. Surprisingly, despite changes in their personal circumstances, their views concerning work, conditions and salaries hardly changed over this period. Interviews were also carried out with labour activists and exporters. A number of focus group discussions were also held with workers in both the formal and informal sectors. In the following section, I first outline the experience of informal sector workers engaged in subcontracting for various export houses in New Delhi, followed by a discussion of formal sector workers' livelihoods. This is then contrasted with the perspectives of exporters who envisage the growing opportunities in the post-MFA global order, while continually asserting the need for workers to be more flexible. Finally, I consider instances of workers challenging their conditions within the informal sector of the industry.

Gender relations and political contexts vary in these two field sites giving rise to different expectations. In Kolkata there has been a long history of labour struggles; until recently a ruling coalition of leftist parties was in power for three decades. Among the labour activists, there are both men and women involved in mobilizing the women workers. The husbands and fathers of striking women workers remain supportive of their actions. Although there are similarities in both areas of fieldwork in terms of gender ideologies in that husbands are expected to support their wives to remain at home, women's mobility is far more circumscribed in Delhi since they are newly arrived migrants from rural areas. By comparison, Kolkata households are among the established network of the labouring poor in the city.

## Findings

### *Informalization and subcontracting in Delhi neighbourhoods*

In contrast to the labour migration of foreign workers in Southeast Asia (Crinis, this volume), internal migrants make up the bulk of the labour force in Indian garment factories in the EPZs and garment clusters of New Delhi. The composition of this labour force is primarily centred on what Ghosh refers to as the 'weakest possible segments' (CEC 2004), including women factory- and home-based workers, migrant workers and minority labour. Piece-rates as opposed to set wages or 'time rate contracts' further diminish their power. Alongside this, the feminization of the garment labour force is difficult to calculate given that women workers often constitute the highest proportion of casual and subsidiary garment labour (CCC and CEC 2006; CEC 2004; Hirway 2008).

In her study of women home-based garment workers in Ahmedabad, Kantor reiterates existing research that shows 'earnings from home based work are often irregular and low paid due to skill requirements, high levels of competition among workers and family intervention in decisions about how much work is done' (Kabeer 2000 cited in Kantor 2003: 429). Workers can view home-based work as not 'real' work given its proximity to other home-based activities, namely, unpaid domestic duties. Dispersal and isolation of workers also hinder labour rights and earnings because of 'producers' independent contracts' (Kantor 2003: 443). Additionally, Kantor found that subcontracting relations are exploitative because men tend to have greater knowledge of how enterprises operate (2003: 443).

Many of these patterns are reflected in my findings. The vast majority of women in my study had come to New Delhi with their husbands from the resource-poor agricultural districts of the northern Indian states of Bihar and Uttar Pradesh. Most were engaged in informal sector work and were married with school-age children. They had been living in New Delhi between two and 20 years and most lived in nuclear households surrounded by a network of kin.

In some families all the women were engaged in the same work, but more commonly it was the older, mature mothers – of pre-teen and teenage children – who combined home duties with home-based subcontract work. Predominantly work was eagerly sought in families where men were employed only periodically or did not work due to severe work injuries or substance abuse. Women were providing finishing touches to garments produced in factories such as floral embroidery, bead work, and cutting excess thread and cloth from seams. They were not engaged in machine embroidery, because the costs of a sewing machine, as well as electricity, are prohibitive for both the worker and the contractor. Typically, labour contractors recruited women from nearby villages. It was not uncommon for contactors to mock women to get them to consent to work. The following vignette illustrates the women's contradictory attitudes to work. These attitudes are framed by feminine ideologies of 'not working outside the home', which is widespread in north Indian patrilineal cultures.

Amirka Devi said that

> the contractor asked us, why are we sitting idle? He told us to work instead. He asked us to make productive use of our spare time and make money. Otherwise, we would never look out for work in the market or ask anybody for work.

Seemingly blasé attitudes about a requirement not to work prevailed among a number of women. Frequently, they would claim 'if we get the work, then it is fine, if we don't get the work we just stay at home'. Yet, with persistent questioning by the researcher, this was contradicted on a number of occasions. When asked why some women sought out the contractor, Amirka Devi explained that in lean times, the contractor provides piece-work to his kinfolk or to women of neighbouring families. Women then send their male children or other young male family members to the contractor for more work. Therefore, their claim that 'we would never go looking' depends on prevailing conditions.

Undoubtedly it seems the sheer volume of available work during peak times has resulted in most women believing that work always comes to them.

By observing women in neighbouring households, wives of recently arrived labour migrants cut cloth and threads on finished garments, cut cloth from patterns, do bead and embroidery work, and complete hems – the last two require more skill. Those with basic tailoring skills are recruited quickly. For a few women, the customary practice of returning to the natal family for the birth of the first child gave them the opportunity to acquire these skills.

Home-based garment work is carried out in nearly every household, depending on the family's needs. When a young family moves into the area, they are encouraged by neighbours and contractors to take on work to supplement the household income. A degree of negotiation takes place between the women and the subcontractor and without knowledge of the cost of the final product, the rate is set at anywhere between 50 paisa and INR1 (US$0.00755 to 0.0151). Accidental damage to apparel results in a pay cut. Subcontracting means that at times payment is delayed, sometimes up to a month. Despite this, women continue to trust the contractor because he lives in the vicinity. The contractor often justified this delay by claiming that he had not been paid on time, which the women cannot verify. Also, there is some flexibility, wherein the contractor will make an advance payment to a woman in need. Such flexibility contributes to building trust.

In general, women's average income is INR600 (US$9.06) per month for sewing around 200 pieces. Most women can earn anywhere between INR1000 and INR1500 (US$15.1 and US$22.65) per month. The rates and their earnings vary according to the complexity of the garment. For cutting thread they are paid ten paisa (US$0.0015) per garment, while for a complicated item, which can take two days to complete, they are paid INR25 (US$0.38) per piece. Such exploitative rates are sustained first by community attitudes that women must not work in factories, and second by the absence of government or NGO agents assisting in enforcing legal wage rates. Health-care costs are very high. Working in insufficient light affects women workers' eyesight and some have even had to discontinue work due to poor vision. Accidental piercings and injuries from the fast-paced sewing are also common. Prolonged sitting in the same posture causes knee and other joint pain. Apart from women's own complaints, during fieldwork local clinicians and chemists added that they had been administering large quantities of pain killers to combat such ailments.

The women interviewed were aware that the garments they worked on came from Okhla industrial area, situated in south Delhi, and were destined for export. Curiously, however, they were not interested in the value of the final product. Despite repeated questioning, most laughed, 'We only wear the sari. Why would we want to know how much rich people pay for these clothes?' This response is a contrast to that of formal sector workers who at times were embittered.

There were also women who spent approximately four hours a day on piecework. In the winter months, they sat together outside their dwellings. During the excessive heat of summer, despite poor lighting and the isolation of working alone, they remained indoors. Arduous hours of domestic chores made it difficult to seek factory work. The following is a typical conversation when women were asked why they did not pursue work in factories:

RESPONSE: Our husbands do not like us to work in the factory. We can work from home. A lady from Bihar would never go to the factory to work!
QUESTION: Have you ever tried to ask your husband if you can work in a factory?
R: No. My husband will never allow me.
Q: What would be his reason for that?
R: He does not like me to work outside of my home.
Q: What explanation would he give?
R: He will ask me to manage with whatever *he* [original emphasis] earns.
Q: If you say to him that's difficult, what would he say then?
R: He will say that it is foolish to have big dreams.
Q: What about you? What do you think? Suppose you get an opportunity to work in a factory, will you work there?
R: In a factory you have fixed working hours. We have to manage house, look after the children, wash clothes and cook for the family, and especially for the husband before he goes out for work. If we work in the factory, we have to work according to the working hours of the factory. Who then will handle our household responsibilities? Here we can manage our house as well as work in our spare time.

In contrast to the predominance of migrant workers in the Delhi export-garment sector, among its counterpart in Kolkata a substantial portion of the manufacturing is carried out by the established local community, the *dorji samaj*, who are mostly Muslim Bengalis. A vast pool of women workers are employed on an 'informal' basis. Many belong to the family, clan, caste and neighbourhood of the job providers. They sew buttons and cut threads. As elsewhere in India, family ideologies frequently reinforce the notion of women, whose work is unpaid, as mere 'helping hands' to the male workers. Men run the sewing machines and do the ironing. Male workers earn around INR400–500 (US$6.04 to US$7.55) per week. They are pushed into the unorganized and uncertain world of home-based production. The following vignette highlights their precarious existence and the ways employers can exert power over vulnerable workers. Md Abdul Kalam, a well-known manufacturer at Haji Ratan, Garden Reach, said, 'Till recently, 7 or 8 of the 20 odd workers in my unit were women. Now, I do not take women workers [because] they have many disadvantages. They become mothers too often and have regular health problems'. When asked how much they earned, at first, the answer was, 'Equal to the men, of course!' On repeated questioning, his reply changed to, 'I used to ensure that they earned INR150–200 a week'. That is half the male workers' wage. Working in the informal economy means that statutory benefits for women, such as maternity leave, are not available. Significantly, in lean seasons no work is equivalent to no pay.

*Indian export garment industry* 131

### The formal sector and factory-based employment

In New Delhi, workers in the formal sector were recruited for interview from several well-known exporting companies including Gaurav International, Myra International, Orient Fashion, Panex Overseas Pvt. Ltd, Pearl Global, Richa International and Usha Fab. A combination of export destinations and items manufactured is outlined in Table 7.1.

*Table 7.1* Workers recruited from ten exporter companies

| Type of garments | Countries | Brands |
| --- | --- | --- |
| Children's wear | USA | GAP |
| Women's wear | UK | Walmart |
| | China | JC Penney |
| Sportswear | USA | GAP |
| Menswear | Germany | |
| Women's wear | Greece | |
| | Other European countries | |
| Knitwear | USA | JC Penney |
| Women's wear | Germany | GAP |
| Children's wear | Other European countries | |
| Women's wear | Hong Kong | Belk |
| Children's wear | England | GAP |
| Nightwear | South Korea | Tommy Hilfiger |
| | USA | |
| | Canada | |
| Women's wear | France | Zara |
| Menswear | Germany | Forecast |
| | Spain | Tintoretto |
| | Holland | Didi |
| Children's wear | USA | GAP |
| Women's wear | Japan | Impulse |
| | Spain | Tribal |
| | | Corner |
| Women's wear | USA | GAP |
| Children's wear | UK | Avenue |
| | | Alta |
| | | George |
| Children's wear | USA | GAP |
| Skirts, shirts | UK | |
| | Germany | |
| Women's wear | USA | GAP |
| Children's wear | Canada | |
| | Netherlands | |
| Menswear | Italy | GAP |
| Women's wear | UK | |

Source: Fieldwork data.

## 132  *R. Ganguly-Scrase*

## Women in the formal sector

Women working in the EPZs of Noida, a satellite town of New Delhi, migrated there with their families from the eastern state of Bihar or the northern province of Uttaranchal. The majority interviewed were married with older children. Most had completed middle-school education with some training in tailoring or sewing, and they were all drawn from traditional tailoring communities. Some entered garment work through informal contacts established during training or formal recruitment while others gained entry through their husbands, fathers, or fathers-in-law who worked in garment factories. They worked in a chain system where about 50 operators were involved in completing one garment. None of the women interviewed worked in the sampling departments, where a complete item is made and the pay is higher. These tasks are the preserve of men. At the time of the fieldwork, the maximum salary a woman earned was INR5000 per month.

While some young women acquired their sewing skills after leaving middle school and before marriage, others entered the workforce after marriage. Many decided to work in factories because there was not enough home-based work available. More importantly, unlike those in the informal sector, they were literate and thus could gain basic training. The number of employees in the factories ranged between 1000 and 5000 (US$15.1 and US$75.50). In Kolkata, such factories are considered large, while in Delhi they are small. Many women noted the strict discipline and the frequent verbal abuse, which they considered acceptable. Sangeeta exemplifies their views:

SANGEETA: There are usually 2–3 masters per 1,000 workers. Since he is responsible for getting the things done by us, he *has* [original emphasis] the right to scold us if things are not done according to his instructions.

RUCHIRA: Does this happen often?

S: Yes it always happens, till we become expert workers. Suppose we get a target of 20 pieces per hour and if our production falls short to say 15 or 18 per hour, then the master will scold us and ask for an explanation for our reduced output. He can issue a token against you and won't allow us to go to the bathroom and ask us to keep sitting there and do the work.

R: Is it common for the supervisor to tell you off?

S: Yes, yes, everybody gets scolded sometime or the other.

R: So how do you feel when you are scolded?

S: We realize our mistakes, and try to improve and work better. We waste less time; we go to drink water once instead of two times and save time and try to maximize production.

R: What happens if you are late for work? Are there any deductions for coming late?

S: We have about 5–10 minutes' grace; if we are late by 5 minutes, then wages are deducted for half an hour.

Scholars such as Chakravarty (2007) criticize the inherent docility of women in export garment factories, but given their precarious employment, it is not surprising that many accept their situation. Tara summed up the trade-off in working for Sara Enterprises where surveillance and discipline was intense:

TARA: The job is more or less secure. Sara does not lay off their workers, which is why mostly us ladies work for Sara Exports. They don't give us forced breaks if there is no job.

RUCHIRA: Other companies lay off their workers for 2–3 months when there are no orders with the company. Is that right?

T: Yes, that is correct. That is why we put up with their strict expectations. Here we get money for working on holidays, we get bonus; we have PF [Provident Fund], ESI [employee insurance] facility. A lady worker gets 3 months' paid maternity leave. We have a crèche at our factory.

## Male formal sector workers

In Delhi most migrant worker accounts revealed that they had come there because of limited opportunities in rural and provincial areas. In contrast to the women's attitudes of perseverance, the men were sad, angry and frustrated. This was in part due to leaving their families behind. They described their conditions as miserable, devoid of personal fulfilment except earning much-needed cash to send back home. Their cost of living was high, with most paying INR600 (US$9.06) in rent, not including electricity and water charges, for a shared room. Sonu, from the Punjab, elaborated:

Get up in the morning, go to work, come back in the evening, cook, eat food, and then sleep—this is the life here. The life in the village is much better than in the metro[politan centres]. If employment is provided in villages, village life would be far better, but this is not the case. In the village, we used to get Rs 50 per day, but here we get Rs 150 per day and any overtime that is available.

Therefore, the trade-off between not having an adequate income in the village and working long days and living in difficult circumstances is marginal. As one man sarcastically remarked:

To stay alive in Delhi, the most important thing you have to have is money. We can live without air for sometime in Delhi, but not without money.

Their incomes ranged between INR4000 and INR6000 (US$60.40 and US$90.60) per month, depending on their skill level and where they worked. Additionally, they would receive 3–4 hours' overtime per day. Most complained about the lack of superannuation or health insurance. Though a number of respondents mentioned their cordial relationship with the supervisor, at times, their wages were cut if they were late even by five minutes.

Workers were unanimous in conveying their need for pay increases given the high inflation rate and rising cost of living. However, they were afraid of making

## 134   R. Ganguly-Scrase

any demands on their employers. The following comment by Abdhesh Kumar from Bihar captures the sentiments of most respondents:

> We are not satisfied with our working condition. The salary is not proportional to the amount of work we have to do. But we need the money. We don't say anything and just mind our own business. We have no alternative, but to listen to the supervisor. If we speak out, we are simply thrown out...

Many interviewees welcomed the opportunity to earn extra whenever possible and none reported falling sick due to overwork. However, throughout my fieldwork, NGO representatives, labour activists and trade unionists reported workers collapsing due to exhaustion from overwork, and, sometimes, even dying. In 2010, two organizations launched formal enquiries and court cases are pending regarding workers' deaths in export garment factories.

Ever-present threats of dismissal coupled with the casualized nature of work underpin migrant workers' inability to take collective action against employers. The following is a case in point:

> We try to maintain a good relation with the supervisor, and we don't interfere in other people's business.... We have a healthy relation with our co-workers. All of them are good people and we have got some unity. Yet, we can't raise our voices against exploitation. This is because there is so much unemployment. If anybody raises his voice, he is simply thrown out.

Meanwhile, attributing industry problems to labour issues, exporters tend to invert the vulnerability of workers into a state of being held to ransom:

> Our workers expect a rise in wages with general inflation, which you can anticipate and increase wages and salary year after year, which means unless you keep changing them with your wages, [the] bill is always shooting up.

Their complaints centre on the inefficiency of small-scale production, which is seen as resulting from workers' demands. Consequently the blame for the unwillingness of exporters to adopt economies of scale is shifted to the workers. For example, one exporter commented:

> Unfortunately in our country we cannot fight with attitudes of so many of these types of people. Otherwise, we could have thousands of people under one shed. Our entrepreneurs are scared of having too many people under one roof whereas in other countries they can have 5,000–10,000 people working. This way, they can reduce overheads also. Here, we can't think of handling more than 600 people in one single factory. That is why we have small–small factories. Just like in the fields, in foreign countries, you see bigger farms. We have small fields and that increases your cost of operations. If we have one big operation; we don't have to have two managers on

one floor. It would have been good if we have one large shed where all the operators would have been working and you can imagine the saving in aspects like transportation, manpower cost and so many other things because every single rupee adds to the cost.

I alluded previously to the problems of the SMEs. This is reinforced by Ramaswamy's (2004) findings, which highlight that despite investment in sophisticated machinery, lower productivity continues since employers spread the manufacturing over several units in order to circumvent labour regulations.

While industry-oriented reports emphasize high rates of absenteeism in the Indian apparel sector compared with other Asian exporters (Padhi *et al.* 2004: 11), infrastructure problems such as power shortages, road connectivity and inadequate port facilities, are also major concerns across the industry (Das 2007: 77–8; Doshi 2006: 5; Khan 2009: 66–7), as mentioned earlier in this chapter. For example, Doshi found that compared to the new international standard of 30–35 days, required 'lead times (from procurement to fabrication and shipment of garments)' in India are 45–60 days (2006: 5).

Two major trends have emerged in India post-MFA. On the one hand, increasing casualization of work and precarious employment dominates the lives of garment industry workers, while on the other, many exporters have capitalized on high-end, value-added designer fashion. In an interview, Mr Rajiv Vaishitha, vice president of Maral Exports, emphasized the need for value adding:

> Future of the apparel industry is very bright provided we as the players in the industry shift away from merely provider of basic production to supplier of highly value added product. With growing affordability all across the world the *mantra* [original emphasis] is value addition, be it apparel industry or for that matter, any industry or any product you may talk about. Without value addition you are bound to fade away. India is a huge storehouse of natural resources, *low cost labour* [emphasis added] which all should be channelized [*sic*] for creating value added product ranges.

Similarly, Dipankar Adhya, vice chairman of the Textile Association of India and a consultant textile engineer, is optimistic about India's ability to reap benefits of the new quota-free world order. However, this vision of 'India' does not distinguish between labour and capital; instead, concerns are largely framed in terms of the 'national economy', 'exports' and foreign exchange. The producer has little control over labour and market power lies with the retailing companies located in the industrialized countries of the North. In Kolkata, I found both manufacturers and traders engaged in export. Overseas importers/buyers prefer those known as 'merchant exporters', since they have the flexibility of outsourcing to fulfil requirements, as well as versatile contacts – both horizontal and vertical – in the export regime. This increasing number of merchant buyers in the region is no longer considered 'middlemen', but rather 'market facilitators', expediting the process of procurement, quality control, as well as safe export.

136   *R. Ganguly-Scrase*

Exporters in New Delhi deal directly with retailers, claiming they have become responsible, vertically integrated companies, which can be relied on. In addition to their well-known primary customers such as Marks & Spencer, Banana Republic, Benetton and others, they also cater for private labels, whereas in Kolkata, many export houses only supply boutiques due to their low output.

## Trade unionism

Arguably, the small- and medium-scale industry base which has created fragmentation of workers means less access by unions, and that the needs and rights of workers vary according to their work environment. This is coupled with an overall decline in trade-union activities (see De Neve 2008: 235) that results from the increase in women and migrant workers who are not inclined to join unions (Chakravarty 2007; De Neve 2008: 226; Hirway 2008). An inevitable consequence of the increasingly competitive multilateral environment is the 'insecurity and the threat of deteriorating conditions' for garment and textile workers (Hale 2002: 33). Hale and Willis (2005: 9) also argue that in order for workers to secure rights, they should be involved in political processes and organizations that move beyond the workplace, and include global and national networks of activists, particularly the combined efforts of trade unions and NGOs. During my fieldwork, I encountered a number of organizations that have adopted the strategy of visiting migrant worker neighbourhoods. While this resembles the tactics of political parties, activists were careful to downplay this view. They focused on dissemination of information, through magazines such as the local monthly *Faridabad Majdoor Samachar*, raising broader issues for workers' families and children. Even the person who played a leading role in publishing this magazine and lived in the workers' neighbourhood refused to be labelled a leader or activist, or even as being in an NGO, since the magazine was produced by volunteers. Other NGOs, such as the Delhi-based CEC, have attempted working collaboratively with unions, culminating in a series of studies and seminars concerned with labour rights, incorporating both local and national trade union organizations, and local and international NGOs.

De Neve (2008), in his study on the garment cluster in Tirrupur, shows that the political economy of labour framework requires elucidation and that labour struggles must be contextualized according to their historical and political settings. He says that even in the realm of particular models of analysis, including 'global value chain analyses', there has been a weakness in 'looking at labour and in particular at workshop-based labour politics within global commodity chains' (De Neve 2008: 217). He argues that the focus has been on the structure and economics of these global chains rather than on agency, politics and power, labour organization and resistance in the particular contexts.

I now consider the actions of a group of women in a small export manufacturing company producing jeans in Kolkata. While the manufacturers frequently cite the 'labour problem' as a major cause of the industry's decline in the late 1980s, the export-oriented garment industry in its new avatar thrives on unethical/illegal labour practices. It is important to note that until 2011, the state of West Bengal was governed by a coalition of Left parties, with the Communist Party of India as its dominant partner for over 30 years. During this period there was widespread labour activism. Yet even now, there are virtually no unions, no wages fixed by collective bargaining and certainly no agreements in the garment industry. Given these conditions, the actions taken by this group of women is indicative of the possibilities of Hale and Willis's (2005: 9) proposition.

Despite having worked in the factory for 18 to 20 years, the monthly income of these women ranged from INR1200 to INR2500 (US$18.12 to US$37.75). They had no superannuation, employee insurance and/or workers' compensation. A long-time employee who drafted a pamphlet about their oppressive conditions explained:

> Our factory owner Mr Ajay Khemra is a terrific guy! He doesn't bother with any government regulations. Whenever we have broached the issue of wage rises or other employee rights, he has promptly replied—'if you don't like it here, go somewhere else'. And as a bonus he has gifted us with many abusive words.

Since the management made no effort to engage in dialogue concerning their rights, the women formed the 'Jeans Factory Workers Union'. The owners refused to listen to their complaints and instead, transferred eight to ten employees to another unit. Faced with lock-out, the women mobilized workers in nearby factories and neighbourhoods. Together they went on strike for 33 days and subsequently secured their right to ESI and a better wage structure. They have also made considerable progress towards gaining a Provident Fund (superannuation). Most importantly, they unanimously declared that their greatest achievement was gaining a sense of dignity. The following excerpts from their pamphlets distributed at the May Day rally of 2011 indicate their views:

> Previously we never had any experience of undertaking such a big struggle, we were isolated. Through our struggle we have formed a strong unity and have built an organisation. We have come to understand that without an organisation and being unified it is not possible to claim our rights.... From our experience of the 33 day fight we have learnt that we can gain the support of other fighting forces when we struggle for reasoned demands, dignity and rights. When we saw that workers from other factories stood beside us, supported us financially, gave us moral support that is when we understood the real strength of worker unity. When we saw that people from other walks of life stood beside us, gave us unqualified support, that is when we realised how important it is for worker–citizens to unite.

While forming a coalition of unions is not novel, the notion of the citizen–worker alliance reflects a new imaginary in the landscape of labour unions.

## 138 R. Ganguly-Scrase

## Conclusion

In this chapter I have demonstrated that since the demise of the MFA the Indian garment industry has accrued considerable benefits. However, workers have been largely excluded from reaping economic rewards brought about by the success of the export garment sector. Faced with more competition from other Asian exporters in the global market, Indian manufacturers and exporters have lowered production costs through increased casualization and informalization of the labour force, particularly in the form of subcontracting and home-based production. This precarious situation poses a threat to building core labour standards and sustaining worker rights. The latter is further complicated by the nature of labour laws, since guaranteed protection applies to those in units of more than 100 workers. While large-scale production units are the norm in the globalized garment industry, with few exceptions Indian exporters prefer smaller units. Indeed, many tend to split production centres into smaller units to bypass labour laws and other regulations.

In order to challenge these employer strategies some labour activists have moved beyond shop-floor activism to campaigns building alliances with unions across the global garment chains, as well as adopting the strategy of trade unionism in industrial clusters. If carried out on a broader scale, the actions outlined above would have a positive influence on labour rights in the garment industry, however, it would be naïve to assume that this can happen in the short term. Social conventions, including formidable patriarchal and hierarchical forms of authority and submission, may well be an important element in understanding women garment workers' unwillingness to unionize, alongside their tendency to be involved in casual labour. While I have presented an example of a partially successful outcome in a small factory, the problems are far reaching and cannot be easily resolved, even in the limited realm of increasing levels of unionization.

## Note

1 The Centre for Asia Pacific Social Transformation Studies (CAPSTRANS) research on the Asia-Pacific Ports project (see Hill and Scrase 2012) shows some of the difficulties presented by liberalization of Calcutta's port. Inadequate infrastructure in ports poses serious problems for the garment industry, as firms are unable to maintain delivery schedules for the global market.

## References

Barrientos, S. and Smith, S. (2007) 'Do workers benefit from ethical trade? Assessing codes of labour practice in global production systems', *Third World Quarterly*, 28(4): 713–29.

Bhavani, T. A. (2002) 'Small-scale units in the era of globalization: problems and prospects', *Economic and Political Weekly*, Special Articles, 37(29): 3041–52.

Centre for Education and Communication (CEC) (2004) *Understanding the Indian Garment Sector in the Post MFA Context: A Brief Report*, New Delhi: CEC.

Chandrasekhar, C. P. and Ghosh, J. (eds) (2004) *The Market That Failed: A Decade of Neoliberal Economic Reforms in India*, New Delhi: LeftWord.

*Indian export garment industry* 139

Chakravarty, D. (2007) 'Docile oriental women and organised labour: a case study of the Indian garment manufacturing industry', *Indian Journal of Gender Studies*, 14(3): 439–60.

Chatterjee, U. (2004) 'The need for labour reforms', www.domain-b.com/industry/textiles/20041229_labour_reforms.html (accessed 21 January 2012).

Cividep (2009) *Richer Bosses, Poorer Workers: Bangalore's Garment Industry*, New Delhi: Cividep-India & SOMO.

Clean Clothes Campaign (CCC) and Centre for Education and Communication (CEC) (2006) 'Global campaigning, local action', Clean Clothes Campaign and Centre for Education and Communication, New Delhi, 19–21 January.

Das, K. (2007) 'SMEs in India: issues and possibilities in times of globalisation', ERIA Research Project Report 2007 No. 5: ASEAN SMEs and Globalization, Senayan: ERIA.

Das, N. (2004) 'Low employment growth: reviving labour intensive manufacturing', *Economic and Political Weekly*, 39(29 May): 2192–4.

De Neve, G. (2008) 'Global garment chains: local labour activism: new challenges to trade union and NGO activism in the Tiruppur garment cluster, South India', in G. De Neve, P. Luetchford, and J. Pratt (eds), *Hidden Hands in the Market: Ethnographies of Fair Trade, Ethical Consumption, and Corporate Social Responsibility*, Bradford, UK: Research in Economic Anthropology, Emerald, pp. 231–40.

De Neve, G. (2009) 'Power, inequality and corporate social responsibility: the politics of compliance in the South Indian garment industry', *Economic and Political Weekly*, 44(22): 63–71.

Doshi, G. (2006) 'Indian textile exports: post-MFA scenario opportunities and challenges', http://ezinearticles.com/?Textiles-Exports:-Post-MFA-Scenario-Opportunities-and- Challenges&type=sv&id=372738 (accessed 21 January 2012).

Fair Wear Foundation (2003) Minutes of the Workshop 'Code of conduct implementation and local partners', Mumbai, 16–17 January.

Fibre2Fashion (2009) 'Program to bridge skill development in apparel sector', www.fibre2fashion.com/news/textile-company-news/newsdetails.aspx?news_id=80844 (accessed 21 January 2012).

Franck, A. (2008) *Key Feminist Concerns Regarding Core Labor Standards, Decent Work and Corporate Social Responsibility*, Brussels: WIDE.

Ganguly-Scrase, R. (1995) 'Global manufacturing and Indian leather workers', in D. Smith and J. Borocz (eds), *A New World Order? Global Transformation in the Late 20th Century*, Westport, CT: Praeger, pp. 163–79.

Ganguly-Scrase, R. (2013) *Global Issues, Local Contexts: The Rabi Das of West Bengal*, 2nd edn, New Delhi: Orient BlackSwan.

Geertz, C. (1973) *Interpretation of Cultures*, New York: Fontana.

Ghosh, J. (2005) 'Waiting for the boom', *Frontline*, 22(3), www.flonnet.com/fl2203/stories/20050211002309500.htm (accessed 21 January 2012).

Hale, A. (2002) 'Trade liberalisation in the garment industry: who is really benefiting?' *Development in Practice*, 12(1): 33–44.

Hale, A. and Shaw, L. M. (2001) 'Women workers and the promise of ethical trade in the globalised garment industry: a serious beginning', *Antipode*, 33(3): 510–30.

Hale, A. and Willis, J. (eds) (2005) *Threads of Labour: Garment Industry Supply Chains from the Workers' Perspective*, Oxford: Blackwell.

Hashim, D. A. (2004) *Cost and Productivity in Indian Textiles: Post MFA Implications*, New Delhi: Indian Council for Research on International Economic Relations.

140  *R. Ganguly-Scrase*

Hirway, I. (2008) 'Trade and gender inequalities in labour market: case of textile and garment industry in India', Paper for the International Seminar on Moving Towards Gender Sensitization of Trade Policy, UNCTAD, New Delhi, 25–27 February.

International Labour Organization (ILO) (2005) 'Promoting fair globalization in textiles and clothing in a post-MFA environment', Geneva: Sectoral Activities Programme, www.ilo.org/public/english/dialogue/sector/techmeet/tmtc-pmfa05/tmtc-pmfa-r.pdf (accessed 21 January 2012).

Jha, P. (2001) 'A note on India's post-independence economic development and some comments on the associated development discourse', Institute for World Economics and International Management, www.wiwi.uni-bremen.de/publikationen/pdf/b070.pdf (accessed 21 January 2012).

Kantor, P. (2003) 'Women's empowerment through home-based work: evidence from India', *Development and Change*, 34(3, June): 425–5.

Kashyap, S. P. (1988) 'Growth of small-size enterprises in India: its nature and content', *World Development*, 16(6): 667–81.

Khan, R. S. (ed.) (2009) 'The readymade garment sector in India', in *Export Success and Industrial Linkages: The Case of Readymade Garments in South Asia*, New York: Palgrave Macmillan, pp. 57–82.

Kolben, K. (2006) 'The new politics of linkage: India's opposition to the Workers Rights clause', *Indiana Journal of Global Legal Studies*, 13(1, Winter): 225–59.

Manicandan, G., Mansingh, P. and Kumar, P. (2006) 'Transformations and labour in the Indian garment industry: a study on wages and structural changes in garment industry in Delhi and NCR region', CEC Working Paper, New Delhi: CEC.

Mezzadri, A. (2010) 'Globalization, informalization and the state in the Indian garment industry', *International Review of Sociology*, 20(3): 491–511.

Ministry of Textiles, India (2009) 'Note on Indian textiles and clothing exports', www. texmin.nic.in/sector/note_on_indian_textile_and_clothing_exports_intl_trade_section. pdf (accessed 21 January 2012).

Ministry of Textiles, India (2010) 'Export division: frequently asked questions', www. texmin.nic.in/faq/faq_exports.pdf (accessed 21 January 2012).

Mukherjee, A. and Zhang, X. (2005) 'Rural non-farm development in China and India: the role of policies and institutions', DSGD Discussion Paper No. 24, Washington DC: International Food Policy Research Institute.

Nathan, D. and Kalpana, V. (2007) 'Issues in the analysis of global value chains and their impact on employment and incomes in India', A Development Agenda for Employment and Decent Work in India, Discussion Paper Series No. 183, International Institute for Labour Studies, Mumbai, 10–11 August.

Osakwe, E. (2009) 'Cotton fact sheet: India', Nagpur, Maharashtra State Co-op Cotton Growers Marketing Federation, www.mahacot.com/pdfs/cottonfactsheet.pdf (accessed 21 January 2012).

Padhi, A., Pauwels, G. and Taylor, C. (2004) 'Freeing India's textile industry', *McKinsey Quarterly, Special Edition, What Global Executives*, Think, 9–11 July.

Pande, R. (2007) 'Gender, poverty and globalisation in India', *Development*, 50(2): 134–40.

Ramaswamy, K. V. (2004) 'Global opportunity and domestic constraints in textile and apparel industry in South Asia: analysis and strategic response of firms in India', in M. Bhattacharya, R. Smyth and M. Vicziany (eds), *South Asia in the Era of Globalization: Trade, Industrialization and Welfare*, pp. 131–43, New York: Nova Science Publishers.

Ramaswamy, K. V. and Gereffi, G. (2000) 'India's apparel exports: the challenge of global markets', *The Developing Economies*, 38(2): 186–210.

Rao, V. (2010) 'Distance education for the garment industry in India', *Asian Journal of Distance Education*, 8(1): 53–62.

Singh, J. N. (2007) 'Strategies for realising vision 2010 of Indian textile and apparel industry', *Journal of the Textiles Association*, January–February: 228–35.

Sluiter, L. (2009) *Clean Clothes: A Global Movement to End Sweatshops*, London and New York: Pluto Press.

Tewari, M. (2006) 'Adjustment in India's textile and apparel industry: reworking historical legacies in a post-MFA world', *Environment and Planning*, 38(12): 2325–44.

Tewari, M. (2008) 'Varieties of global integration: navigating institutional legacies and global networks in India's garment industry', *Competition and Change*, 12(1, March): 49–67.

UNCTAD and Government of India Centre for WTO Studies (2011) 'The Indian Textile and Clothing sector: An overview', *Potential Supply Chains in the Textiles and Clothing Sector in South Asia: An Exploratory Study*, Geneva, http://unctad.org/en/docs/ditctncd2011d3_en.pdf (accessed 15 December 2014).

van der Meulen Rodgers, Y. and Berik, G. (2006) *Asia's Race to Capture Post-MFA Markets: A Snapshot of Labor Standards, Compliance, and Impacts on Competitiveness*, Department of Economics Working Paper Series, Working Paper No. 2006–02, Salt Lake City, UT: University of Utah.

Verma, S. (2002) *Export Competitiveness of the Indian Textile and Garment Industry*, Working Paper No. 94, November, Indian Council for Research on International Economic Relations, New Delhi, http://62.58.77.238/downloads/conference%202002/1.2%20Samar%20Verma.pdf (accessed 13 January 2012).

Vijayabaskar, M. (2002) 'Garment industry in India', in J. Gopal (ed.), *Garment Industry in South Asia: Rags or Riches?* New Delhi: South Asia Multidisciplinary Advisory Team (SAAT), ILO, pp. 39–91, http://ilo-mirror.library.cornell.edu/public/english/region/asro/newdelhi/download/garment.pdf (accessed 13 January 2012).

Weiner, M. (1996) 'Child labour in India: Putting compulsory primary education on the political agenda', *Economic and Political Weekly*, 9(16 November): 3007–14.

World Trade Organisation. (2014) 'International Trade Statistics 2015', www.wto.org/english/res_e/statis_e/its2015_e/its2015_e.pdf.(accessed 6 April 2016).

# 8 Child labour and gender discrimination in the garment industry of Kong Pisei, Cambodia

*Melanie Beresford, Ivan Cucco and Laura Prota*

> Mary, a young village woman, who wanted to work in a garment factory, asked the commune officials if it was possible to get an ID before the administrative round of certification. It turned out it was not possible as Mary could not afford the fee of 50 US$ and as the next certification round was in three years Mary missed her opportunity, by then she would be 22 too old to start work in a garment factory.
>
> (Translated interview with young women in Sala Kruas Village, Peah Nipean, 14 December 2010)

The career of a Southeast Asian garment worker is notoriously short, often starting at around age 15 and ending in the mid to late 20s. Over the past four decades the literature has well documented the preference of garment employers for young, usually single, women who can be paid low wages and tend to leave (voluntarily or not) their employment upon marriage and childbearing. Among the many reasons put forward for this phenomenon most either refer to the internal processes of the firms or to structural conditions of the labour and capital markets. Both explanations leave the workers with little ability to bargain for better pay and conditions or improved career prospects.

Examples of the 'internal process' argument include employer preferences for 'nimble fingers' or a supposedly docile workforce, or piece-rate regimes that lead to 'self-exploitation' and early ill health (Chand 2012). Rather more convincing are the more 'structural' arguments that rely on the footloose nature of highly labour-intensive production, the abundant supply of cheap labour among young village women, and an international division of labour organized through 'buyer-driven' GVCs (Gereffi and Korzeniewicz 1994) which gives low-wage countries a comparative advantage in garment production (Rasiah 1993).

The introduction of monitored labour standards through various programmes known as CSR targets the structural processes of firms in response to a growing segment of developed-country consumers who demand 'sweat-free' labour, whether for purely ethical or for protectionist reasons. BFC, a programme established in 2001 under the auspices of the ILO, is one of the most influential attempts at creating a transparent and independent monitoring system for improving labour standards in global supply chains.

*Child labour and gender discrimination*   143

The BFC programme has been regarded as highly successful, particularly in its initial phase between 2001 and 2006 (Chiu 2007; Berik and Rodgers 2008; Beresford 2009; Polaski 2004). Not only have labour standards improved but – with the exception of the period of the GFC from late 2008 through 2009 – garment exports from the country have continued to grow. Although not exempt from criticism, the undeniable impact of the BFC programme on Cambodian labour standards appears to lend support to the structural thesis by suggesting that pressures originating in the global sphere have been the driving force behind its successful implementation. In other words, demand from western consumers transmitted either through buyers within the global garment value chain or by protectionism of developed-country manufacturers (Beresford 2009) has led to improved labour standards in Cambodia. Explanations rooted in the nature and functioning of global supply chains focus however on the assessment of labour conditions in the factory, while little consideration is given to the wider institutional and social context in which factory-level monitoring programmes operate. Furthermore, structural explanations lack an important gender dimension which would enable us to understand why so many women leave work at such a young age, while men in the low-wage labour market do not.

Bearing these elements in mind, it is worth asking whether there are also factors in the lives of garment workers outside the factory environment that influence the implementation of labour standards. In order to investigate this question, we surveyed 396 households in Kampong Speu province and asked household members about their careers in the garment sector. Most garment workers in the surveyed villages were commuters rather than migrants; this offered us the opportunity to look more closely at the interactions between the monitoring system implemented in the factories and the social, economic and institutional context in the rural sending communities to which workers return on a daily basis. We examine two cases for which, during the fieldwork, it became clear that BFC monitoring was not as successful as claimed in the synthesis reports. First, we look at the impact of the monitoring system on one of the ILO's core labour standards – the elimination of child labour (ILO Conventions 138 and 182) – and also on labour which might be considered detrimental to the development and education of young people. Second, if one of the aims of implementing labour standards in the garment industry is to end the phenomenon of the 'youthful and short' career and to provide women with more stable and remunerative employment opportunities, we investigate the reasons why women have left the factory workforce. The effective protection of the two core rights of the programme – the elimination of child-labour and gender-based discrimination – for which high compliance rates are generally assumed (Robertson 2011; Polaski 2006) are therefore the focus of our analysis. Fieldwork results are compared with BFC reports and other evidence available in the literature on Cambodia's labour standards.

We found that: (i) the falsification of ID certificates is a widespread practice among minors, allowing them to bypass the requirement demanded by factories of being 18 years old; and (ii) caring duties remain the main reason why women

144   *M. Beresford* et al.

leave the factory. These results make clear how, notwithstanding the improvement in the factory-level implementation of labour rights, the eradication of child labour is far from complete and gender relations still strongly discriminate against the career prospects of rural women. In both cases, the persistence of practices in contrast with core BFC labour standards suggests that factory-level monitoring alone is not able to improve structural conditions in the sending communities.

Previous studies have already suggested that the interaction between the factory and the wider society is not always positive (Kabeer 2004). In an earlier paper, Prota and Beresford (2012) argued that hierarchical relations in the factory environment influenced village relations via the system of factory recruitment, leading to changes in power and wealth within the village. In this chapter we take the argument a step further by proposing that factory owners are able to take advantage of the underdeveloped nature of Cambodian villages in ways that simple monitoring of factory conditions cannot pick up. We suggest that there might be structural conditions of the rural Cambodian labour market that militate against the proper application of labour standards in garment factories, and that these conditions are particularly mediated by gender relations. Indeed, to put the case even more strongly, conditions in the rural areas might work actively against the sustainability of labour standards monitoring.

The remainder of the chapter is organized as follows: Section 2 provides a brief introduction to the development of the Cambodian garment sector and discusses different evaluations of the BFC programme. Section 3 describes fieldwork locations and the data collection process; we also discuss the context of the study and particularly the perspective of commuter villages, their institutions and their discourses. In Section 4 we examine the issue of child labour, while in Section 5 we investigate the relation between job termination and child caring. Overall conclusions are presented in Section 6.

## The garment sector and Better Factories Cambodia

Since the mid-1990s, the garment sector has been one of the main drivers of Cambodia's economic growth. In 2012 garment and footwear exports (valued at almost US$5 billion) accounted for about 35 per cent of the country's GDP and for about 80 per cent of its total exports. The industry has also significantly contributed to the expansion of non-agricultural employment: as of 2013, about 400,000 of the country's 660,000 industrial workers were employed by factories registered with the GMAC.[1] The Cambodian garment sector presents two unique features: first, it has arisen from an economic vacuum (Beresford 2009); and second, its development has been praised by the international community as a 'fair model of globalization' that can be transferred to other developing countries.

Unlike other Southeast and East Asian countries, where export-oriented clothing industries grew in the 1970s and 1980s after a period of import-substituting industrialization, Cambodia had little industry to speak of before the 1990s

*Child labour and gender discrimination*   145

(Vickery 1990; Heintz 2007). The first garment factories were established in 1994 by Asian investors. At the time the global garment and apparel trade was regulated by the MFA, a multilateral framework that had been in effect since 1974. The MFA departed from standard GATT rules in allowing participating countries to bilaterally negotiate (or, under special conditions, unilaterally impose) country-specific quotas. After the end of the Uruguay Round in 1994, the MFA was replaced by the WTO ATC, a transitional instrument that stipulated the gradual abolition of the quota system and its eventual phasing out in 2005. The end of the ATC meant the lifting of all protections on the international trade of garments and apparel, opening up domestic industries to the competition of low-cost, labour-abundant developing countries. This posed concerns not only to western economies, where labour rights would have become too costly and unsustainable (the 'race to the bottom argument'), it was also seen as dangerous by small developing economies, such as Cambodia, considered still too weak to face the competition with China. To limit the impact of the liberalization process, the US and the EU agreed with China on a safeguard policy to restrict its exports until 2008 (Lee 2011).

Cambodia, being a latecomer, was not part of the MFA and only joined the WTO in 2004; it was therefore exempt from the trade restrictions stipulated under both multilateral frameworks. The Cambodian government, recognizing the country's potential advantage in global garment chains, provided generous tax and duty exemptions to foreign investors. The combination of national incentives, cheap labour costs and preferential access to world markets made Cambodia an attractive location for garment manufacturing.

The development of the garment industry was in this first phase very rapid, and the seven factories established in 1994 had already become 189 by 1999 (Dasgupta *et al.* 2011: 3). Exports to the US, Cambodia's main market, grew to the point that 'in 1998 the domestic US textile and apparel industries called for import restraints' (Polaski 2006: 920). Requests for interventions also came from US trade unions, which supported burgeoning Cambodian union militancy, and from civil society groups alarmed by reports of abuses against workers in Cambodian factories, including debt bondage, forced overtime and failure to pay the minimum wage (Polaski 2004; Dasgupta *et al.* 2011).

In response to these pressures, the bilateral US–Cambodia Trade Agreement on Textiles and Apparel (TATA), signed in 1999, set an explicit connection between labour rights and trade policies. The agreement posed a positive incentive to enhance labour conditions by rewarding the country with increasing export quotas in the US markets, provided that labour conditions were enhanced. Progress in the implementation of labour standards was to be monitored twice yearly, and on positive assessment the country would be granted an additional 14 per cent quota increase on top of the regular annual quota growth.

As a direct result of the agreement, an independent system of monitoring of Cambodian labour rights was set up in 2001 by the ILO under the name of BFC; all export factories had to enrol in the programme and agree to be monitored. The ILO, GMAC and the Cambodian trade union movement were all directly

146    *M. Beresford* et al.

involved in the programme (Sibbel and Borrmann 2005; Beresford 2009). The BFC monitoring process is based on unannounced visits to the factories, in the course of which monitoring teams interview managers and workers, check documental records and make direct observations. Assessments are measured against a 52-point checklist that includes 21 'Critical Issues' and 31 'Low Compliance Issues' (BFC 2014a). The issues cover core national and international labour standards in areas like compensation, contracts, discrimination, child labour, forced labour, working hours, occupational safety and health, freedom of association and collective bargaining (BFC 2014c). The programme also provides training to managers and workers in areas related to labour rights implementation, and offers one-year advisory services to help factories address the issues that emerge during the assessments.

The BFC programme was an attempt to reconcile the development of the labour-intensive garment industry with the protection of labour rights and with the rising demand of ethical trade (Hale and Shaw 2001). By catering to the increasing awareness of western consumers, it was hoped that BFC would provide Cambodia with a comparative advantage in 'sweat-free' garment production. The ensuing developments in the Cambodian garment sector seem to prove that this was the case. Notwithstanding the end of the ATC and the phasing out of restrictions on Chinese garment exports, in the 2000s the sector maintained double digits growth rates, outperforming the regional average (Economic Institute of Cambodia 2008). In 2008, however, the GFC severely hit Cambodia; more than 70 factories closed and some 60,000 workers lost their jobs, at least temporarily (ILO 2009). An even more serious effect of the GFC was the loss of overtime work due to reduced demand, making it hard for employed workers to cope with basic needs (CAMFEBA and BDLINK 2010). The garment industry managed to recover from the crisis (Beresford 2009), but serious structural vulnerabilities still affect the sector.[2] According to Rasiah (2009), the long-term sustainability of the Cambodian garment sector will largely depend on its ability to upgrade from the low-skilled Cut-Make-Trim phases of production to higher value-added segments of the chain.

There is little doubt that BFC has helped Cambodian garment manufacturers carve out a reputational niche as 'sweat-free' producers, thus sustaining the global competitiveness of the sector. Particularly in its first half-decade, the programme has been regarded as successful on account of its independent and credible monitoring (not in-house by buyers with a vested interest in promoting sweat-free products to consumers); its transparency (until 2006 non-compliant firms were named and shamed); and the fact that its focus was on encouraging suppliers through rewarding them with increased exports, rather than relying on buyers to become compliant. It has generally achieved good results in key areas such as wage payments and union density (Berik and van der Meulen Rodgers 2010; Beresford 2009; Polaski 2004, 2006; Chiu 2007; Wells 2006). The BFC is being proposed by international organizations as a 'fair model of globalization' that should be transferred to other developing economies (Polaski 2006; Robertson 2011; Sibbel and Borrmann 2007; Brown *et al.* 2012). It has become the

*Child labour and gender discrimination* 147

blueprint for the ILO/ International Finance Corporation (IFC) Better Work programme, currently implemented in nine countries involved in global garment supply chains.

Assessments of BFC's impact on the promotion of labour rights are however more mixed, and the structural weaknesses of the programme are becoming more evident as time passes. A recent study by the Stanford Law School (Sonnenberg and Hensler 2013) highlighted that health, job security, collective action and wage levels are among the areas that improved the least under the BFC programme. A first reason for the poor record in these areas is the programme's limited coverage. The large majority of the monitored factories are exporting factories, but these factories regularly outsource part of their orders to non-exporting factories that lie outside the BFC system.[3] The non-monitored subcontracting factories are those where labour rights violations are more likely to happen. The persistence of different labour standards in exporting and non-exporting factories creates challenges for implementing sector-wide trade union organizing efforts (Arnold 2013).

Hughes argued that the programme dis-empowered the emerging labour movement, replacing 'the political framing of grievances with a technocratic "benchmarking" approach in which local power relations were framed out, in favour of international administrative standards' (Hughes 2007: 844). Thus the instances of change and participation of workers remained far from being satisfied. While formal protection is given to workers' freedom of association (the garment sector has a unionization rate close to 60 per cent), genuine collective bargaining is still rare (Nuon and Serrano 2010). The labour force is increasingly casualized, as fixed-duration contracts offering little guarantee against termination have become the norm in the sector since 2005 (Sonnenberg and Hensler 2013; Arnold 2013). The real wages of Cambodian garment workers have substantially decreased in real terms in the last ten years while the programme was in full operation (Sonnenberg and Hensler 2013). Cambodian garment salaries are only higher than in Bangladesh; they remain well below estimated living wages and are insufficient to cope with the daily consumption needs of the growing industrial proletariat. Any savings on the side of the workers are the result of living standards stretched below poverty levels (Chandararot and Danne 2009). The structural dependence on variable overtime for meeting basic needs further exacerbates workers' insecurity (Arnold 2010).

Wage bargaining has polarized class contradictions, leading to assassinations of union leaders (the most prominent case being Chea Vichea) and violent street protests (Arnold 2013; Robertson *et al.* 2009). Last in a long chain of conflicts were the workers' protests in Kampong Speu province in May 2013, where workers requested wage increases. The balance of the conflict was 23 people injured by police and one pregnant woman losing her child. This and other violent confrontations have raised serious concerns about which rights have really been included in the 'ethical package' the BFC programme intends to protect, and how they fit the neoliberal agenda (Hughes 2007; Sonnenberg and Hensler 2013).

148  *M. Beresford* et al.

Finally, several authors have highlighted how the changes in the BFC monitoring system that occurred after the end of the ATC quota regime dampened its transparency as well as its independence, altering the very nature of the programme (Beresford 2009; Sonnenberg and Hensler 2013). First, until 2006 the programme was largely funded by the US government and other international donors as part of the bilateral TATA agreement. Initially seen as a guarantee of independence, donor funding has been reduced since 2006 and now covers only 36 per cent of the costs of the programme. The remainder is funded by GMAC, the Cambodian government and Cambodian trade unions; buyers are also required to contribute more to financing the programme through service fees (BFC 2013b). As one of the earlier concerns with labour standards monitoring elsewhere was the lack of independence – and therefore credibility – of monitors, the shift in funding of BFC means that these interested parties may try to use their financial clout to influence the process. Not only the ILO, but other major stakeholders might have an interest in making the programme look successful.

Furthermore, while in the preceding years the ILO synthesis reports published the names of non-compliant firms, since 2006 full reports on individual firms are only accessible with payment of a fee and with the permission of the monitored company. While this change may have been aimed at compelling buyers to contribute to the financing of monitoring, it also represents a large loss of transparency. Managers are unlikely to give permission to anyone other than current or potential buyers, while costs are too high to encourage a wider audience. Importantly, Cambodia's garment trade unions could be effectively excluded from obtaining this information, along with international NGOs and journalists who were previously involved in exposure of abuses. BFC has responded to pressures for reinstating the name-and-shame practice, and it has recently launched the BFC's Transparency Database (BFC 2014b) where the names of non-compliant factories are publicly disclosed.

## Study location and methodology

Cambodia is divided into 23 provinces, plus the special administrative area of the capital city Phnom Penh. Each province is further divided into districts, with a total of 159 administrative districts. Within districts, communes (*sangkat*) and villages (*phum*) represent the smaller administrative units. Given our intention to focus on the relation between conditions in rural areas and the effective implementation of labour standards in the factories, we purposefully selected two communes that hosted villages characterized by high overall rates of migration and by a relevant proportion of female migrants.[4] The two communes selected for the study, Preah Nipean and Angk Popel, are located in Kong Pisei district, Kampong Speu province, about an hour's drive from Phnom Penh. Kong Pisei district had among the highest proportion of migrants working in the factory sector in the country, with an average migration rate of 11.2 per cent (Ministry of Planning 2008).

*Child labour and gender discrimination*   149

Along with two other provinces that border Phnom Penh (Kandal and Kampong Cham), Kampong Speu is one of the three provinces providing a large majority of Cambodia's garment workers. Instead of migration, however, we found that the majority of those engaged in factory work were in fact commuting on a daily basis.[5] More than 30 per cent of the households in Preah Nipean commune had at least one household member employed at the factory. Of these, about 90 per cent commuted every day from the village, while only 10 per cent lived in Phnom Penh.[6] Angk Popel was one of the district's poorest communes and about 60 per cent of the households had access to factory work.

Factory work was the main source of income for households in the selected communes. Agriculture was, by contrast, very poorly developed. Rice farming was the main agricultural activity – with subsistence-level production of traditional varieties, due to lack of irrigation, averaging only 1–1.5 tonnes/ha in a single season. Some villagers produced watermelon, cauliflower and Chinese kale during the dry season. There were no resident traders or millers, indicating the poor development of agricultural markets. Cattle were raised for draught power and a few pigs, but livestock was generally regarded as risky and the livestock market was almost non-existent. The median landholding was 0.5 ha. Some villages also had a large number of households engaged in crafts like basket weaving and pagoda tile production. Despite the connections in place for marketing these handicraft products, they were poorly paid and represented a minor source of income for the population.

Given the lack of viable alternative economic activities, the main aspiration for the young people was to work at the factory. The pressure of families against migration is, however, very high, particularly in relation to young women. Young women were discouraged with the argument that 'city life is dangerous and it is easy to get into trouble'. The need to follow family advice was a *leitmotif* of our interviews to explain why commuting was convenient despite the fact that migration could be more profitable.[7] In reality, by remaining under the influence of the family, commuters are perceived as a more reliable source of savings and less likely to 'run away' from their family obligations.[8] On the contrary, male migration raises no issues within the family, as it is simply explained as a matter of logistics. Migrant males are usually construction labourers and they are scattered throughout multiple locations, which makes daily commuting impossible.

The decision to commute is however not solely an individual or household choice. Commuting requires first of all the creation of a complex logistic system enabling the workers to reach their workplace according to the overtime schedules imposed by the factories. For this reason, in almost every village a cattle truck has been transformed into a bus, collecting workers from their homes and bringing them to specific factories located along Highways 3 and 4. Commuters have to depart as early as 5 am and they return around 7 at night. The trip took on average one hour and 20 minutes. The organization of effective transport is particularly difficult and expensive given the irregular patterns of overtime demanded by the factories on the basis of their contracts. The need to share

150    *M. Beresford* et al.

transportation makes it important for those living near one another to be working in the same factory. Thus, the truck drivers can adapt their schedules to the pattern of overtime. Fares for daily transport by truck cost US$8–15 per month from a basic wage of US$61. When the factory requires overtime beyond the standard two hours, workers can no longer rely on this system. To comply with exceptional overtime schedules, individual workers may need to find temporary accommodation near the factory. These extra costs constitute an important reduction in the real wage and they are entirely borne by the workers, as no public transport is available.

The survey was conducted between December 2010 and January 2011 as part of an ARC grant (DP0771350), in collaboration with Agricultural Development International (ADI). After identifying the two communes, we randomly selected 11 villages (seven in Preah Nipean, which was bigger; four in Angk Popel). To these, we added the two villages originally identified on the basis of overall/female migration rates reported in the Commune Village Database (see note 5). Thus, fieldwork was conducted in 13 villages.

In each village, we randomly sampled about 15 households with factory workers and about 15 households without factory workers; the latter were to be used as a control group. The sampling was based on rosters provided by the village chief.[9] A total of 396 households were sampled for the study (237 in Preah Nipean, 159 in Angk Popel) and they all participated in the survey. If there was an adult garment worker in the household we interviewed that worker; if there was no garment worker we interviewed another adult member of the household. Data was collected on all household members, so that if there was more than one garment worker information was obtained about all of them. Information about young people (below 18 years) working in the garment sector was gathered indirectly by interviewing parents and adult siblings and not directly from young workers.[10]

On average, households had 5.4 members, with a median of 5. Information was collected on 2108 individuals; of these, 358 were currently employed in the garment sector and 163 were former garment workers. Thus, information was collected on a total of 521 current and former garment factory workers. The share of children under 15 was 27 per cent and for people aged 60 and over it was 8 per cent, meaning that 65 per cent of the individuals that information was collected on were within the legal working age. We deducted the age respondents first entered their employment retrospectively, by asking how long they had been employed in the garment industry.

## Entering the factory: child labour and ID falsification

Finding the balance between economic utility and ethical concerns is the main argument debated in the literature on child labour. On the one hand, child labour is seen as a means of subsistence for poor households; on the other hand, premature work is considered inimical for the economic and cultural prospects of new generations, setting the conditions for persistent poverty to become the norm.

*Child labour and gender discrimination* 151

The World Bank found no evidence that child labour in Cambodia is related to extreme poverty. On the contrary, there was a positive correlation between children's work rates and households' land ownership (World Bank *et al.* 2006). In the case of Cambodia, therefore, child labour cannot be explained as the consequence of extreme poverty.

Looking at the relation between child labour and education in Cambodia, Kim (2009) found that the tacit support given to child labour among those under 18 and even among those under 15 was indeed detrimental to children's education prospects (Kim 2009).[11] Kim's (2009) findings show that work was the main reason for children not attending or irregularly attending school. These data explain the national increase in the proportion of children leaving school prematurely between 1999 and 2004. Among children not attending school, there was a sharp rise at ages 12–14 in those citing as the main reason the need to work, either earning income or in household chores (Kim 2009). Moreover, according to the national Child Labour Survey of 2001, while there was little difference by gender in the proportion of economically active 15–17 year-olds, 62 per cent of boys in this age group were still attending school, but only 42 per cent of girls were (World Bank *et al.* 2006).

In sharp contrast with this alarming data, the BFC monitoring reports had for long found virtually no minors working in the garment factories. In nine of the 12 six-month periods shown in Table 8.1, one or no underage workers were confirmed. In the three years when child labourers where found, they were scattered within a few factories.

Based on the evidence reported by monitors, the eradication of child labour is considered by authors such as Polaski (2004) as one of the main goals achieved

*Table 8.1* Child labour detected in Cambodian garment factories

| Report date | No. factories monitored | Factories with underage workers | No. underage workers confirmed |
|---|---|---|---|
| April 2012 | 136 | 10 (7%) | 30 |
| Oct 2011 | 169 | 5 (3%) | 7 |
| April 2011 | 186 | 0 | 0 |
| Oct 2010 | 131 | 0 | 0 |
| April 2010 | 157 | 0 | 0 |
| Oct 2009 | 172 | 1 | 1 |
| April 2009 | 175 | 1 | 1 |
| Oct 2008 | 205 | 1 | 1 |
| April 2008 | 200 | 0 | 0 |
| Oct 2007 | 227 | 1 | 1 |
| April 2007 | 223 | 1 | 1 |
| Oct 2006 | 212 | 4 (2%) | 13 |

Source: BFC synthesis reports, various years.

Note
While it is not explicitly stated, we assume, based on other BFC documents, that confirmed underage workers are under 15.

152    *M. Beresford* et al.

by the programme, it being an essential requirement for international buyers to invest in Cambodia:

> The near-absence of child labor was a positive discovery, because child labor can impose damaging costs on the child's development and that of the country. It also poses a particularly strong threat to buyers' reputations in a world of instant communications and consumer sensitivity to such abuses. Before the advent of the ILO monitoring project, a British Broadcasting Corporation (BBC) program had presented two ostensibly underage workers in a factory that supplied apparel products to Nike. Although many knowledgeable observers questioned the accuracy of the program, Nike ended its contracts with the factory and left Cambodia. After the ILO began its monitoring program and issued its first report, Nike returned to place orders in Cambodia once again, demonstrating the value of the ILO's credibility to global firms.
>
> (Polaski 2004: 11)

How is it possible, we ask, that school attendance dropped due to child work while no children were found working in the factories? Is it possible that agricultural work absorbed all the child labour force, even in places surveyed where agriculture was almost completely abandoned?

Respondents to our survey were adamant that gaining employment in the garment industry required a minimum age of 18. However, to obtain the required age certification was a major problem for prospective workers. On the one hand, frequent errors and losses of village registries made ID certificate inaccurate or unavailable – in one of the villages surveyed, for instance, all the official registries went lost due to a flood. On the other hand, the current system of certification obliged people to wait as long as three years to obtain the required document.

Currently, ID certificates are issued every three years by the police in collaboration with the commune office with a formal payment of 2000 Riel (equivalent to US$0.5) per certificate. This three-year lag system implies that an 18-year-old entitled to work has to pursue alternative ways to enter the labour market immediately. In order to avoid losing up to three years of work, an informal system of certification has emerged. It is a widespread practice to pay local authorities US$50 to obtain the certificate at any time. This alternative system has also ended up being widely used by people aged 15 (or less) in order to start working sooner. The US$50 capital required to buy the ID before the three-year round was considered by villagers as the main barrier to access work, and not being able to afford the fee was seen as a sign of extreme poverty. The widespread falsification of IDs implies that Better Factories' inspection results with regard to child labour may be seriously compromised.

It is important to note that the Twenty-Seventh Synthesis Report explicitly acknowledged the existence of this widespread ID falsification regime (BFC 2012b). Despite this recognition, no concrete action was taken at the time by the

*Child labour and gender discrimination* 153

BFC to measure the extent of the distortion induced by ID falsification on the reported levels of child labour, nor to increase awareness on the limits of the ID certification system. The policy adopted by monitors to detect child labourers was instead limited to performing first, visual checks of the workers; and second, targeted and random inspections of employment records. Both these remedies however continued to ignore the links between the factory floor and the society at large. We argue that these links are important to make rights effective. In an inversion of this tendency of minimizing the importance of distortions in reporting, the Thirtieth Synthesis Report monitoring factories from 1 November 2012 to 30 April 2013 for the first time stated that the rate of child labour monitored at the factory was not reliable given the widespread use of ID falsification (BFC 2013a). A consultant was hired to further investigate the issue of ID falsification, but as yet no study has been published on the topic.

In our analysis of child labour we adopted BFC's distinction between child workers (less than 15 years old) and young workers (between 15 and 18).[12] We avoided interviewing minor workers directly; rather, we asked adult workers how long they had been working in the factory. Then, we took the person's age at the time of the interview and subtracted the total number of years worked in the garment sector to obtain their commencement working age. This calculation probably underestimates the extent of underage employment by assuming that workers have been continuously employed in the garment sector. People who underwent periods of unemployment or temporarily retired from factory work could have started working at even an earlier age than estimated through our method.[13] Information on current employed minors was gathered from parents or other adult relatives.

In Figure 8.1 the current age of all female and male garment workers in the sample is plotted against the age they were first employed. In the graph black dots indicate workers who commenced working as children (aged below 15 years of age); dark grey dots indicate workers commencing work between 15 and 17 years of age (young workers); light grey dots indicate workers who were first employed after 18 years of age. For reference, a vertical line has been added corresponding to 18 years of age on the axis reporting first employment ages.

We found that about 39 per cent of the workers in the sample (139 out of 358) commenced working in the factory as minors (under 18 years of age). The great majority of these (106 people) were aged between 15 and 17, though it is clear from interviews that all these workers had obtained false documents stating that they were 18. Moreover, about 9 per cent of the workers (33) had begun working in a garment factory when they were under 15; of these, four were under 12 (in contrast with ILO Convention 138), with the earlier commencement age being nine years (two cases reported). It is noteworthy that all workers who started working before they turned 15 were women; no men in the sample began working at such an early age and a much smaller proportion had commenced before the age of 18 (Figure 8.1).

These data are in striking contrast to the claim that child labour has almost been abolished in Cambodia (Robertson 2011; Sibbel 2007; Polaski

154  *M. Beresford* et al.

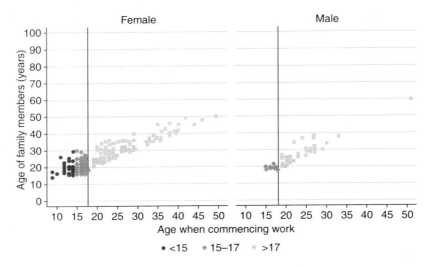

*Figure 8.1* Graph plots of female and male garment workers' current age against first employment age.

Source: Fieldwork data. Preah Nipean and Angk Popel, Kong Pisei District, Kampong Speu Province Cambodia 2010.

Notes
The data refer to all the garment workers in the sample.
Colours represent age classes: black = child labourers; dark grey = young labourers; light grey = adult workers.
A vertical line indicates workers had their first employment at 18 years of age.

2006), indicating the incidence of false ID certificates among factory workers is not scattered, but systemic and relevant.

After accounting for ID falsification, a temporal analysis of the data highlights the very little difference BFC has made for child labour. In Figure 8.2 the percentage of active garment workers under 15 (child labour) and aged between 15 and 17 (young workers) was calculated for each year between 1995 and 2010. The data presented in Figure 8.2 also report the percentage of workers who ceased being employed in the garment sector each year.

Results suggest that the employment of young workers in the garment sector has been steadily increasing since 2002, peaking at about 24 per cent between 2007 and 2009 (roughly corresponding to the GFC period). Only in 2010 did the percentage of young workers decline to about 15 per cent, which however is twice the figure estimated for 2001 (7.5 per cent), when the BFC programme was first implemented. As for the incidence of child labour, this would also appear to have been increasing after the start of the BFC programme. In 2001, 1.2 per cent of the employed garment factory workers in our sample were under 15. This figure reaches a maximum of 4.6 per cent in 2007 and only falls below the pre-BFC level in 2010 (0.5 per cent).

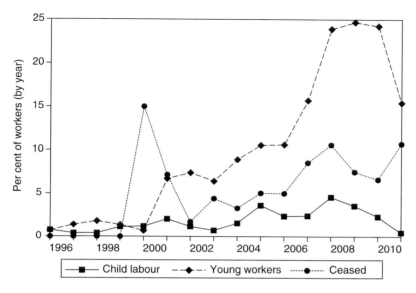

*Figure 8.2* Incidence (per cent) of child labourers, young workers and ceased workers per year (1995–2010).

Source: Fieldwork data. Preah Nipean and Angk Popel, Kong Pisei District, Kampong Speu Province Cambodia 2010.

Note
Squares = child labourers; diamonds = young workers; circles = ceased workers.

Given the relative importance of young labourers in the sample, we further explore the conditions of employment defined by the law for these minors, and how these conditions are implemented in practice. The legal definitions both in Cambodia and from international organizations are unable to univocally identify age boundaries and working loads for young workers. The Cambodian Ministry of Labour and Vocational Training (MOLVT) distinguishes 'child labour' that inimically affects the mental, physical, social or moral progress of the child, from 'child work'.[14] The latter is legally permitted as far as it helps to educate or train the child for future occupation. As Kim (2009) points out, no guidance is provided in the law as to the type of work that helps to educate or train the child for future occupation or what type and how much work is 'inimical' to a child's progress.

Starting from this very ambiguous foundation, a number of contrasting norms and interpretations regulate the minimum age and the workload of young workers. The minimum working age (Art. 177) set by Cambodian law is 15 years. However, Art. 173 specifies that a child under 16 years may not be hired in any enterprise other than a family business (World Bank *et al.* 2006). In apparent contrast with these rules, in its Guide to the Cambodian Labour Law

156  *M. Beresford* et al.

the ILO (2005) points out that minors aged from 12 to 14 years may be hired to do light work. In the absence of a specific definition of 'light work', the World Bank adopted a 14 hours per week maximum (World Bank *et al.* 2006). Children aged 15–17 who work more than 43 hours per week are considered together with those involved in hazardous work by the interagency report on *Children's Work in Cambodia* (World Bank *et al.* 2006). The same report shows that for females aged 15–17 in manufacturing the average weekly hours were 49.6 in 2001 – in other words a full working week plus a little overtime. Finally, the ILO Convention 138 prohibits work in the formal sector for children below the age of 12, prescribes only 'light work' for children aged 12–14, and bans all children below the age of 18 from work that is detrimental to 'health, safety and morals' (ILO 1973).

We asked our respondents to indicate average weekly overtime hours in the course of the previous year. The median overtime work for all workers in our sample was ten hours per week, within the legal limit set for adults at 12 hours per week. About 15 per cent of the sample reported average overtime hours well beyond the legal limit of 12 hours per week, ranging from 14 to 40 hours per week.[15] A question arises about the extent young workers are involved in overtime. Figure 8.3 shows the percentage histogram of average weekly overtime

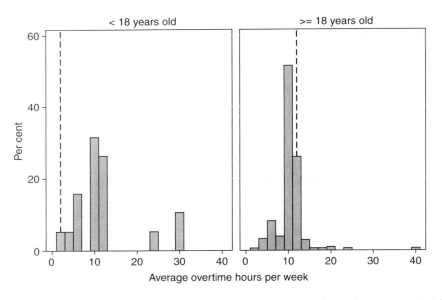

*Figure 8.3* Percentage distribution of average weekly overtime hours for young and adult workers.

Source: Fieldwork data. Preah Nipean and Angk Popel, Kong Pisei District, Kampong Speu Province Cambodia 2010.

Note
Bars indicate the percentage of observation in each category. A vertical line indicates the legal limits of overtime for each age group.

*Child labour and gender discrimination* 157

hours in the sample for current minors and adult workers. A vertical line was added to indicate the legal overtime limit for each age group. It should be noted that there is no significant difference in the working practices of currently employed minor workers. Young workers follow exactly the same workload as adult workers, including very long working days during peak production periods.[16]

Data on overtime make it clear why many factories stipulate that workers must be at least 18 years old. In practice it would be very inconvenient for managers during peak production periods to distinguish between 'young workers' and adult workers in order to exclude the former from work extending after 10 p.m. On the one hand, the high-pressure peaks of the garment industry encourage the system of corruption to obtain false IDs; on the other hand, the rapid growth in employment post-GFC, leading to labour shortages (BFC 2012c), means that employers may be more willing to turn a blind eye or fail to keep proper records. Indeed the Twenty-Eighth Synthesis Report does record an 11 per cent drop in compliance on document maintenance (BFC 2012c) from 98 to 87 per cent. Empirical evidence collected from commuter workers in their villages very clearly explains why BFC monitoring reports are unable to capture the effective extent of child labour in the garment factories. By overlooking the relation linking child labour with the falsification of IDs, the BFC programme can only describe the formal side of child employment.

## Leaving the factory: gender discrimination and caring duties

One of the common explanations for the short career of the garment worker is explicitly gender related and pertains to the caring responsibilities of women. From a theoretical perspective Kabeer argues that, 'maternity benefits and child-care facilities help to offset pre-existing distortions in market forces which do not factor in the cost of women's unpaid work in caring for their children and family' (2005: 192). In her study of Bangladeshi workers, for example, she found that absence of support for women who become pregnant and/or have childcare responsibilities led to loss of employment.

Therefore, at the core of the effectiveness of gender policies is the ability of women workers to gain support for their reproductive roles. Once this is achieved it should become possible for them to benefit over the longer term from the high wages (relative to farming) and stability of employment offered by factory work. If young women are more likely to report improvements in intra-household relations as a consequence of their factory work, the ability to retain such employment over the main child-raising years only ought to enhance this effect.

Kabeer (2004) cites several studies from other countries referring to the relative freedom conferred by garment employment where workers are living away from home. Women migrant workers are more likely to report improvements in intra-household relationships and to report help in domestic work and sharing decision-making with male members. Factory work comprises only one part of a worker's life and it is this link between the factory and life beyond the factory gate that constitutes the gender-specific element in the application of labour standards. In the case of commuters this higher degree of inter-household equality can be more difficult to achieve given the influence of patriarchal relations at the village (Prota and Beresford 2012).

The BFC programme has certainly tackled the issues of maternity leave, childcare and employer discrimination against pregnant women within the garment sector. However, as in the case of child labour, the focus on the factory shop floor might have provided a rather limited understanding of the reinforcing mechanisms shaping the roles of women at work and in their families.

The levels of compliance of monitored factories to the items indicating gender discrimination, childcare provision and maternity leave seem to support the impression that BFC has, at least partially, achieved its objectives of providing women workers with improved opportunities to continue their career after childbirth. By law, factories should either provide a childcare centre or pay the costs of childcare for their employees. A rather high, but diminishing, percentage of factories does not meet this standard on provision of childcare. Figure 8.4 shows the percentage of non-compliant factories for childcare recorded in the BFC Synthesis Reports from 2006 to April 2012. Data are not always complete, as they are available in the reports only when the issue is among the top ten non-compliance issues for a particular reporting period. It would appear from what is available that, after dropping quite rapidly during 2006–7, the level of non-compliance for childcare provision stabilized in the 55–8 per cent range during 2010–12. In Chiu's (2007) study of Hong Kong firms in Cambodia, with data from 2006, only five of the 24 firms did not provide childcare as required under the Cambodian law.

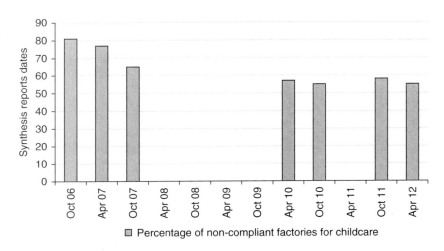

*Figure 8.4* BFC reported percentage of non-compliant monitored factories on childcare provision from October 2006 to April 2012.

Source: BFC synthesis reports.

Similarly, there are high compliance rates for maternity leave reported by the BFC. The graph in Figure 8.5 shows the percentage of compliant firms reported by BFC over time. Payment of maternity leave shows a marked decline after the middle of 2008. The GFC hit Cambodian exports in the third quarter of that year and it seems likely that payments were reduced in response to lower demand, especially from the US. However, maternity leave payments have shown little tendency to recover as the industry and exports recover. By the reporting period for November 2011 to April 2012, employment in the Cambodian garment industry was back to the levels of early 2008, but maternity leave payments remained significantly lower. Despite this reduction, even at the peak of the GFC on average at least one out of two factories was compliant. It is important to specify that being compliant includes paying the full amount due for maternity leave, including the entire period of continuous employment when determining workers' entitlements to maternity leave, paying attendance bonuses, seniority bonuses and/or annual leave.

Chiu (2007) reports even higher compliance rates among Hong Kong factories. Almost all (22 out of 24) surveyed firms included maternity leave in the collective bargaining agreement, while the other two provided it anyway. Interestingly, 17 firms also included paternity leave, which is required by Cambodian labour law. Nineteen firms provided a childcare centre, as required by law.

The progress monitored by BFC reports is supported by reported falling rates of discrimination. The Synthesis Reports note that discrimination typically

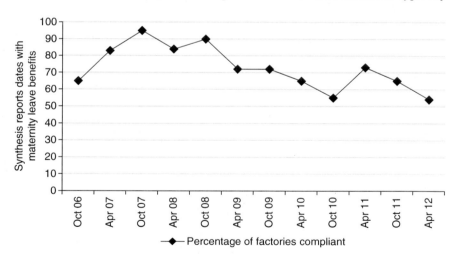

*Figure 8.5* BFC reported compliance levels of maternity leave from October 2006 to April 2012.

Source: BFC synthesis reports for the relevant periods.

Note
Compliance levels are calculated by summing two compliance questions: payment of half of wages and benefits, and payment of only half wages during maternity leave. The graph includes both amounts.

involves either unfair treatment of pregnant workers (for example, dismissal or non-renewal of contracts when they become visibly pregnant), or unfair treatment of men (for example, failure to hire men because they are perceived as more likely to lead workers to strike). Since women form 90 per cent of the workforce, we can assume that the majority of cases fall into the former category. Figure 8.6 shows that, although gender-based discrimination remains an issue in a minority of factories, there was a tendency for the level to rise after the GFC. Between 2006 and 2012 the percentage of non-compliance factories almost doubled, going from about 10 per cent to about 20 per cent.

Gender discrimination in our fieldwork results are also in striking contrast to the picture illustrated by the BFC reports. As mentioned above, we collected information about 163 former garment workers (128 females and 35 males). Table 8.2 reports the reasons for quitting the job by gender. Caring responsibilities are, by far, the main reason for quitting for workers of both sexes. However, caring is indicated as the cause of termination by 77.3 per cent of female workers and only by 51 per cent of males. Furthermore, 28.6 per cent of male workers left their factory job for what could be called 'voluntary' reasons (because they found better opportunities or because they didn't like the job), while the same was true only for 10 per cent of females.

Figures 8.7 and 8.8 show how the decision to leave the job for caring responsibilities strongly relates to the birth of the first and of the last baby in the household; data are again divided by gender. In both graphs, the horizontal axis reports the number of years before (negative values) or after (positive values) the birth of the first/last baby (indicated with 0) where workers left the job for caring responsibilities.[17] Not surprisingly, for female workers caring responsibility

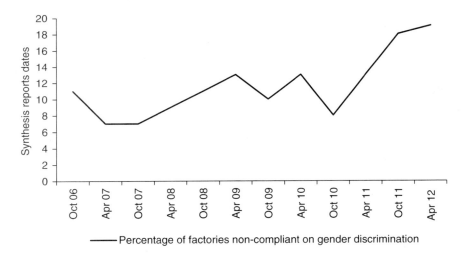

Figure 8.6 BFC reported percentage of non-compliant monitored factories on gender discrimination from October 2006 to April 2012.

Source: BFC synthesis reports.

*Table 8.2* Reasons for quitting garment factory work

| Reason for quitting | Females | Males |
|---|---|---|
| Caring responsibilities | 99 (77.3%) | 18 (51.4%) |
| Firing/dismissal | 11 (8.6%) | 5 (14.3%) |
| Didn't like the job | 9 (7.0%) | 7 (20.0%) |
| Found better job | 4 (3.1%) | 3 (8.6%) |
| Other | 5 (3.9%) | 2 (5.7%) |
| Totals | 128 (100%) | 35 (100%) |

Source: Fieldwork data.

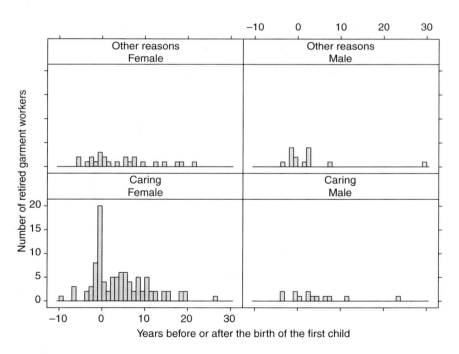

*Figure 8.7* Job cessation and birth of the first child.

Source: Fieldwork data.

Note
The horizontal axis reports the number of years before (negative values) or after (positive values) the birth of the first baby (indicated with 0) in which workers left the job for caring responsibilities.

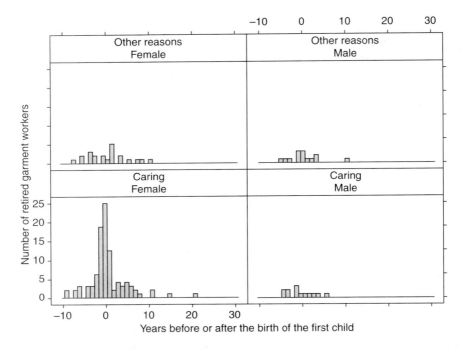

*Figure 8.8* Job cessation and birth of the last child.

Source: Fieldwork data.

Note: The horizontal axis reports the number of years before (negative values) or after (positive values) the birth of the last baby (indicated with 0) in which workers left the job for caring responsibilities.

becomes incompatible with work one year after the birth of the first child (Figure 8.7). Similarly, Figure 8.8 shows that the chances of quitting the job for caring responsibilities increase again one year before and after the birth of the last child. These data suggest that the working cycle of female garment workers is still very much interwoven with their reproductive cycle.

While our data are not representative for all Cambodian factories, as they only describe labour conditions in the Kong Pisei District, they are however unlikely to represent an exceptional case. It seems more reasonable that job cessation due to caring might be under-reported at the factory by workers who, either consciously or not consciously, might consider it 'normal' to quit when pregnant.

Direct fieldwork observation and discussions with workers suggested a widespread strategy to cope with discrimination was rolling employment from one generation of women to another, thus creating a cyclic replacement of productive and reproductive roles. As one woman in the household becomes pregnant and needs childcare for the newborn baby, either an older woman retires from work for caring, or a younger woman prematurely enters the factory allowing the new mother to quit. Through this cyclic replacement of women in their double roles of workers and carers, the household is able to maintain a stable stream of income. Should this cycle be broken due to the lack of an appropriate replacement, the economic condition of the household would suddenly fall into poverty. This harmonization of productive and reproductive cycles within the household is beneficial both to the village patriarchy and to the factory hierarchy. The former is not endangered by women's empowerment and changes in inter-household roles; the latter is lifted from bearing the costs of providing an effective solution to gender discrimination.

We argue that effective improvements in women's rights will not be achieved by linking 'specific requirements to orders', as suggested by Chiu (2007). Effective monitoring will come from an increased awareness of the links between the factory and the wider social context of Cambodia. Monitoring the factory floor, even when accompanied by sanctions against non-compliant firms, cannot by itself overcome the cultural norms that associate the work of caring with women. Instead, the very weakness of the concepts of labour rights and gender equality in the society as a whole influences the lives of women garment workers in ways that tend to counteract the effect of BFC standards.

## Conclusions

The aim of this study is to examine the factors in the lives of garment workers outside the factory environment that can influence the implementation of labour standards. The study reports evidence from two commuting villages located in Kong Pisei District. Commuters offered us the opportunity to look more closely at the interactions between the monitoring system implemented in the factories and the social, economic and institutional context in the villages that workers return to on a daily basis. We focused on two rights that BFC's supporters often cite as largely attained: the abolition of child labour and the sharp reduction in gender discrimination.

Our results lead us to question the reliability of BFC results, as the reports are based on a partial representation of what can formally occur on the factory shop floor. We argue that the effective application of labour standards is instead often denied by mechanisms rooted within the wider social context where the industry develops rather than in the factory itself. Sustainable improvements in working conditions require changes that go beyond the factory floor and beyond the single sector of traded goods.

First we analysed the age that the careers of garment workers start. We found that a widely adopted system of ID falsification allowed prospective workers to obtain a legal document certifying they were 18, regardless of their true age. The falsification of documents involved a high fee (US$50) and the 'help' of the commune/village chief and police. Through this back door, child and young workers enter the labour market in Cambodia on a large scale (39 per cent in our sample). These data highlight how formally improved labour rights, far from protecting workers, have instead produced a second market for age certificates.

164   *M. Beresford* et al.

Currently, the commodification of age represents an ethical clearance for the full inclusion of minors in the workforce. Being formally registered as adult workers, minors are called to bear the same workload as adults, including long night shifts of overtime. A prompt change in the age certification system is needed to make the system transparent and monitoring reliable.

The second issue we investigated was the correlation between quitting jobs and caring responsibilities. We found that 77.3 per cent of female workers in our sample left work at the factory because of caring. Our analysis suggests that a cyclic replacement of women at work links generations within the household. As one woman gets pregnant and needs to care for the newborn baby, her mother retires from work or a younger woman in the family prematurely enters the factory. This hypothesis will be statistically examined in future work looking at the correlation between job cessation, child labour and reproduction within the household life history.

While our sample is not representative for all garment workers in Cambodia, it describes the key features of the garment industry in Kong Pisei District well. It would be interesting to reproduce the study in other garment districts of Cambodia, to evaluate differences and similarities. The study highlights the importance of adopting a more comprehensive approach to labour rights that is able to frame them in Cambodia's social and economic context. The main recommendation of the study is an immediate reform of the ID certification system and a full check of other key certification systems, such as driving licences, that might be suffering similar distortions.

## Notes

I wish to thank the ARC for providing funding (DP0771350) that made this research possible. We thank Mr Sok Muniroth and all the staff at Agricultural Development International (ADI), Phnom Penh, for helping us to finalize the questionnaire and collect the data. Particular acknowledgements go to the late Tim Purcell, director of ADI, whose work on Southeast Asian rural development we will always remember as an extraordinary source of inspiration.

1  Not all garment factories operating in Cambodia belong to the GMAC. While exporting factories and a few large non-exporting factories register with GMAC, smaller establishments – particularly informal subcontractors – are often not registered.
2  The literature points in particular to the lack of adequate infrastructure, the absence of forward and backward linkages, and the dependence on raw materials imported from China, Taiwan and Hong Kong. Furthermore, with only 7 per cent of the factories owned by Cambodian investors, local involvement in ownership and management remains minimal (Arnold 2013; Beresford 2009; Heintz 2007; Yagamata 2006). It also appears that positive spill-overs from the garment industry to other sectors of the economy are rather limited (Economic Institute of Cambodia 2007; Kobayashi *et al.* 2009).
3  As of April 2013 (the end of the monitoring period covered in BFC Thirtieth Synthesis Report), the number of workers employed in the 412 monitored factories was 394,262 (BFC 2013b). In the previous year, Ken Loo (Secretary-General of the GMAC) reported that an additional 200,000 workers were estimated to be employed in garment factories that supplied exporters but did not have export licences (quoted in MacIsaac 2012).

*Child labour and gender discrimination*   165

4 The two communes were identified using secondary data from the Commune Village Database (Ministry of Planning 2008). For each village in Cambodia, we first calculated the ratio of migrants over the working-age population (15 to 65 years). We then calculated the gender migration ratio as the proportion between female and male migration rates in the village; values close to 1 indicate that females have the same odds of migrating as males, while higher values correspond to a higher propensity of females to migrate compared to males. After inspecting the data, we decided to concentrate on villages with overall migration rates above 33 per cent and a gender migration ratio between 1 and 2. Among the villages that simultaneously satisfied the two conditions, two (Sayav and Svay Teab) were located in the same district (Kong Pisei), which offered the additional advantage of being easily accessible from Phnom Penh. The two villages were respectively located in Preah Nipean and Angk Popel communes, and for this reason the two communes were selected as the study location.

5 This observation calls for some caution in using the Commune Village Database, since it conflates migrants who had left the village with workers who commuted on a daily basis. Since in our case the selection of villages was aimed at identifying locations characterized by high rates of employment outside the village (irrespective of the continued residence of workers in the village), we believe that this conflation has not significantly biased our sample selection.

6 Along with their high migration rates, it is possible that Kandal and Kampong Cham provinces also provide large numbers of commuter-workers. According to the district chief in Kong Pisei (Kampong Speu), only female workers from more distant areas are likely to migrate than commute. In one household that had migrated to Kong Pisei from the Takeo province, the wife was commuting to work in Phnom Penh. We do not, however, have further data to support the hypothesis that migrant workers might form a minority in the factory population.

7 According to our interviews, the monthly transport costs can be as much as double that of shared rental accommodation in the city.

8 Escaping misery and family obligations for many women means to flee, to seek an alternative life in the city, or even further away in, for example, Malaysia. Several young mothers we interviewed, unable to work at the factory because of their childcare obligations or their age, and under the pressure of debts, had settled on the dramatic resolution of leaving their children and relatives for an unknown future somewhere else. Other interviewees informed us about abandoned children who were desperately ill or had even died.

9 Whenever village-level registers reported information about households with members engaged in factory jobs, we used the register as the sampling frame. If detailed registers were not available, we collected this information from knowledgeable local informants (generally village chiefs). In smaller villages the sample was close to a census; therefore, the proportion between households with and without migrants in the sample could vary to some extent across villages. In the end, 243 households (61 per cent of the sample) had at least one garment worker.

10 All interviews were undertaken at home at a time chosen by respondents. Interviewers were all experienced Cambodian researchers, thus interviews were held in the local language after clearly introducing the scope of the research and clarifying that data would remain anonymous. Respondents were also clearly informed about the possibility of not answering questions or of dropping out, at any time, from the interview. At the time of the interview, informants on the household's members were therefore adults, or were at least certified as older than 18 years of age.

11 National-level survey results from the Cambodia Socio-Economic Survey of 2004 (cited in Kim 2009) showed that 3.9 per cent of all children and 4.7 per cent of girls aged 10–14 were in paid employment, while 4.3 per cent of all child workers in that age group and 5 per cent of girls were working in manufacturing (including the

166 *M. Beresford* et al.

non-garment industries). This figure compares with a global figure for the year 2000 of 4 per cent (Edmonds and Pavcnik 2005).

12 BFC (2012a), in contrast to Convention 138, describes the 15–17 age group as 'young workers' rather than as children.

13 This calculation method is based on the consideration that garment factory workers rarely remain unoccupied for long periods during their youth. Interviewed ex-factory workers reported that while it is common to move from one factory to another during your career, it is difficult to go back to work after a long period of unemployment or retirement. The total years worked, therefore, should broadly correspond to a continuous working period. The commencement date obtained by subtracting this period from the current age should provide at least a reasonable indication of the real phenomenon.

14 The MOLVT definition of 'child labour' recalls the notion of 'worst forms of child labour' as defined in Article 3(d) of ILO Convention No. 182 and Article 3 of ILO Recommendation No. 190.

15 The BFC report for the relevant period (November 2010 to April 2011) noted that 75 per cent of factories were not in compliance with the overtime standard (BFC 2011). By April 2012, this figure was 86 per cent.

16 A t-test confirms that there is no significant difference in means between the two groups.

17 The number of years before or after the birth of the first/last baby in the household was calculated by subtracting the year the worker left the garment sector from the year the baby was born.

## References

Arnold, D. (2010) 'A fair model of globalisation? Labour and global production in Cambodia', *Journal of Contemporary Asia*, 40(3): 401–24.

Arnold, D. (2013) *Workers' Agency and Re-working Power Relations in Cambodia's Garment Industry. Capturing the gains*, Working Paper 24, Maastricht: Maastricht University.

Beresford, M. (2009) 'The Cambodian clothing industry in the post-MFA environment: a review of developments', *Journal of the Asia Pacific Economy*, 14(4): 366–88.

Berik, G. and Rodgers, Y. van der Meulen (2010). 'Options for enforcing labor standards: lessons from Cambodia and Bangladesh', *Journal of International Development*, 22(1): 56–85.

Better Factories Cambodia (BFC) (2011) *Twenty Sixth Synthesis Report on Working Conditions in Cambodia's Garment Sector*, April, Phnom Penh: Better Factories Cambodia.

BFC (2012a) *Child Labour Guidance: Methods to Prevent Child Labour at your Workplace*. Phnom Penh: Better Factories Cambodia.

BFC (2012b) *Twenty Seventh Synthesis Report on Working Conditions in Cambodia's Gar Sector*, January, Phnom Penh: Better Factories Cambodia.

BFC (2012c) *Twenty Eighth Synthesis Report*, July, Phnom Penh: Better Factories Cambodia.

BFC (2013a) *Thirtieth Synthesis Report on Working Conditions in Cambodia's Garment Sector*, July Phnom Penh: Better Factories Cambodia.

BFC (2013b) 'How we're funded', http://betterfactories.org/?page_id=71 (accessed 5 December 2013).

BFC (2014a) 'Transparency database, low compliance introduction'. Online at: www.betterfactories.org/transparency/widespread_noncompliance/introduction (accessed 21 July 2014).

*Child labour and gender discrimination* 167

BFC (2014b) 'Transparency database fact-sheet', www.betterfactories.org/transparency/pages/view/18 (accessed 21 July 2014).

BCF (2014c) 'Monitoring', www.betterfactories.org/?page_id=90 (accessed 21 July 2014).

Brown, D., Dehejia, R. and Robertson, R. (2012) *Retrogression in Working Conditions: Evidence from Better Factories Cambodia*, Better Work Discussion Paper 6, Geneva: International Labour Organization.

CAMFEBA and BDLINK (2010) *Understanding the Impact of the Global Economic Crisis on the Cambodian Garment Sector. Final Survey Report*. 26 April, ILO & AFD, Cambodia. On line at: http://apps.ubmasia.com/files/mediaobjects/Files/25/PSF/10%20ILO%20Global%20Eco%20Crisis%20on%20Cambodian%20Garment.pdf (accessed 5 December 2013)

Chand, A. (2012) 'At the bottom of a global commodity chain: how different really are hourly wage rates and piece rates?', *Industrial Relations Journal*, 43(2): 171–91.

Chandararot, K. and Danne, L. (2009) *Living Wage Survey for Cambodia's Garment Industry*, Commissioned Report for the Community Legal Education Center, Cambodia Institute of Development Study and Friedrich Ebert Stiftung, Cambodia.

Chiu, C. C. H. (2007) 'Workplace practices in Hong Kong-invested garment factories in Cambodia', *Journal of Contemporary Asia*, 37(4): 431–48.

Dasgupta, S., Poutiainen, T. and Williams, D. (2011) *From Downturn to Recovery: Cambodia's Garment Sector in Transition*, Phnom Penh: International Labour Organization.

Economic Institute of Cambodia (2007) *Export Diversification and Value-Added Addition for Human Development*, Phnom Penh: Economic Institute of Cambodia.

Economic Institute of Cambodia (2008) *Cambodia's Labor Market and Employment. Background Paper Prepared for the World Bank*, Phnom Penh: World Bank.

Edmonds, E. V. and Pavcnik, N. (2005) 'Child labor in the global economy', *Journal of Economic Perspectives*, 19(1): 199–220.

Hale, A. and Shaw, L. M. (2001) 'Women workers and the promise of ethical trade in the globalised garment industry: A serious beginning?' *Antipode*, 33(3): 510–30.

Heintz, A. (2007) 'Human development and clothing manufacturing in Cambodia: challenges and strategies for the garment industry', *The Good Society*, 16(2): 65–72.

Hughes, C. (2007) 'Transnational networks, international organizations and political participation in Cambodia: human rights, labour rights and common rights', *Democratization*, 14(5): 834–52.

Gereffi, G. and Korzeniewicz, M. (1994) *Commodity Chains and Global Capitalism*, Westport CT and London: Praeger.

International Labour Organization (ILO) (1973) 'C138 – Minimum age convention 1973 (No.138)',www.ilo.org/dyn/normlex/en/f?p=NORMLEXPUB:12100:4306538611189757::NO:12100:P12100_INSTRUMENT_ID:312283:NOwww.ilo.org/dyn/normlex/en/f?p=NORMLEXPUB:12100:4306538611189757::NO:12100:P12100_INSTRUMENT_ID:312283:NO(accessed 21 June 2012).

ILO (2005) *Guide to the Cambodian Labour Law for the Garment Industry*, Phnom Penh: International Labour Organization.

ILO (2009) 'ILO Better Factories Cambodia 22nd synthesis report: garment factory working conditions generally remain good, despite continuing pressure due to the global economic slowdown', www.ilo.org/asia/info/public/pr/WCMS_113136/lang-en/index.htmwww.ilo.org/asia/info/public/pr/WCMS_113136/lang-en/index.htm(accessed 14 June 2012).

168   *M. Beresford* et al.

Kabeer, N. (2005) 'Labour standards and women's rights', in S. G. Indrani (ed.), *Human Rights of Minorities Women*, pp. 192–230, Dehli: Isha Books.

Kim, C.-Y. (2009) 'Is combining child labour and school education the right approach? Investigating the Cambodian case', *International Journal of Educational Development*, 29: 30–8.

Kobayashi, S., Tanji, H., Saito, K., Huang, W. and Tada, M. (2009) 'Industrial structure of Cambodia and the role of agriculture and fishery in its development', *Japan Agricultural Research Quarterly*, 43: 309–16.

Lee, J. J. (2011). 'An outlook for Cambodia's garment industry in the post-safeguard policy era', *Asian Survey*, 51(3): 559–80.

Ministry of Planning (2008) *Commune-Village Database*, Phnom Penh: Ministry of Planning.

MacIsaac, V. (2012) 'Garment industry at crossroads', *The Phnom Penh Post*, 7 February 2012. Online at: www.phnompenhpost.com/special-reports/garment-industry-crossroads (accessed 21 July 2014).

Nuon, V. and Serrano, M. (2010) *Building Unions in Cambodia. History, Challenges, Strategies*, Singapore: Friedrich-Ebert-Stiftung Office for Regional Cooperation in Asia.

Polaski, S. (2004) 'Cambodia blazes a new path to economic growth and job creation', online at: www.carnegieendowment.org/files/cp51polaskifinal2.pdfwww.carnegieendowment.org/files/cp51polaskifinal2.pdf (accessed 26 May 2012).

Polaski, S. (2006) 'Combining global and local forces: the case of labor rights in Cambodia', *World Development*, 34(5): 919–32.

Prota, L. and Beresford, M. (2012). 'The factory hierarchy in the village: Recruitment networks and labour control in Kong Pisei District of Cambodia', *Institutions and Economies* (formerly known as *International Journal of Institutions and Economies*), 4(3), 103–22.

Rasiah, R. (1993) 'Competition and governance: work in Malaysia's textile and garment industries', *Journal of Contemporary Asia*, 23(1): 3–23.

Rasiah, R. (2009). 'Garment manufacturing in Cambodia and Laos', *Journal of the Asia Pacific Economy*, 14: 150–61.

Robertson, R. (2011). *Apparel Wages Before and After Better Factories Cambodia*, Better Work Discussion Paper no. 3, Geneva: International Labour Organization.

Sibbel, L. and Borrmann, P. (2007) 'Linking trade with labour rights: the ILO Better Factories Cambodia project', *Arizona Journal of International and Comparative Law*, 24(1): 235–49.

Sonnenberg, S. and Hensler, B. (2013) *Monitoring in the Dark. An Evaluation of the International Labour Organization's Better Factory Cambodia Monitoring and Reporting Program*, Stanford CA: International Human Rights and Conflict Resolution Clinic, Stanford Law School and Worker Rights Consortium.

Vickery, M. (1990) 'Notes on the political economy of the People's Republic of Kampuchea (PRK)', *Journal of Contemporary Asia*, 20(4): 435–65.

Wells, D. (2006) '"Best Practice" in the regulation of International Labor Standards: lessons of the US–Cambodia Textile Agreement', *Comparative Labor Law and Policy Journal*, 27: 357–76.

Yamagata, T. (2006) *The Garment Industry in Cambodia:Its Role in Poverty Reduction through Export-Oriented Development*, Discussion Paper 62, Tokyo: Institute of Developing Economies.

World Bank, UNICEF and ILO (2006) *Children's Work in Cambodia: A Challenge for Growth and Poverty Reduction*, Inter-agency Research Cooperation Project: Understanding Children's Work, Report no. 38005, December, Washington DC: World Bank.

# 9 Asian women doing home-based garment manufacturing in Sydney, Australia

*Elissa Sutherland*

When I first came to Australia I worked in a factory making ladies' underwear. I was very bored because the work was too easy. I preferred to do sophisticated jobs, not these basic designs. After that time I became an outworker, making formal suits and gowns at home. I also tried to get work making leather clothing because this was more of a challenge. At that time the money was OK – I was earning similar to the Award rate.

(Ruby, an outworker in Sydney, reflecting on her work in the 1990s)

Home-based women workers have played a central role in the Australian clothing industry's workforce. These workers, involved in garment manufacturing, are referred to as 'outworkers' in Australia and 'homeworkers' internationally. Homework is usually sewing work paid at low piece-rates, most often performed by migrants (mostly from south-east Asia in the Australian context), and by women working in their home-spaces but using industrial sewing machines. In Australia's capital cities, widespread networks of home-based workers and the middle-men, or makers-up, who often employ them, offer large retailers, manufacturers and fashion houses both a low-cost, relatively unregulated alternative to factory-based manufacturing, and a domestic alternative to cheap offshore production.

In the first half of the chapter, I discuss how the Australian clothing industry faces continued restructuring pressures and has made increasing use of home-based workers to maintain production and profit levels. This sets the context for an overview of attempts at assessing the number of home-based workers in garment production in Australia. The difficulty in quantifying these workers highlights the marginal status of this work, and the propensity for it to be exploitative and 'off-the books'. Drawing on four years of fieldwork, I then outline some of the experiences and voices of Chinese, Cambodian/Khmer and Vietnamese women in Sydney doing home-based garment manufacturing from the late 1990s until 2002. Issues of gender, migration and the fact that work occurs in private home-spaces have shaped the marginal status, policy and regulation of the work form. Central themes explored are exploitation, as well as livelihood and empowerment.

## 170   E. Sutherland

Before looking at the extent to which garment manufacturing in Australia is reliant on home-based workers, it is important to place outwork in the context of a rapidly globalizing industry, facing significant domestic, regional and international pressures.

## Restructuring of the Australian clothing industry

The Australian clothing industry has restructured in response to globalizing forces. Increasing imports, falling tariffs, declining factory employment, retail concentration and formularized industry policy plans are all forces shaping the industry. Since the phasing out of the 1974 MFA and its integration into the 1994 Uruguay GATT, trade barriers to the flow of clothing have been slowly phased out. As a result of early adoption of trade liberalization – the Whitlam government adopted an across the board 25 per cent reduction on all tariffs – Australian tariffs on imported clothing have dropped significantly. More recently, between 1990 and 2015, tariffs on clothing imports have declined by 50 per cent. These tariff reductions, along with the impact of exchange rate movements, have led to more than a quadrupling of clothing imports into Australia in that same period (Green 2008 vol. 1: 50–1).

Industry policy has been integral to reshaping the Australian clothing industry. Since the Whitlam Labor government, and except for the Fraser Liberal government that followed it, tariffs, quotas, bounties and duties have been lowered in various phased processes under each successive TCF industry policy plan. Representations about an emerging global economy began to colour industry policy language in the early 1970s and, in response, each Australian government viewed the domestic industry as backward and in decline, and unable to respond to global challenges. A new direction toward internationally competitive industries, efficiency and 'comparative advantage', was therefore set in motion along with very high rates of 'effective rates' of industry assistance particularly from 1980–7 (Jayanthakumaran 2008). Deregulation of trade barriers and the facilitation of export trade have continued to be the central tenets of policy though assistance has declined.

Although international trade in clothing has increased, the patterns of that trade are intra-regional, reflecting market concentrations and connections as well as bilateral agreements between nations (Dicken 2003: 323–5). Australia has close associations with Asian markets, particularly garment manufacturing in China and Hong Kong; with signatories to the South Pacific Regional Trade and Economic Cooperation Agreement (SPARTECA) such as Fiji; as well as with New Zealand, owing to long-standing reciprocal and non-reciprocal agreements. This is reflected in the sources of Australia's imported clothing. However, with the increased value of the Australian dollar, high-end fashion imports from Italy and France have also, in value terms, come to flavour clothing imports, particularly in the last decade (Green 2008).

Increasing imports have had a direct impact on lowering recorded domestic employment in the clothing industry. Following the reduction in tariffs in 1974,

*Home-based garment manufacturing* 171

clothing factory employment between 1974 and 1976 experienced its steepest fall – a considerable 25 per cent (Peck 1992: 673, based on Australian Bureau of Statistics (ABS) Census 1986). Moreover, from 1974 to 1997, there was a general decline in employment of 60 per cent (ABS 8221, and unpublished data (DISR 1999: 35)). The 2008 Review of the Australian Textile Clothing and Footwear Industries found that between 1995/6 and 2005/6, employment in clothing manufacturing declined by 38.7 per cent, from 33,600 to 20,600 workers (Green 2008 vol. 1: 23, 26).

A gender-based division of labour in the clothing industry has been widely documented (Bennett 1986; Coyle 1982; Fincher 1991; Frances 1986; Johnson 1990, Van Acker 1995; Yeatman 1992), with the majority of jobs being held by women sewing machinists. It was hardly surprising, therefore, that when a decline in official employment figures in the Australian clothing industry occurred; the greatest impact was felt by women.

Women's labour in factories could be undercut by lower wages in offshore sites as well as by migrants in Australia willing to work for low piece-rates doing homework. Yet the decline in factory employment is not a clear indicator of absolute decline in the industry:

> …while employment numbers in the industry may appear to decline, in reality clothing production will merely be shifted 'off the books'. If this occurs, the problems associated with outwork, ranging from tax evasion, non-compliance with awards, social and industrial isolation, alienation, powerlessness, exploitation and inequality (especially among women and migrants), will intensify, even though statistics might indicate that the industry is dying. All that would have died in reality is clothing industry unionism and award conditions.
>
> (Greig and Little 1996: 117)

This assessment by Greig and Little agrees with most analyses that the Australian clothing industry has taken a 'low road' to labour adjustment as part of a significant restructuring process. To some extent the debate has tended to centre on just which low road has been taken: homework or offshore production? Obviously both have played a part, but the difficulties associated with accounting for labour content (whether domestic or overseas) of clothing sold in Australia has made it close to impossible to know the significance of each strategy to the Australian clothing industry.

Overall, the Post-Fordist, trade liberalization era of intraregional flows of apparel has seen a new, dual pattern of organization emerge for Australian clothing manufacturing (Greig 1992; 2001). First, since increasing trade liberalization, the movement of much low-end fashion repetitive sewing work has been moved to low-cost offshore locations like China and Fiji. Second and simultaneously, the continued need for fashion-led segments of the market to be time responsive has seen an increasingly concentrated retail market use organized networks of low-cost small-scale home-based working women instead of relying

172   *E. Sutherland*

on factory-based workers within Australia. Thus, home-based work, like off-shore production, offers retailers and manufacturers low-cost, flexible and relatively unregulated labour. However, it is difficult to quantify the Australian industry's reliance on home-based workers. Nevertheless, estimates of the number of people who may be affected are crucial in order to appreciate the significance of home-based work, the many women and their families, mostly from migrant backgrounds, who do this work, and the issues they face.

## The significance of home-based working women

Since the earliest days of settlement in Australia, the sewing of garments has relied on individual women in domestic spaces, craft-based artisans and workshops where hand-sewing was undertaken by women paid low wages relative to the male wage. The development of relatively affordable sewing machines after the 1900s, and especially into the middle of that century, resulted in machine sewing replacing hand-sewing in domestic as well as workshop and factory spaces, and still undertaken predominantly by women.[1]

By the Fordist 1950s to 1970s, much garment sewing in Australia was done within larger factories, reflective of import-protected manufacturing in Australia's post-war long-boom period. Women, again, were considered the 'natural' operators of sewing machines, overseen by male management structures that favoured scientific management of the women's work to increase efficiency. In the post-war era of high levels of migration, the women sewing in factories were predominantly of southern European origin (Alcorso 1989; Tierney 1996). Factory work, though diminishing in importance, continues to play a role today, and the cultural background of its mostly women workers has changed to reflect the altering intake of migrants into Australia. Post mid-1970s, with the effects of reduction of tariffs and other trade barriers as well as regional conflicts, Vietnamese and Cambodian women began to make their mark on the industry, mostly through their home-based work. In the 1990s and 2000s, Chinese women migrants from both mainland China and Hong Kong working in their homes as well as factories have played an integral role in the Australian clothing industry.

As mentioned previously, the number of home-based workers involved in Australian garment manufacturing is difficult to quantify due to the often clandestine nature of the work in domestic spaces, as well as lack of reporting in union, tax and other figures. Census data has been notoriously unhelpful given the high levels of under-reporting of this type of work, and over the last two decades has estimated outworker numbers to be between almost 2500 and some 3000 workers.

This low figure seems at odds with the Senate Inquiry into Outwork in the Garment Industry (1996) which found that a key factor for the survival of clothing manufacturers, in an increasingly competitive and deregulated environment, is a dependence on low-cost labour, so much so that the industry is now characterized by home-based work:

*Home-based garment manufacturing* 173

...manufacturing has moved from a factory based workforce to home-workers. Outworking is now so prevalent that it is not just a characteristic of the industry, the entire industry is structured around it.

(SERC 1996: xi)

While there have been many estimates of the number of clothing outworkers in Australia, all are questionable given concerns that outworkers are under-reporting their work practices due to possible contravention of industrial relations, immigration, tax, social welfare and even local planning laws and regulations. Poor questionnaire design, small sample sizes and dispersed sampling methods, which are unable to accommodate geographic concentrations of outwork, also hamper measurement.[2] The 1991 Census figure of 2483 clothing outworkers is therefore widely considered unreliable.[3]

The Productivity Commission, in its 1997 Draft Report on the TCF industries, estimated 23,650 full-time homeworkers and concludes that '...it appears likely that the total pool of TCF homeworkers[4] is somewhat less than 330,000 but probably greater than the Australian Tax Office (ATO) estimate in 1994 of 50,000 individuals' (Productivity Commission 1997: Vol. 2, D12–D13).[5] The ATO's conservative estimate was based on an analysis of the total turnover in the industry, known clothing company audits, profit margins and reported value of sales. From this, the ATO surmised that there were 1500 major makers-up, 20,000 subcontractor makers-up and 50,000 individual homeworkers (not full-time equivalent) in the clothing industry.

Geographical concentrations of outworkers, according to the relevant industrial registrars of outwork and community-based organizations, are in inner to outer western suburbs of Sydney and Melbourne.[6] Again, these estimates are unconfirmed. Nevertheless, community groups and the union research agree that outwork became the dominant work category in the clothing industry from the mid-1980s and into the 1990s. In the report, *The Hidden Cost of Fashion* (TCFUA 1995), the Textiles Clothing and Footwear Union of Australia (TCFUA), estimated that there were over 329,000 home-based workers in the clothing industry working intermittently, and most on a casual and part-time basis. The numbers of outworkers in each State are estimated to be: Victoria: 144,000, NSW: 120,00, Queensland: 25,000, South Australia: 25,000, Western Australia: 15,000[7]

However:

The union later made an important qualification to their 329,000 outwork estimate, stating that the estimate was '... the approximate pool of home-workers ... it does not assume that all 329,000 workers would be full time employed and working everyday.

(PC 1997: D11–D12)

The union estimation was seen as taking into account the intermittent nature of outwork based on seasonal demand and the role that other family members

174    E. Sutherland

(including children) might play at various times in home-based clothing production. Regardless of the veracity of these claims made by the union about outwork numbers, policymakers have frequently adopted the '329,000 clothing outworkers' and it a widely quoted estimate.

Academic and commissioned researchers criticized the union figures as likely to be exaggerated (Peck 1992: 673; Evatt Foundation 1998: 9) and some of their research has drawn more conservative estimates of the number of outworkers. The Evatt Foundation's report, based on an analysis of the Productivity Commission's estimates and methods, says:

> It is reasonable to conclude: that around 100,000 people are engaged in homework at any particular time; that the total TCF homework work-pool is in the order of 150,000; and that they could be being assisted by a further 50,000 unpaid family members. Many of these family members would be children.
>
> (Evatt Foundation 1998: 10)

The Evatt Report concludes, '...it is impossible to develop any estimate with a high level of confidence' (Evatt Foundation 1998: 10), and calls for the development of more accurate reporting and statistical measurement of the extent of outwork. Likewise, the 2008 *Review of the Australian Textile Clothing and Footwear Industries* concludes its discussion of the difficulty of assessing numbers of home-based workers with an estimate that there are over 25,000 equivalent full-time outworkers, which therefore exceeds factory-based employment by 25 per cent (Green 2008 vol. 1: 34–5).

While the inaccuracy of figures for homework in Australia is a significant issue, the lack of transparency surrounding this type of work is a function of deep structural issues of potential exploitation and marginalization of migrant women workers.

## The marginal status of home-based workers

Gender, marginal citizenship status, non-English language skills, underdeveloped social networks, diminished socio-economic resources and the fact that they work in unregulated private home-spaces makes exploitation more likely for home-based workers. Indeed, most women only receive work intermittently from a few makers-up or middlemen (requiring them to rely on social welfare payments when they are available to them),[8] and when they do work, the piece-rates are often low and the workload is high resulting in time-pressured work in their home-spaces.

Kosack (1976) and Morokvasic (1980) describe the exploitation of women in home-based garment production as 'triple oppression', that is, 'oppression as worker, as woman and as migrant' (quoted in Phizaklea 1982: 99). Yet other research suggests that the heightened exploitation of women doing home-based work can result in radical (read: positive) transformations in the household division of labour even if patriarchal ideologies remain intact:

Although women's income earning usually results in a double shift for women, the extreme work pressure on women can also become a motivation for men's participation in housework, especially where men are present at the site of women's double burden. The fact that they literally observed the load of piecework to be completed, along with the unwashed dishes, led some men to help with domestic tasks and softened engendered divisions of work in the family.

(Miraftab 1996: 76)

Nevertheless, help given to homeworkers by their children, who also see the double burden their mothers and fathers may face, is far from a positive transformation of household division of labour and can instead be viewed as a further layer of exploitation (Clark 1996: 721).

It is clear that outworkers are marginal to the economy proper and face difficulties due to the unregulated nature of their work and the multiple marginal positions they occupy at various times. Home-based working women in Australia remain relatively unprotected by labour laws despite recent improvements to their legal status as employees (see Sutherland 2007). Yet, in the literature their contributions to the clothing industry can be devalued for some of the same reasons. They are often viewed as faceless labour input and demand-side analyses of the need for migrant labour are a common theme in discussions of home-based garment work.

## Women-centred understandings of home-based work

Discussions of the many reasons that women decide to begin and continue home-based garment manufacturing have tended to centre on themes of limited choice. For most home-based working women in the industry this is the case, however, whether this predetermines the role of that work as *only* exploitative is a view that has not yet been fully explored in the literature in a critical manner. Most important to the analysis here, is a need to depart from seeing these women as a faceless and homogenous category of marginal worker and instead to view the differential impacts, to varying degrees empowering and exploitative, that home-based work can have on their lives. In the following section, the voices and experiences of the women I encountered 'in the field' over four years of research into home-based work in Sydney's western suburbs are placed centrestage so that their accounts can be better understood and the complexities of their work situations better appreciated.

## The research context

Over four years, I recorded focus groups with Chinese, Cambodian and Vietnamese home-based worker groups, I was an activist for an organization called Fairwear, which, alongside other community organizations, successfully lobbied the New South Wales (NSW) government for changed regulations in relation to

176   *E. Sutherland*

homework, and I was a volunteer rights-based English teacher through a community NGO in Sydney which provided English language classes to Asian migrant women doing homework and hospitality work. Over this period, I developed relationships with the home-based workers, especially through the weekly English classes.

The context of these classes is important for understanding how relationships with individual homeworking women were initially framed. Volunteering as an English teacher involved preparing classes on relevant topics. Some weeks this meant learning how to speak and understand basic English in relation to banking, shopping or applying for rental properties. The women also wanted to learn how to deal with bosses and negotiate their work: to negotiate better pay and time extensions to complete work, to ask for more work or to deal with a dispute. Over 40 women took these classes and I formed strong associations with 12 of them, two of whom became community NGO organizers. I present their voices and my understandings of their experiences gained through participant-observation work that involved keeping fieldwork diaries throughout the four years.

There are two themes that highlight the reasons behind the varied experiences of these women doing homework in Sydney. Migration histories as well as different understandings of what constitutes 'women's work' are first explored in order to better understand the women's circumstances and valuings (or not) of their home-based work. The chapter then turns to the diverse experiences of homework. These experiences, seen through the eyes of the migrant women encountered throughout the fieldwork, are presented via excerpts from my diary, vignettes edited from my diary and also in their own words. This helps address the often-unanswered question: what is home-based work in Australia's garment industry like? As Prügl argues:

> On the one hand, homework appears as a universal phenomenon and the experiences of homeworkers around the world are remarkably similar. On the other hand, feminist theorists have come to reject universalizing explanations and argue that research that is relevant to the everyday struggles of women requires interpretations in historical and cultural contexts. How can a practice emerging in countries around the world under conditions of global capitalism be understood in a way that values the particular understandings of homeworkers?
>
> (1996: 114)

## Diverse migration histories

It is clear that different migratory experiences are particularly crucial in shaping these women's attitudes to home-based work, informing the decisions to begin, continue and move between it and other forms of work. During the participant-observation fieldwork in interviews, home visits, English classes and focus groups, I caught glimpses of women's experiences of migrating to Australia. These

*Home-based garment manufacturing* 177

perspectives of Vietnamese, Cambodian/Khmer and Chinese women suggested that some culturally specific generalizations could be made about how migration experiences affected their practices of home-based garment manufacturing.

The history of Australian immigration policy, as it coincided with world events, is a wider backdrop for situating the women's experiences. For instance, the Vietnam War, the Cambodian War and the Tiananmen Square massacre had a significant bearing on Australian immigration policy and welfare provision for newly arrived Asian migrants. After the Tiananmen Square massacre, for example, the Hawke Labor government allowed Chinese students already in Australia to stay for four years as non-permanent residents, after which time they could become permanent residents and Australian citizens. Only a small number of these Chinese students were outworkers but, as outworkers, they had to make enough money to support themselves, because, unlike the earlier group of Vietnamese refugees, they were restricted access to welfare benefits. I reflected on this in my diary:

> ... the Vietnamese and Cambodians came earlier and mostly as refugees and so the government at that time gave widespread information to these people about how to access social security payments. Therefore, Vietnamese–Australians have been more ready to utilise the welfare system and built it into the way they feel about and do paid work. [Community NGO worker] suggested that therefore many Vietnamese women see outwork as an essentially poorly paid job that requires subsidisation through social security, whereas the Chinese women doing outworking were not necessarily more reticent about talking about the Centrelink issue – rather, they are less likely to have contact with it – as it is not as built into their system of work.
>
> (Diary entry, 24 January 2000)[9]

Likewise, Chinese and Vietnamese or Cambodian women who came to Australia through a family reunion immigration pathway, and undertook home-based garment production, also had restricted access to welfare benefits. As a result they relied on family members for assistance in periods of economic hardship.

At the time of the fieldwork between 1998 and 2002, the largest group of recent migrants and those arriving under family reunion categories came from China and Hong Kong and they approached outworking in a particular way:

> Chinese outworkers that [community NGO] deal with have mostly fallen into the category of migrants who could not easily access welfare benefits. [Community organisation worker] argues that it is generally for this reason that Chinese outworkers were more likely to seek out better pay – they just could not afford to work for appallingly low pay in the same way [and subsidise it with welfare payments as Vietnamese-born outworkers in Sydney had been more likely to do] and so the Chinese outworkers are a strong group of outworkers in the Sydney community with a business-like approach.
>
> (Diary entry, 24 January 2000)

178   *E. Sutherland*

However, even these generalizations are fractured by the differences between Hong Kong Chinese and mainland Chinese women's experiences of home-based work in Sydney, on which I again reflected in my diaries. During a focus group and English classes with Chinese women, general differences emerged. The women from Hong Kong had generally been able to generate better incomes from home-based garment production than the mainland Chinese women and were more likely to speak about it in small business entrepreneurial terms. The women from Hong Kong were generally also more conversant with their rights as employees than the women from mainland China. This variation in Chinese women's experiences of outworking in Australia probably reflects the exposure that each group had first, to a market-led economy and, second, to a Common Law system of regulation of the wage-relation in their countries of origin.

## Women's various perspectives of homework

Different cultural understandings of 'women's work' shape the meanings and values that individual women attach to home-based garment manufacturing. These gendered valuings impacted the women's ability to imagine and practice more empowering versions of home-based work. They also informed an understanding of outworking as supplementary income or as essential livelihood.

Among many of the Chinese women I had most contact with, husbands were commonly working alongside their wives. Nevertheless, most of these women viewed home-based garment production as a valuable occupation that belonged to them and not to their husbands. Joan[10] and her husband, for instance, viewed outworking as her job and he merely 'helped' in the business by dealing with makers-up, making deliveries, cutting off long threads and doing overlocking work:

> Joan and her husband work together although they both see him as the 'helper' despite the fact that this seems to be his occupation as well ... I was aware very much of a sense [while talking to Joan and her husband] of this being Joan's work, her machines, her room and the end product – designer jackets and skirts (black) at the time of writing – are seen by them both as her creation and as a result of her high skill level.
>
> (Diary entry, 11 March 1998)

In front of their husbands and partners, many of the Chinese women, including Joan, seemed to enjoy telling stories of being the main breadwinner – 'he just helps me to get the work done'. These stories were frequently infused with a strong sense of mischief and husbands played along with the role reversal joke, often laughing encouragingly at hearing their wives speak like this with pride about their work.

In a very general sense, the Vietnamese and Cambodian/Khmer women I encountered viewed outworking as the most appropriate form of work for them to do, expressing their feeling that it is very important for women to remain at

*Home-based garment manufacturing* 179

home with children and to look after the house. By contrast, the Chinese women were less inclined to define their motivations for outworking as a need to stay at home for children. Although they would often say that their limited English prevented them from working in a restaurant or elsewhere outside the home, they frequently used the experience of homework to go on to establish other businesses.

Perceptions of homework as livelihood or supplementaty income (pin-money) are integral to how the women I encountered viewed their work. Does home-based work enable personal empowerment through contribution to household income; does it enable greater personal independence; do the women view the work as an extension of their identities via career pathways or as an extension of their role as homemakers? What is homeworking like? The answers to these questions provide a more in-depth understanding of the differences between the women and how they encounter and incorporate home-based work into their lives.

Most of the women described their work as 'boring' and repetitive. Three women who attended my English classes were sewing T-shirts and tracksuits and spoke of outwork in these terms. Four were sewing children's and infants' clothing and described their work in similar tones. All but one of these women were from mainland China and had children. They were paid low piece-rates, were asked to fulfil large orders and saw the work as a temporary measure lasting five to ten years to contribute to the family income during a settling in period. Most had dreams of pursuing their vocations.[11] Their careers, in teaching for instance, were curtailed by their migration to Australia.

For some like Ruby, the monotony of the work was short-lived or interspersed with more challenging jobs:

> When I first came to Australia I worked in a factory making ladies' underwear. I was very bored because the work was too easy. I preferred to do sophisticated jobs, not these basic designs. After that time I became an outworker, making formal suits and gowns at home. I also tried to get work making leather clothing, because this was more of a challenge. At that time the money was OK – I was earning similar to the award rate. This was 12 years ago.
>
> (Copy of Ruby's written statement for a Justice and Faith, Uniting Church, gathering, given to the author 26 October 2001)

Ruby also writes about her satisfaction at finishing each garment order, and a sense of pride in her work when she completed sophisticated jobs that allowed her to 'show off' her skill. This image is far removed from those of factory discipline and deskilling that Braverman (1974) paints of Taylorist work practices: practices that divide the creative process of work into separate tasks performed by individual workers on assembly lines. By contrast, Ruby managed her own workload and was often the sample maker, so was also somewhat a master of a creative process, taking pride producing the full garment that everyone else

## 180    E. Sutherland

would work from. The keys to her success in being able to manage her home-based work were her high skill level, confidence and flair for the work, as well as relatively good English. Other women were similarly empowered by their experiences. When visiting Joan, one of my English students, I saw her work and felt that it was rewarding for her:

> Overall, there was a sense of industry about Joan and her husband, that they work together as a team and she has a separate room overlooking the back above-ground pool. In this room are three machines set up near big windows with a lot of natural light. I got the impression that Joan likes her work and has a strong sense of pride about her work – when she showed us the suits she makes she was very proud of them and showing them off – holding them up and looking – admiring them herself, while we did the same.
>
> (Diary entry, 11 March 1998)

Jess, who attended the English classes, told me her reasons for sewing. She expressed a pride in her work that I rarely heard communicated so powerfully.[12] Jess recalled being 15 years old and getting work in a factory in Hong Kong where she fixed mistakes in garments. She remembered with pride how quickly her peers in the factory acknowledged her as the best mender. She told me she started dreaming about and imagining holes, split seams and faults in material, and how she could fix them. As a young girl in Hong Kong, her parents had always encouraged her to develop her already advanced sewing skills. Later, in class when we discussed outworking, Jess referred in passing to her high level of skill in quality control and referred back to her factory experiences in Hong Kong to demonstrate this aptitude.[13] Some of the women in the class were out-workers but had backgrounds in accounting, nursing, teaching and music. In response to this audience, Jess was perhaps distinguishing herself from the other outworking women. She valued her work in clothing manufacturing as a career, but seemed to be devaluing the other women's outworking as being temporary or low-skill work. Jess seemed to be demonstrating that her needlework and sewing were as much a passion in her life as their former occupations had been to them.

Almost all the Chinese women I had contact with saw home-based garment manufacturing as a livelihood, with their families relying on the income. This supports Mitter's argument that

> It would be wrong to assume that immigrant women work for 'pin-money'. In a changed economic situation, when the level of unemployment is particularly high among immigrant men, a woman homeworker can be a major, if not sole, earner in the family.
>
> (1986: 63)

However, for most of the Vietnamese women in Cabramatta with whom I had contact, it was apparent that they viewed outwork as a supplementary income,

*Home-based garment manufacturing* 181

not just to husbands' and other family members' income, but also to welfare payments.

The following are vignettes providing different life contexts and practices of home-based work of five Chinese women – Mia, Joan, Huan, Mary and Nina. They are counterpoints to the narratives of Jess and Ruby discussed above (although some develop the theme of empowerment). They are constructed from the diary entries I wrote after I visited the women (often with a community worker who also knew them and who acted as translator) in their homes in Sydney. I edited the vignettes to reduce their stories to make them more access-ible for the reader. I do so in order to develop the concept of variety, along a continuum from extreme exploitation to tentative notions of empowerment, and thereby answer Prügl's call for a variegated sense of the work form.

## Vignettes

### *Mia*

Mia and her husband (an English teacher in China) and her daughter (12 years old) migrated to Australia in 1996 and had been living in Australia for two years when a community worker and I visited. Mia had been a primary school teacher in [city four hours by train south of Shanghai in mainland China] and also had some experience working in a clothing factory. Not long after their arrival, Mia found she was pregnant and her second daughter was born. In order to look after her baby at home and with limited English speaking skills (though she could read English with a fair level of comprehension) and Chinese teaching qualifications not recognized in Australia, she decided to do home-based work while her husband began teaching Mandarin part time. Mia was sewing Seafolly swimsuits on the day we visited. She said she was being paid about $7 per hour and did not show any signs of indignation when the community worker said this amount was just over half the national award rate of pay. Not long after the birth of their second daughter, Mia and her husband helped her parents migrate to Australia and the extended family were living together in a three-bedroom flat in Auburn in Syd-ney's inner western suburbs. Mia's work area was in the sparsely furnished main living area, near a window that looked on to a balcony. Mia said she didn't work any later than 11 p.m. She was very aware of her neighbours below and above and worried about the noise the machines made. Mia said she only took jobs if she thought she would be able to finish them before 11 p.m., while still having some time with her family. She told the story of turning down work for this reason and then the boss paid her one month late for the next job. Mia said she thought the boss withheld payment as a way of punishing her for exercising some freedom.

### *Joan*

Joan, her husband and two daughters, migrated to Australia from mainland China in the early 1990s. Joan and her husband had been accountants in

## 182 E. Sutherland

Shanghai. In Australia, both were involved in producing and delivering designer clothing from their suburban home in Auburn in Sydney's inner west. They lived in a well-maintained, three-bedroom fibro home on a quarter-acre block common in the area. Both mentioned that their mortgage was almost paid off. When we visited them in 1999, they were saving to buy a news agency. Joan mentioned that their daughters were at school (an exclusive girls' school in North Sydney) and that their turnover was barely enough to maintain their children in their current lifestyle. They said that after they came to Australia they found it very difficult to learn English and that with the children and needing to make a living, Joan's husband had only been able to take some of the 520 hours of free English tuition entitled to him. Joan didn't go to English classes and instead stayed home looking after the children and doing industrial sewing. Joan's husband said he decided to stop going to English classes in order to earn income and because he felt guilty not earning money for the family. He began doing more negotiating with the bosses for Joan's sewing work and did all the deliveries. They both spoke of his responsibility in 'the business' in a support role and as a negotiator because he could speak better English than Joan. It was clear that they viewed Joan as having the creative and technical sewing skills, while both she and her husband had the financial acumen to make the business sustainable. They spoke of slowly learning who the best bosses were and that this understanding had been formed from a variety of positive and negative experiences with more than 100 bosses over about ten years. They felt they were now in a much more comfortable position than when they first began and were even able to afford to pass on some work to other outworkers – often just the button holing or pressing tasks. Joan was proud of her designer creations and said they sold in exclusive boutiques in Sydney. She told us that they were paid about $27 per hour for sewing the designer suits but then had to subtract $5 for each garment for button holing and pressing. When Joan first joined the English classes she said she was making t-shirts for 40 cents each and was able to do 30–40 per hour ($12–$16 per hour). From the words that Joan and her husband used, it was obvious that they saw their work as a business and that there was a sense of industry about them.

### Huan

Huan had been in Sydney only six months when I first met her in English classes. She had migrated with her husband, child and mother from mainland China while pregnant and was living in a small, dark, two-bedroom flat in Lidcombe in Sydney's western suburbs. They had very little furniture and many of their treasured belongings were propped on packing boxes. Huan had given birth to her second child one month before we visited and was very tired from looking after her sick newborn and attending English classes for three hours a day twice a week, while her mother helped with the children. Although parts of the conversation between the community worker and Huan were not revealed to me, I was led to believe that Huan's second pregnancy played a role in expediting their

*Home-based garment manufacturing*  183

migration to Australia given the strict one-child policy in China. Until he could find another job, Huan's husband was earning some money working for a relative. Huan said travel time added to her time away from home when she went to English classes and when she went to a friend's house to do outworking. Her friend paid her approximately $2 per hour to help with some large orders and was teaching her to sew the garments. Huan said she was sewing t-shirts and said she couldn't keep pace with her friend. Though Huan was always cheerful in our company and in English classes, the strain on her was obvious and the community worker steered discussion away from topics that would highlight her difficulties. We talked about a Buddhist teaching she had on her living-room wall and Huan and the community worker translated parts of it for me as we talked. Essentially the teaching was about keeping the appearance of happiness even when things are difficult because this allows true happiness to flow to you. To show such feelings to the outside world would put undue strain on friendships and families. Huan seemed to be living according to this mantra.

### *Nina*

Nina moved with her husband and child from southern mainland China to Hong Kong and then Australia in the mid-1980s. They lived in a large, double-brick home in Auburn that she said they were 'paying off'. On the day we visited Nina, her husband and his friend were playing mahjong in the kitchen and Nina later mentioned that her husband had been made redundant from his job working as a carpenter in a factory. With the $2000 redundancy payment he was planning to start doing carpentry in the back garage. We left the men playing mahjong and moved to a large room at the back of their home so we could talk with Nina. She said she was unable to find a job in China and had stayed at home looking after their child. She had her second son after they arrived in Australia and soon after his birth discovered he was profoundly disabled. Nina had spoken to the community worker about feeling guilty that she could not care for her son and that he was being looked after in a nearby care centre where she could visit him often. The community worker directed discussion towards other topics such as her work. Nina said she had learnt to sew on a [household model] Chinese sewing machine and could already make her own clothes when she and her family came to Australia. Nina said she got a clothing factory job in their first 20 days in Australia, without even being able to say 'yes' or 'no' and she taught herself to use the industrial sewing machines. Nina said she was glad she had learnt this skill as she felt she would have been bored only looking after her family. She mentioned that she was pleased she had come to Australia because here she had a job. In contrast, she said her mother had never learnt to sew and always complained about being 'bored'. Nina said she had bought her sewing machine at the Katie's factory closing down sale and had paid $2500 cash for it. Before she was able to afford to buy her own machines (she had one overlocker and two sewing machines), she had borrowed one from an employer. Nina said that he paid very low wages at that time and when she asked for better pay he said it was low because she was using his machine. He also told her to register her own business name before he would give her work. Her current employers considered Nina's sewing skill level so high that she was always asked to make the samples – the first full garment of an order that everyone else worked from. She said that originally she would get $25 per tailored jacket sample (taking up to two hours), whereas making them in a long order she was only paid $12 for each one and it often took an hour and a half to complete. Nina was aware that in most cases, each jacket cost approximately $140 in the shops. Nina told us that many of her bosses were Chinese and she usually worked for four to five bosses at any one time. This meant that at least one boss had work to give her. She recalled only one boss who had been very good to her, who had paid above the award rate and who praised her work although she said she was 'not looking for praise' she was 'just looking for good pay'. Nina was about to begin working for this boss in their factory making Qantas uniforms and was happy that she could do work outside the home because she would have a set schedule. Nina also said she felt confined in her home because she could not speak to anyone – even when her neighbour said 'hello' to her she was embarrassed because she had such limited English and she would run inside.

### Mary

Mary, her husband and three daughters, migrated to Australia from Hong Kong in late 1996 before the British hand over in July 1997. They left because they were worried about Chinese rule and they saw an opportunity to help extend a family business into the Australian market. Mary's brother had migrated to Sydney several years before and travelled back and forth between Sydney and Hong Kong, organizing large shipments of clothing to Sydney. Mary fixed any faults in the garments before the whole family sold them at the Saturday and Sunday markets. Another family member who remained in Hong Kong helped coordinate the clothing orders. Mary said it was cheaper for the garments to be made in Hong Kong and that it was easy to organize because the family business was based there. Mary's brother sponsored her family's migration to Australia. Mary's husband drove taxis at night and Mary also had income from looking after neighbours' children. Mary and her family lived in a large, new, three-storey townhouse near Lidcombe in Sydney's inner west. It had three bedrooms and two bathrooms as well as a large basement for storing the imported clothing. Mary was very house proud and gave us a tour when we arrived. She had two overlockers and an industrial sewing machine in the basement but said that much of her work needed to be done by hand. She worked in the family's clothing factory in Hong Kong for many years and she said she found the work she was doing at home quite enjoyable in comparison, but mentioned that it could be very busy looking after neighbours' children, picking up older children from school, cooking, shopping and maintaining the house. Mary had not previously learnt English and attended the English classes because she wanted to be able to talk to customers at the markets where they sold the clothes.

*Home-based garment manufacturing*   185

Joan and her husband paid off their mortgage not long after we visited them. Huan became active in the community NGO and though she and her family continued to struggle for many years, she had friends who supported her while she made a small income from home-based garment work and other work. Nina moved to factory work not long after the interview and also maintained contact with the community NGO for many years. Mia continued outworking while looking after her young child, but also attended a Technical and Further Education (TAFE) English class. Mia and her husband were able to buy a small suburban block of land in Sydney's outer western suburb of Blacktown and in 2002 were saving to build a home there. Mary continued to be integral to the intraregional family business and remained active in the community NGO for a number of years, though she stopped going to English classes. To varying degrees, home-based work was wearying and difficult for the women and their families. However, these vignettes also show the diverse nature of outworking: it can be an extension of an existing clothing business, a means of saving money for another business, such as a news agency or restaurant, or a livelihood relied on in difficult times immediately after migrating. Home-based work can also be a stepping stone into another form of employment in a clothing factory.

Continuing and remaining an outworker is not necessarily an undesirable outcome either. It can also be a means of alleviating marginalization, in Young's (1990) terms, by providing work opportunities and livelihood that may not otherwise exist (for Mia, Nina and Huan). Outworking can also provide a sense of economic autonomy, alleviating feelings of economic powerlessness for women who might have been forced to rely on welfare payments or a husband's and family income (for Mia and Nina).

Ruby and Jess's accounts and perspectives point to the strategic ways that some women go about their homework, see it as potentially more empowering than factory work, or as an extension of their careers across national borders. Their voices were nevertheless somewhat exceptional and cannot be read as a possibility for all home-based workers in this industry. The particular circumstances of their previous work experience enabled them to negotiate decent piece-rates and do more interesting work than the majority of homeworkers.

With a working knowledge of some 30 women's stories, and a detailed knowledge of more than 10, I have chosen these five stories from my diary because they offer the widest variety and they could be easily edited into instructive vignettes. Even if I presented more stories, I could not generalize about the experience of homework, and nor do I wish to. I therefore acknowledge both the limited nature of this account as well as my role as mediator between my diary and the text presented here. In doing so, I am not constructing an argument for generalizing these women's situations nor am I accounting for all differences between women doing home-based work. Rather, I am consciously forwarding an agenda that their understandings give us incomplete but new glimpses of the work form.

## Conclusion

The phased removal of Australia's trade barriers has resulted in increased clothing imports and a more competitive industry, but one prone to 'taking the low road' in relation to domestic labour practices. It has resulted in more home-based garment production in Australia's capital cities. There are difficulties such as the marginal and clandestine context within which home-based work in the industry tends to operate, as well as in obtaining verifiable numbers of outworkers. The marginalization of migrant women into a work form peripheral to the economy proper, given its lack of regulation, enables easy exploitation of these women, though it cannot presuppose this outcome. The majority of literature on home-based work in this industry has concentrated on demand-side analyses and tends not to present homeworking women's perspectives. In this chapter, how the Asian women I came to know in western Sydney experience home-based work is placed centre-stage so as to inform a more diverse and complex understanding of the work form.

The different experiences of outworking women contain overlapping themes and processes. Varying migration histories, altered understandings of 'women's work' and many other factors will change how women experience and make sense of outwork over time. Future research on experiences of new migrant groups will produce new understandings.

While the act of migrating to Australia is formative in shaping strategies of home-based work, other factors, in tandem and independently, affect how the work is understood, performed and experienced. Raising and educating children, buying homes, setting up businesses, surviving on small incomes, helping other family members migrate, juggling different work commitments, learning English, expressions of business acumen or whether the family are still in survival mode post migration are also important.

The variation in experience, perception and adaption to home-based garment production by the women cannot be explained by heterogeneous understandings of migration, nor patriarchal gender relations, nor the sense that work in home-spaces is devalued. As a result, not all women will experience a form of oppression, or the same oppressions, when they offer their labour. Overall, the experiences of women doing home-based garment manufacturing are highly situated and particular, and lead to diverse employment and business possibilities, constraints and attitudes, offering fresh insights about the 'triple oppressions' as well as possibilities for empowerment.

## Notes

This chapter draws on work published in Sutherland (2009).

1 This is an example of an exception to the trend for males to dominate work where technology was introduced.

2 For instance, the Census data that records industry of employment as well as outwork only includes 'each person's main job' and only work performed in the person's own home rather than homework performed in another's home. The reliability of ABS

*Home-based garment manufacturing* 187

'Person's Employed at Home' supplements to the Population Surveys conducted in 1989, 1992 and 1995 are hampered by small sampling sizes that are inherent in a survey that covers all Australian statistical and geographic divisions. These surveys failed to accurately represent the concentrations of home-based clothing work in certain geographical areas.

3 The veracity of the Census figure is so widely criticized that the Evatt Report was able to unequivocally dismiss it (1998: 8).

4 Again, this estimate is not solely for clothing but also for textiles and footwear.

5 These estimates are based on incomplete statistical analysis given that they rely on the ABS *Manufacturing Survey*, which draws its sample from the Business Register, which excludes two crucial groups: small self-employed or owner-operator businesses and all homeworkers. The Productivity Commission's estimates are extrapolated from the total turnover of the TCF businesses on the Business Register, a turnover that therefore excludes the value of homework production (Evatt Report 1998: 9). The Productivity Commission estimates are then derived from a division of the total turnover for local clothing manufacture by an estimate of the average turnover per employee. This average turnover per employee was based on confidential information given to the Industry Commission Inquiry by 'some local clothing manufacturers (some of whom use outworkers)' (Productivity Commission 1997 vol. 2: D13).

6 The Australian Industrial Relations Commission's (AIRC) registrar and the state industrial registrar of outwork contain very limited data on home-based work in the industry. These registration records have limited statistical use given that the numbers of outworkers registered by their employers (as is required by the Clothing Trades Award in Australia, clauses 26 and 27) is so low. Only 79 companies had registered as using outwork with the AIRC by 1995. In South Australia registrations were as low as 5 to 1995, despite conservative ATO estimates that there were as many as 435 companies employing outworkers there (Productivity Commission 1997 vol. 2: D15) and according to Peck (1992) in Victoria, registrations between 1988 and 1989 were 255. These registrations constitute such a small proportion of the likely size of the real clothing outwork population that these figures cannot be relied on.

7 These estimates were based predominantly on a National Outwork Information Campaign involving a multilingual phone-in for outworkers that received approximately 3000 calls over eight weeks in 1994. The estimate of outwork also relied on union lists of suppliers to large retailers, lists of contractors for clothing manufacturers, registered clothing manufacturers, companies reported to the union by outworkers, a small sample of contractors and subcontractors in Melbourne and 'companies respondent to the federal Clothing Trades Award' (Productivity Commission 1997 vol 2: D11).

8 According to Liu (2007), Australia social welfare payments, after 1997 were only available to migrants two years after entering Australia (except in the case of humanitarian migrants).

9 Centrelink is the Australian government agency that services the unemployed and underemployed.

10 All names used are pseudonyms.

11 These Chinese women, based on a culture of valuing factory work as better paid and more stable in the Chinese context, viewed their more vocational careers in teaching, for example, as done in order to fulfill personal beliefs rather than to seek monetary advancement.

12 Jess and I caught the train back to central Sydney together after many of the classes and we shared our thoughts on topics like family, children, relationships, cooking, work, migration and racial discrimination.

13 In a sense, Jess's understandings and valuing of her skills by reference to her factory work rather than outworking demonstrates that skills and experience are generally viewed as only being acquired in formal workplace settings.

188    *E. Sutherland*

## Bibliography

Alcorso, C. (1989) *Newly Arrived Immigrant Women in the Workforce*, Wollongong NSW: Centre for Multicultural Studies, University of Wollongong, pp. 10–24.

Australian Bureau of Statistics (ABS) 8221.0, Manufacturing Industry, Australia, 1986.

Bennett, L. (1986) 'Job classification and women workers: institutional practices, technical change and the conciliation and arbitration system 1907–72', *Labour History* 51: 11–23.

Braverman, H. (1974) *Labor and Monopoly Capital*, New York and London: Monthly Review Press.

Clark, C. (1996) 'Child labor and sweatshops', *Congressional Quarterly Researcher* 6(31): 721–44.

Coyle, A. (1982) 'Sex and skill in the organization of the clothing industry', in J. West (ed.), *Work, Women and the Labour Market*, pp. 10–26, London: Routledge & Kegan Paul.

Department of Industry, Science and Resources (DISR) (1999) *Textiles, Clothing, Footwear and Leather Industries: Profile, Sectoral Information Group*, April, Canberra: Australian Government Publishing Service.

Dicken, P. (2003) *Global Shift*, 4th edn, London, Thousand Oaks, New Delhi: Sage Publications.

Evatt Foundation (1998) *Reforming Homework: A Statistical Profile and the NSW Code of Practice*, a report prepared by The Evatt Foundation for the NSW Minister for Public Works and Services, May 1998, Sydney.

Fincher, R. (1991) 'Caring for workers' dependents: gender, class and local state practice in Melbourne', *Political Geography Quarterly* 10: 356–81.

Frances, R. (1986) 'No more "Amazons": gender and work process in the Victorian clothing trades, 1890–1939', *Labour History* 50: 95–112.

Green, R. (2008) *Review of the Australian Textile Clothing and Footwear Industries: Building Innovative Capability, Vols 1–2*, Commissioned by Department of Innovation, Industry and Science, www.industry.gov.au/TCFReview (accessed July 2010).

Greig, A. (1992) 'Sub-contracting and the future of the Australian clothing industry', *Journal of Australian Political Economy* 29: 40–60.

Greig, A. (2001) 'The struggle for outwork reform in the Australian clothing industry', *Journal of Australian Political Economy* 49: 5–23.

Greig, A. and Little, S. (1996) 'The (unintended) consequences of Australian Labor's TCF Industry Policy, 1983–1996', *The Journal of the Textile Institute* 87(3): 107–18.

Jayanthakumaran, K. (2008) 'Trade reforms and the survival of the textile, clothing and footwear industries in Australia', in C. Harvie and B. Chye-Lee (eds), *Small and Medium Sized Enterprises in East Asia: Sectoral and Regional Dimensions*, pp. 332–46, Cheltenham: Edward Elgar.

Johnson, L. (1990) 'New patriarchal economies in the Australian textile industry', *Antipode* 22: 1–32.

Kosack, G. (1976) 'Migrant women: the move to western Europe – a step toward emancipation?', *Race and Class* 17(4): 369–79.

Liu, P. (2007) *Welfare Policy and Labour Outcomes of Immigrants in Australia*, www.ecosoc.org.au/files/File/TAS/ACE07/.../LiuP.pdf (accessed July 2011).

Miraftab, F. (1996) 'Space, gender, and work: home-based workers in Mexico', in E. Boris and E. Prügl (eds), *Homeworkers in Global Perspective: Invisible No More*, pp. 63–80, London: Routledge.

*Home-based garment manufacturing* 189

Mitter, S. (1986) *Common Fate, Common Bond: Women in the Global Economy*, London: Pluto Press.

Morokvasic, M. (1980) 'Yugoslav Women in France' F.R.G. and Sweden, Unpublished Report, Paris, Centre National Recherche Scientifique.

Peck, J. (1992) ' "Invisible threads": homeworking, labour market relations, and industrial restructuring in the Australian clothing trade', *Environment and Planning D: Society and Space* 10: 671–89.

Phizaklea, A. (1982) 'Migrant women and wage labour: the case of West Indian women in Britain', in J. West (ed.), *Work, Women and the Labour Market*, pp. 99–116, London: Routledge & Kegan Paul.

Productivity Commission (1997) *The Textiles, Clothing and Footwear Industries Draft Report Volumes 1 and 2*, Canberra: Australian Government Publishing Service.

Prügl, E. (1996) 'Home-based workers: a comparative exploration of Mies's theory of housewifization', *Frontiers* 17(1): 114–27.

Senate Economic Reference Committee (SERC) (1996) *Inquiry into Garment Industry Outwork*, Canberra: Commonwealth of Australia.

Sutherland, E. (2007) 'An epidemic of community, union and government induced reform? Mapping the "tipping point" for ethical governance of home-based apparel work in NSW, Australia' in D. Buttigieg, S. Cockfield, R. Cooney, M. Jerrard and A. Rainnie (eds), *Trade Unions in the Community: Values, Issues, Shared Interests and Alliances*, Melbourne: Heidelberg Press.

Sutherland, E. (2009) *Exploited or Entrepreneurs? A Study of Home-based Working Women in Australia's Clothing Industry*, Berlin/UK/USA: VDM Verlag.

Textiles Clothing and Footwear Union of Australia (TCFUA) (1995) *The Hidden Cost of Fashion: Report on the National Outwork Information Campaign*, Sydney: TCFUA.

Tierney, R. (1996) 'Migrants and class in postwar Australia', in R. Kuhn and T. O'Lincoln (eds), *Class and Class Conflict in Australia*, Melbourne: Longman.

Van Acker, E. (1995) 'Winners and losers: industry policy and gender concerns in the clothing industry', *Australian Journal of Political Science* 25(4): 45–58, 523–44.

Yeatman, A. (1992) *Non-English Background Women and Award Restructuring: A Case Study in the Clothing Industry*, Canberra: Department of the Prime Minister and Cabinet Office of Multicultural Affairs.

Young, I. M. (1990) *Justice and the Politics of Difference*, Princeton NJ: Princeton University Press.

# Appendix

Table A1.1 Vietnamese worker interviews conducted in Batu Pahat and Johor in 2008

| Name | Sex | Place of origin | Clothing factory | Working in factory |
|------|-----|-----------------|------------------|--------------------|
| Kim | Female | Vietnam | Sing Lun | 2 yrs |
| Chung | Female | Vietnam | Sing Lun | 1 yr |
| Huong | Female | Vietnam | Grimmell | 3 yrs |
| Thanh | Female | Vietnam | Grimmell | 9 mths |

Table A1.2 Vietnamese and Nepalese worker interviews conducted in Penang in 2009

| Name | Sex | Place of origin | Clothing factory | Working in factory |
|------|-----|-----------------|------------------|--------------------|
| San | Male – 26 | Nepal | Esquel Malaysia | 2yrs/10 mths |
| Chi | Female – 40 | An Giang: Viet | Esquel Malaysia | 2 yrs/2 mths |
| Pham | Female – 23 | Ha Giang: Viet | Pen Apparel | 11 mths |
| Phuong | Female – 23 | BacNinh: Viet | Pen Apparel | 3 yrs extend to 4 yrs |
| Xuan | Female – 22 | Son La Province | Pen Apparel | 3 yrs |

Table A1.3 Vietnamese worker interviews conducted in Batu Pahat in 2010

| Name | Sex | Place of origin | Clothing factory | Working in factory |
|------|-----|-----------------|------------------|--------------------|
| Mei | Female | Vietnam | Hon Sin | 1 yr 11 mths |
| San | Female | Vietnam | Hon Sin | 1 yr |
| Tien | Female | Vietnam | Hon Sin | 1 yr 11 mths |
| Phuong | Female | Vietnam | KL | 10 mths |
| Oanh | Female | Vietnam | KL | 10 mths |

*Appendix* 191

*Table A1.4* Nepalese and Vietnamese worker interviews conducted in Kuala Lumpur in 2010 and 2013

| Name | Sex | Place of origin | Clothing factory | Working in factory |
|---|---|---|---|---|
| Vijaya | Male – 25 | Nepal | Kiko Com | 2 yrs |
| Narayan | Male – 30 | Nepal | Kiko Com | 2 yrs |
| Bahadur | Male | Nepal | Wel Pekes Enterprises Com | 8 mths |
| Kesher | Male | Nepal | Sweet Hearts Garments | 2 yrs |
| Dev | Male | Nepal | Royal Baby Industries | 1 yr |
| Davic | Male | Nepal | Leader of Gefont | 2 yrs |
| Rita | Female | Nepal | Imperial Garments | 1 yr |
| Janek | Male | Nepal | Factory | 8 yrs |
| Su | Male | Vietnam | Detention inmate | 2 yrs |
| Dong | Male | Vietnam | Factory worker | 2 yrs |
| Tan | Male | Vietnam | Restaurant worker | 3 yrs |

# Index

Page numbers in **bold** denote figures, those in *italics* denote tables.

abuses 148, 152; human rights 35; labour
32, 38, 93; migrant workers 87–8, 94n8;
substance 128; verbal 132; workers 49,
91, 145
access 87; to factory work 149; to garment
traders 126; to higher wage rates 109; to
markets 43, 64, 121, 145; to welfare
benefits restricted 177
accessories 4, 8, 77n3, 103
activists 17, 76, 126; anti-sweatshop 31,
33–4; labour 3, 10, 25–6, 37, 75, 127,
134, 138; left-wing 60; Malay female
27; middle class female 31; networks
125, 136; scholar 4
advocacy 86; community 87; organizations
89
Agreement on Textiles and Clothing
(ATC) 4, 145–6, 148
agricultural activity 149; background 28;
districts of the northern India 128;
modernization 122; sector 63; work 152
Agricultural Development International
(ADI) 150, 164
agriculture 120, 149, 152
Ahmed, N. 70
American Federation of Labour –
Congress of Industrial Organizations
(AFL-CIO) 65
Amnesty International 87
anti-sweatshop movement 14; activists 31,
33–4
anti-trafficking movement 89
anti-unionism 27
anti-unionists 35
Appelbaum, R. 4, 8
Apple 103, 106–7
Ariffin, R. 27–8

Arnold, D. 7–8, 10–11, 82, 147, 164n2
Asian American Free Labor Institute
(AAFLI) 65, 69
Association of South East Asian Nations
(ASEAN) 43; Committee on Migrant
Workers 94n4
Australia 2–4, 169; Chinese women 178,
181–4, 186; home-based workers 170,
172, 175; homework 174; migrants 171;
outworkers registered 187n6; social
welfare payments 187n8; textiles union
(TCFUA) 173; Vietnamese Update
conference 94n2; women migrants
176–7, 179; *see also* New South Wales
Australian 171; buyers 8; clothing industry
18, 169–70, 172; home-based clothing
work 187n2; immigration policy 177;
market 184; migrant workers 106; Tax
Office (ATO) 173, 187n6; Textile
Clothing and Footwear Industries 174
Australian Bureau of Statistics (ABS) 171,
186n2; Manufacturing Survey 187n5
Australian government 170; agency 187n9;
Department of Industry 18n1
Australian Industrial Relations
Commission (AIRC) 187n6
Australian Research Council (ARC) 38n1,
94n2; grant 150
Awami League (AL) 65–6

Bair, J. 6, 18n3, 80
Bakker, I. 9, 17
Bangladesh 1, 3, 17, 31–2, 34, 39n10, 71,
92, 126; Bank 62; BGWTUC 68, 73;
campaigns against multinationals 33;
clothing export value *5*; clothing
industry 2; diplomatic relations with

## Index 193

Malaysia 87; Embassy in Kuala Lumpur 86; garment salaries 147; INCIDIN 69; Made in Bangladesh Label 61, 64; Nationalist Party (BNP) 66; Paradox 77n6; postcolonial 65; trade unions 67; worker protest 85; worker resistance 11; workers' federations **68**

Bangladesh Center for Worker Solidarity (BCWS) 69

Bangladesh Export Processing Zone Authority (BEPZA) 66, 77n3

Bangladesh Garment Manufacturers Export Association (BGMEA) 62–3, 74, 77n2

Bangladesh Garment Workers Trade Unity Council (BGWTUC) 68, 73

Bangladesh Garments Textile & Leather Workers' Federation 32

Bangladesh Independent Garment Workers Federation (BIGUF) **68**, 69

Bangladesh Labour Act 2006 77n5; (Amendment) Act, 2013 60

Bangladesh Legal Aid and Services Trust (BLAST) 69

Bangladesh Nationalist Party (BNP) 66

Bangladesh Welfare Society Campbelltown (BWSC) 73

Bangladeshi 69; firms 1; garment workers 16, 61; NGOs 69; RMG workers 77n2; state 72; workers 32, 64, 86–7, 157

Bannerjee, S. S. 64, 77n8

Barrientos, S. 6, 14–15, 31, 33–4, 125

Beresford, M. 17, 143–4, 146, 148, 158, 164n2

Berik, G. 124, 143, 146

Better Factories Cambodia (BFC) 142–8, 152–4, 157, 163, 166n12; Synthesis Reports *151*, **158–60**, 166n15; Thirtieth Synthesis Report 164n3

Bhopal, M. 24, 27, 38n2, 39n6

boatpeople SOS 88–9; Vietnamese American 88

Bonocich, E. 17, 18n3, 80

breaches 55, 73, 94n4; of core standards 124; factory-imposed wage ceilings 112; human rights protocols 82; labour 27, 35

British Broadcasting Corporation (BBC) 152

Broadbent, K. 10

Brown, A. 23

Burmese workers 8, 91–2; *see also* Myanmar

Cambodia 3, 34, 148, 165n4; BFC 144, 146; child labour 151–3, **155–6**; clothing export value 5; garment factories 164n1; garment workers **154**, 164; Hong Kong firms 158; improved labour standards 143; labour market 163; Malaysian clothing suppliers 29; migrant workers in Malaysia 81, 87; monitoring programme 17; Socio-Economic Survey 165n11; TATA 145; unions 31, 33; women employed in the clothing industry 2; worker resistance 11

Cambodian 145, 155, 177; exports 159; factories 162; home-based workers 175; investors 164n2; labour standards 143; law 158; Ministry of Labour and Vocational Training (MOLVT) 166n14; Ministry of Planning 148, 165n4; products 17; researchers 165n10; women 169, 172, 178; workers in Thailand 8

Cambodian garment sector 144, 146; factories *151*; industry 159; workers 147

Cambodians 177; in Malaysian clothing factories 80

CAMFEBA and BDLINK 146

capital 3, 15, 23, 46, 135; boundaries of inclusion and exclusion 81; bureaucratic power 70; to buy ID 152; development 39n13; foreign 25, 43, 54; global 11, 33; inflows 44; less dependent on migrant workers 35; Malay accumulation 27; markets 142; private 9; productivity 121; relocation strategies 10; SMEs 123; structural power 56; unions working in interests of 76; workers subordinated 57

capital and labour struggles 12–13

capital-intensive high-tech production 99–100, 113–14; industries 122; organized sector 120; textile production 4

caring responsibilities of women 157, 160, *161*, **161–2**, 164

Catholic Human Resource Development 91

Centre for Asia Pacific Social Transformation Studies (CAPSTRANS) 138n1

Centre for Education and Communication (CEC) 120–2, 124–5, 127, 136

Chakravarty, D. 125, 132, 136

Chan, A. 16, 48–9, 54–6, 80, 106

Chatterjee, U. 121–2

Chief Executive Officer (CEO) 32–3

194   *Index*

child labour 14, 17, 146, 150–1, 153–4, **155**, 158, 164, 166n14; abolition of 163; elimination of 143–4; force 152; in garment factories *151*, 157

China 3, 48, 98–9, 101, 118, 145; automotive sector 108; cost of living 110; elite consumers 15; employment *131*; factories 32; IR 46; increase in jobs 105; IR system 49; Labor Watch 104, 111; labour-intensive industries 107; manufacturing centres 8; membership of WTO 97, 113; migrant workers 16, 18n2, 102–3, 112; National Development and Reform Commission 100; policymakers 114; post-MFA era 120; raw materials from 164n2; Singaporean companies relocated to 30; trade union administrators 106; women migrants 172, 177–9, 181–3; workers from 87; workers strike action 56

China textiles and clothing 97; exporter 62; export manufacturing sector 104–5, 108; export value 4, 5; industry 18n1, 34; industry wages 7; manufacturing 170; sewing work 171; women employed 2

*China Daily* 18n2, 98–101, 103–8, 110–14

China–Australia commodity flows 8

Chinese 24, 27, 48, 55, 101, 111; agricultural markets 149; communism 25; exporters 121; factories 113; garment exports 146; government 4, 108; home-based workers 175; in Malaysian clothing factories 80; manufacturing hub 107; media 98, 104, 110; migrant workers 16, 97, 106; policymakers 114; scholars 99; union leaders 38n2; women 169, 177–81, 183–4, 187n11; women migrants 172; workers 112

Chinese Academy of Social Sciences Institute of Population and Labor Economics 98–9

Chinese Malaysians 25, 27, 30; non-Muslim 94

Chiu, C. C. H. 56, 143, 146, 158–9, 163

Christian advocacy 92; groups 89

Cividep report 125

Clarke, S. 48–9, 56–7

Clean Clothes Campaign (CCC) 33, 120–1, 124–5, 127

Coalition to Abolish Modern-day Slavery in Asia (CAMSA) 88–9

Coats, JP thread factory 29, 39n10; Employees' Union 32

Cold War 23; alliance with US 65

collapse 33; Rana Plaza 60; small manufacturing enterprises 100; workers 1, 134

Collins, J. 1, 3, 7–8, 14, 18n3

colonial legacies 23–4, 64

commodity chain 8, 11, 13; buyer-driven 6, 122; global (GCC) 3–4, 6–7, 13, 60, 80, 119, 125, 136; passive end 15; subcontractors 77n2

compliance 125; corporate 124; on document maintenance 157; of factory workers 93; high rates 143; levels **159**; low 146; monitored factories 158; monitoring 15; with overtime standard 166n15; worker 82

compliant buyers 146; factories **159**; firms 159; workers 12, 82

concessions 1, 122; tax 2

Coordination of Action Research on Aids and Mobility Research (CARAM) 87

corporate social responsibility (CSR) 142; agendas 14; initiatives 31, 87

Cox, A. 10, 15

Cox, R. W. 46

Coyle, A. 7, 171

Crinis, V. 10, 12–16, 18n2, 26–7, 29, 34–5, 81, 87, 127

Cumbers, A. 4, 31

Das, K. 120, 122–4, 135

Das, N. 120, 122–4

Dasgupta, S. 145

De Neve, G. (also DeNeve) 15, 33, 120–1, 125, 136

De Silva, S. R. 45–6, 54, 56

debt 82–4, 165n8; bondage 145; recruitment 12, 35

Dell 103, 106

Department of Industry, Science and Resources (DISR) 171

Department of Statistics Malaysia 18n1, 39n7

deregistered 26

development 9, 13, 18, 27, 63, 122; accurate measurement of outworking 174; affordable sewing machines 172; agricultural 150; agricultural markets 149; Cambodian garment sector 144–6; capital 39n13; child 152; China 99–100, 113–14; dualist 119; economic 23, 25, 56, 98, 105; export oriented 66; human 91; of labour opposition 10; site 11; state projects 4; studies 7; trade unions

*Index* 195

54; trajectories 126; triangle union 37; Vietnam 43, 48–9; of young people 143
developmental trajectories of western economies 7
developmentalism 61
Dicken, P. 6, 170
disposable workers 4, 11, 15–16, 82
Doshi, G. 120–2, 124, 135
Douglass, M. 12

economic 6, 13–14, 31, 66, 113, 143; activities 149, 151; agenda in Vietnam 56; autonomy 185; British infiltration 24; Cambodia Socio-Economic Survey 165n11; changed situation 180; condition of household 163; context 164; cost of return for migrant workers 104; crisis 1; cycle 2; dynamics of Malaysia 28; enterprises 43; environment 3; European problems 107; global downturn 103; global slowdown 121; growth 26, 144; hardship 177; imperatives 119; influences 45; Institute of Cambodia 146, 164n2; issues 81; macro policies 63; neoliberal policies 15; policies 25, 46, 57; political structures 61; prosperity in India 124; recession 12; reform in Vietnam 47; rewards 138; socio-economic resources 174; South Pacific Agreement (SPARTECA) 170; structure in India 122; transformations 8; utility 150; West Pakistani hegemony 65; workplace matters 23; zones 2, 10
economic development 23; area 105; dualistic 98; of Malays 27; means of promoting 56; pathways to 63; policies aimed to foster 122; uneven 9, 25
Economic Institute of Cambodia 146, 164n2
Economic and Political Weekly (EPW) 120
economics 13; of global commodity chains 136; Institute of Population and Labor 98–9
educated 99; into citizenship rights 75; for future occupation 155; management 122; problems of migrant workers 91; women 87; workers 37
education 17, 69, 101, 103; in Cambodia 151; children 186; employees 51; higher 121; middle-school 132; Technical and Further 185; worker 114, 124; of young people 143

education and training 2; tertiary level 121; worker 124
Elias, J. 27–8, 31, 39n4
Elson, D. 7, 9
Employment Act 1955, 1968, 1998 35–6; Restriction 1968 35
Employment of Labour (Standing Orders) Act 1965 72
ethical trade 146
Ethical Trading Initiative (ETI) 34
ethnic 81, 86; communities 14; divisions 27, 93; groups 8, 85; issues 26; ministries 91; restaurants 94n3; tensions 25
ethnicity/ethnicities 7, 16, 24, 34, 37, 80–1, 84–6, 91–3
Euro-American labour history 11
European Union (EU) 4, 145
Evatt Foundation 174
exploit/ed 32; low wages 98; workers 3, 11
exploitation 9, 13, 18, 134, 169, 171, 181; capitalist 57; labour 6, 25, 77n1, 86, 89, 93; of migrants 88, 124; self 142; of women 17, 124, 174, 186; of workers 34, 81
exploitative 169; circuits of labour migration 81; employer restrictions 82; employment 1; factory work 16; home-based work 175; labour conditions 70; processes 3; rates of pay 129; subcontracting relations 128; wages 121
export earnings 2, 44, 62; value *5*
export processing zone (EPZ) 23, 25–6, 28, 39n5, 62, 72, 75, 127, 132
export-oriented factories 80; garment industry 126, 136, 144; industrialization 23; policy 25
exports 1, 43, 62; Cambodian 159; Chinese manufactured 113; clothing 4; footwear 144; garment 143, 146; growth 111; Indian 121, 124–5; Maral 135; re-exports *5*; restricted 145; Sara 133; textile 64, 120

factory workers 11, 150, 154; female clothing 29; garment 166n13; Jeans FW Union 137; Nepalese 85, 89; repressive regulation 93; searching 52; in Vietnam 8, *191*
Fair Wear Foundation 18n1, 124
female workers 2, 11, 13, 15, 17, 23, 28, 34, 82, 126, 165n6, *190–1*; average weekly hours 156; in clothing industries 11, 29, 31; empowerment 63, 67; failure

## 196   Index

female workers *continued*
  of unions to organize 27, 70; garment
  153, **154**, 162; in Malaysia 84; migrant
  64, 69, 148; migration rates 150, 165n4;
  Nepalese 80; reasons for quitting 160,
  *161*, **161–2**, 164; unskilled 7, 62;
  Vietnamese 90
feminist analysts 11; NGOs 28, 87;
  scholars 17; theorists 176
feminists 62
Fibre2Fashion 121
Filipino *see* Philippines
Flanders, A. 45
Ford, M. 10, 23–4, 31, 93
foreign direct investment (FDI) 39n5,
  43–4, 46, 56–7, 66–7
foreign investment open-door policy 43, 66
Foxconn 103, 106–7; young workers 108
Franck, A. 124–5
free trade 23, 63–4, 66; agreements 17;
  ICFTU 25, 38n3, 65; Washington
  Consensus 9
Free Trade Zone (FTZ) 10; Sungai Way 87

Ganguly-Scrase, R. 17, 125
Garment Manufacturers Association in
  Cambodia (GMAC) 144–5, 148, 164n1,
  164n3
garment workers 10, 62, 69–70, 143, 164;
  Bangladesh Trade Unity Council
  (BGWTUC) 68, 73; Bangladeshi 16, 61;
  Cambodian 147, 149; child labour 154;
  federations 67, **68**; female 17, 162;
  female and male 153, **154**; former 150,
  160; home-based women 127; Indian
  export 119; informal sector 2; public
  recognition 75; retired **161–2**; revolt 74;
  Unity Forum 60, 73; women 1, 138, 163
Garment Workers Union Federation
  (GWUF) 68, 72–3
Gefont *see* Nepalese Trade Union
  Congress
General Agreement of Tariffs and Trade
  (GATT) 4, 9, 64, 145, 170
General Statistics Office (GSO) 43
Gereffi, G. 1, 3, 6–7, 18n5, 80, 122–3, 142
Ghosh, J. 121–4, 127
global financial crisis (GFC) 16, 29–30,
  35, 97–8, 100–2, 104–5, 107, 110,
  113–14, 143, 146, 154, 159–60; growth
  in employment post-GFC 157
global production network (GPN) 4, 67, 13
Global Union Federation (GUF) 31, 33,
  37–8, 39n11

global value chain (GVC) 4, 6, 8, 136, 142
Golden Girls of Bengal 62
Green, R. 170–1, 174
Greig, A. 171
Gross Domestic Product (GDP) 1, 13, 23,
  144

Hale, A. 14, 18n2, 80, 124–5, 136–7, 146
Hannan, K. 16, 99, 113
Hashim, D. A. 120–2, 124
Heintz, A. 145, 164n2
Henderson, J. 6, 8
Hewison, K. 56, 82
HIMAL Southasian 77n6
Hirway, I. 120–4, 127, 136
Home Shiffon Garments 29
home-based work 128, 132, 172, 174–5,
  186, 187n6; work sector 18, 23; working
  women 171, 176, 178–81, 185
home-based workers 2, 30, 34, 176, 185;
  Chinese, Cambodian and Vietnamese
  175; marginal status 18, 174; networks
  169; reliance on 170, 172–3; women
  127
homeworkers 169, 173, 175–6, 180, 185,
  187n5
Hong Kong 5, 23, 44, *131*, 164n2; factories
  159; firms in Cambodia 158; garment
  manufacturing 170; migrant workers 180,
  183; migrants from 177; traders 8;
  women migrants from 172, 178, 184
Hughes, C. 147
*hukou* 2, 101
human resource management (HRM) 43
Human Rights Watch 87; Report 75
Hyman, R. 45

ID 142; certificates 152, 154; certification
  system 164; falsification 143, 150,
  152–4, 157, 163
illegal 84; labour practices 126, 137;
  strikes 16, 26, 32, 38, 39n10, 44, 53, 55;
  workers 91, 101
India 3, 121, 123, 135; All India Board for
  Workers 125; clothing export value *5*;
  Communist Party 137; dual
  development strategies 122; economic
  prosperity 124; export production 17,
  119–20; garment industry 2, 18n1;
  Partition 126; unions 65; women unpaid
  130; workers' protest 85
Indian 24, 27, 128; apparel sector 135;
  government 124; labour 121; unionists
  28; workers 91

*Index* 197

Indian garment industry 127, 138; export 119–23
Indians 24, 27, 92
Indonesia 65; clothing export value *5*; government 10; migrants 34, 81; multinationals 33
Indonesian 86; migrants 12, 80; workers 7
industrial relations (IR) 10, 43, 45–6, 50, 56, 62; Act 1967 35–6; Australian (AIRC) 187n6; contravention 173; developing 46; institutions 57; tripartite 23; Vietnamese system 47–9, 54–5
IndustriALL 33, 39n11
insecurity 8, 136, 147; job 2, 24, 64
Internal Securities Act (ISA) 25–6
International Confederation of Free Trade Unions (ICFTU) 25, 38n3, 65
International Convention on the Protection of the Rights of all Migrant Workers and Members of their Families 88
International Finance Corporation (IFC) 44, 147
International Labor Rights Forum 3
International Labour Conventions 35
International Labour Organization (ILO) 14–15, 18n1, 24, 32–3, 37, 44, 60, 67, 120, 124, 142, 145–8, 152; Conventions 143, 153, 156, 166n14
International Migrant Workers Alliance (IMA) 87
International Monetary Fund (IMF) 63
International Textile, Garment and Leather Workers' Federation (ITGLWF) 31–3, 39n9, 39n11
International Trade Union Confederation (ITUC) 38n3
International Union Federation (IUF) 31

Jenkins, R. 6, 15
Jomo, K. S. 24–6, 30

Kabeer, N. 6, 15, 17, 33–4, 128, 144, 157
Kantor, P. 127–8
Kashyap, S. P. 122–3
Kelly, P. F. 6, 8, 13
Kerkvliet, B. 49, 54–6
Khan, R. S. 121–2, 124, 135
Khan, S. I. 67, 6972
Kim, C.-Y. 151, 155, 165n11
Kuala Lumpur (KL) 30, 39n7, 80, 84, 86, 89–92, *190–1*

labour 2–3, 10, 14, 32, 37, 43–4, 48, 52–3, 61, 64, 93, 112, 121, 124, 127, 145;
abuse 38; activism 80, 137; activists 33, 134, 138; administration 49; Bangladesh (Amendment) Act, 2013 60; conditions 1, 70, 77n8, 125, 143, 162; controls over 46; conventions 35; Directorate (DoL) 60, 71; domestic 17, 186; excess 39n13; exploitation 6, 25, 77n1, 86; exporting 94n9; faceless input 175; forced 146; importing 82; Indian 24, 27; intellectuals 34; leaders 66–7, 73–6; legislation 47; management 62; militancy 12; Minister of 26; mobilizations 65, 69; MOLVT 155; NGOs 28, 87, 106; organized 11; protection 119; protective legislation 63; reforms 56; regulation 135; relations 4, 15; resistance 136; rural 99; shortages 36, 98, 157; skilled 122; system 57; trafficking 88–9; unfair system 92; unregulated 172; watch groups 104; World Confederation (WCL) 38n3
labour contracts 49, 51, 54; Contract Law 100; contractors 128
labour costs 1–2, 4, 71, 99–100; cheap 57, 63–4, 142, 145; cheap and flexible 17, 119–21; low 135
labour disputes and strikes 43–4, 50–2, 54, 61, 106; struggles 13, 16, 127, 136; unrest 25, 76
labour division 13; gender-based 7, 171; household 174–5; international 64, 142
labour force 34, 51, 68, 93, 127, 138, 147, 152; feminized 63; migrant 7, 30, 64; unskilled female 62
labour-intensive 100, 124; export manufacturing 105, 112; garment industry 146; global industry 121; industries 44, 87, 107; low-profit-margin 108; manufacture 97, 102, 113; production 99, 114, 142; sectors 43
labour laws 9, 14, 35–6, 44, 119, 121, 125, 138; 1994 47–8, 51, 54; amendments 25–6, 60, 75; Cambodian 155, 159; Contract Law 100; pro-labour 66; unprotected by 175; violations 124
labour market 2, 6–7, 17, 49, 113, 142–3, 152, 163; rural Cambodian 144; theorists 13
labour migrant 7–8, 129, 175; force 7, 30, 64; market 112; NGO 87, 106; programmes 88; resistance 93; migration 81, 91, 127; slave 89
labour movements 17, 24, 37, 93; Bangladesh 65–6; communist expansion

198  *Index*

labour movements *continued*
25; disorganization 26; emerging 147; Indian 27; international 74; national 9; politics 87; regional or national 86; in Southeast Asia 23; unofficial 45
labour organization 136; dis-organization 3; independent 55
labour practices 186; illegal 137; recruitment 71; unfair 37
labour rights 31, 77n1, 92, 94, 124, 144, 146–7, 163–4; activists 76; advocacy 86; Cambodian 145; education 37, 69, 136; fundamental 125; garment industry 10, 138; hindered 128; Indian garment industry 119, 121; in Malaysia 24; race to the bottom 44, 46, 53, 56, 64; trade union protection 48, 67; for women 33
labour standards 7, 143, 145, 147–8, 158, 163; core 14, 138, 144, 146; implementation 17; monitoring 34, 142
labour trafficking 88–9; anti-trafficking movement 89
labour turnover 104, 109; high 64, 70; rapid 102
labour unions 48, 87, 137; appropriation into political movements 65; politicized 66; trade 12; triangle strategy 38; unionization 76; in Vietnam 55
labourers 149; child 151, 153, **154–5**; migrant 14, 81; skilled 121
Latin American countries 34
Law on Foreign Investment 43
Lee, C. H. 53
Lee, S. 7, 11
Lévesque, C. 46, 55
levy 36, 82, 84
LG South Korean-owned plant 110
liberalization 3, 145; of Calcutta's port 138; market 63; trade 63, 170–1
local labour 1; demand 36; laws 14

machinists 7, 171
Mahmud, S. 62–3, 70
Malaysia 2–3, 7, 10, 14, 30, 32, 89–90, 165n8, *190*; clothing industry 12, 28; Department of Statistics 18n1, 39n7; export value 5; investors 94n5; labour migration 81; labour movements 23; labour NGOs 87–8; levels of resistance 11; passport confiscated 93; Prime Minister 26; strike action illegal 38
Malaysia labour unions 23–5, 27; clothing and textile 31; export sector 33; industry-based 29; members 38n1

Malaysia workers 36; dismissed 35; education 37; foreign 16; migrant 34, 38, 80–4, 87, 89–94; migrant NGOs 94n7; repatriated 85
Malaysian 28–9, 32, 81, 86, 89; affiliates 33; Chinese Malaysian SMEs 30; citizens 36; clothing industry 80, 87; Communist Party 38n2; Constitution 35; detention centres 91; government 23, 27, 34, 38, 88, 90, 94n4; labour history 24; standards 37; state 10; strikes 26; suppliers 39n5; Trades Union Congress (MTUC) 25, 38n1; unions 31; workers 39n12, 82
Malaysian Knitting Manufacturers Association (MKMA) 28–9
Malaysian Textile Manufacturers Association (MTMA) 29
Malaysian Trades Union Congress (MTUC) 25, 27–8, 36–7, 38n1, 92; migrant workers 35; Secretary 36
Malaysians 84; Chinese 25, 27; Chinese non-Muslim 94
male workers 7, 130; knitwear factories 77n4; skilled 27; in textile factories 31; voluntary leaving 160
Manicandan, G. 124
marginalization 185; of migrant women 18, 174, 186; of migrant workers 38; of unions 24
memorandum of understanding (MOU) 34, 74, 81
migrant workers 2, 29, 35, 37, 38n1, 86–7, 90–1, 100, 106, 110, 118, 127, 130, 134, 136, 165n6; abuse of 88; after-levy wages 36; Chinese rural 18n2; demanding wage increases 111–12; disposable 16; exploitation 124; in Malaysia 34, 38, 39n12, 80–4, 93; new generation 108; replacement with robots 107; resistance 85; rights of 89, 94n4; rural-to-urban 97, 99, 102–3; second generation 109; shortage of 98, 101, 104, 113–14; support networks 15; transnational 10, 12, 31; women 157
Migrant Workers and Refugees Support Centres 91
migrants 1, 11, 35, 81–2, 91, 94n3, 94n8, 143, 165n4, 165n5, 165n9; Asian 177; in Australia 171–2; authorized or unauthorized 34, 39n13; in distress 88–9, 93; female 148; female rural 64, 69; illegal workers 101; Indonesian 12; job situation in cities 18n2; labour 87,

129; low piece-rates 169; in Malaysia 84, 94; minimum wage 36; networks 16; from rural areas 127; short-term contracts 33; social welfare payments 187n8

Migration News 34, 36, 81

militancy 11–12; Cambodian union 145; labour 10

militant 76; movement 10; unions 25, 66; women workers 12

minimum wage 32, 36, 53, 76; failure to pay 145; higher 73; increase 74; legislation 35, 94

Ministry of Labour and Vocational Training 155, 166n14

Ministry of Textiles, India 121

monitored BFC 159, **160**; child labour 153; company 148; factories 147, *151*, **158**, 164n3; labour standards 142, 145; local factory managers 9

monitoring 15, 143, 163; BFC 146, 148, 151, 157; Cambodian labour rights 145; external 8; factory-level 144; ILO project 152; independent system 142; internationally sanctioned 68; programme 17; reliable 164; Thirtieth Synthesis Report 153, 164n3

monitors 148; corporations codes of conduct 34; to detect child labourers 153; evidence reported 151

Moshrefa Mishu Garment Workers Unity Forum 60, 73

Multi-Fibre Arrangement (MFA) 4, 64, 9, 29, 34, 64, 97–8, 113, 145; abolition 122, 138, 170; post-MFA 119–21, 123, 127, 135

multinational corporations (MNC) 28, 30, 33, 36, 43–4, 63–4, 113; brands 32; Japanese 32, 39n6; labour strikes 50; practices 119; trade unions 49

Murali, R. 86–7

Myanmar 34, 62, 85, 87

Nathan, D. 70, 121, 124

National Awami Party 65

National Office of Human Development (NOHD) 91

Nepal 34, 37, 81, 84–5, 87, 89, 92–3, *190–1*

Nepalese 80, 85; church services 91; Migrant Workers' Support Group 37; mobility 16; pastors 89–90, 92; undocumented 84; workers 7, 37, 83, 86; Workers' Association 92–3

Nepalese Trade Union Congress (Gefont) 37, 92–3, *191*

Nepali Sangati 90

New Economic Policy (NEP) 25, 27

New South Wales (NSW) 173, 175

newly industrialized countries (NICs) 23

Ng, C. 91, 94n8

non-compliance 29, 158, 171; factories 160

non-compliant factories 148, **158**, **160**; firms 146, 148, 163

non-government organizations (NGOs) 3, 8, 12, 14–15, 34, 37–8, 61, 69, 80–1, 86, 88–9, 104; activism 125; agents 129; community 176–7, 185; externally funded 76; Filipino 91; grass-roots 93; international 136, 148; labour 28, 89; Malaysian 94n7; migrant labour 87, 98, 106; reports 85; representatives 38n1, 134; US-based 68

non-registered 67, 69, 164n1

North Atlantic Free Trade Agreement (NAFTA) 4

Occupational Safety and Health Act 1994 35

Ong, A. 10–11, 93

O'Rourke, D. 6, 15, 18n3

Osakwe, E. 120–1

outsource 64, 147; workers 88

outsourcing 11, 17, 86, 88, 135

outworkers 169, 172, 175, 179–80, 182, 185–6, 187n5, 187n6, 187n7; Chinese 177; clothing 173–4

outworking 173, 177–80, 183, 185–6, 187n13

overtime 12, 82–4, 109, 111, 133, **156**; disputes 69; encouraged 107; forced 145; legal limit 157; less or no 54, 84; loss of 146; night shift 164; pay 53, 73; rarely compensated 72; schedules imposed 149–50; standard 166n15; unpaid 98; variable 147

Padhi, A. 121, 135

Pangsapa, P. 10–12

Pearl River Delta 97–8, 100–2, 104, 106, 110–11, 113

Peck, J. 82, 171, 174, 187n6

Penang and Province Wellesley Textiles and Garment Manufacturing Employees' Union (PTGWU) 29–30, 39n8

*Penang Union Newsletter* 29

200 *Index*

Philippines 34, 65; Filipino NGOs 91
plantation estates 24; workers 25
Polaski, S. 143, 145–6, 151–3
Prashad, V. 61, 76, 77n6
pregnant 162, 164, 181; absence of support
157; entitlement to maternity leave 159;
female permit holders 82; migrant
worker 111, 182; women 147, 158;
workers 160
production costs 4; cheaper 29; increased
100; lowered 138; minimize 1; rising
105
productivity 4, 112; of capital 121;
Commission 173–4, 187n5, 187n6,
187n7; gap 111; increased 114; levels
122; low 120, 122; lower 135; lower in
India 119; of migrant workers 114; poor
123
Productivity Commission 173–4, 187n5,
187n6, 187m7
Prota, L. 17, 144, 158
Prügl, E. 176, 181
Pun, N. 6, 14

race to the bottom 44, 46, 53, 56, 64, 145
Rahman, S. 62, 76
Rahman, Z. 65–6, 70–1, 74–5
Rainnie, A .F. 6, 9
Rajasekaran, G. S. M. 26, 36
Ramaswamy, K. V. 122–3, 135
Rana Plaza 1, 60–1; before Rana Plaza 64;
dead and the missing 69; post-Rana
Plaza period 16, 60; post-Rana Plaza
unions 61, 76
Rapid Action Battalion (RAB) 72–3, 75
Rasiah, R. 26, 29, 142, 146
Ready Made Garment (RMG) 62, 67, 74;
workers 77n2
recruit/recruited/recruiting 8, 131; to
Malaysia 90; migrant workers 12, 80–1;
techniques 70; from Vietnam 85;
women 128–9; workers 27, 35, 71–2,
*131*
recruitment 87–8, 144; corrupt process 94;
costs 81–2; debts 12, 35; expenses 107;
firms 80; formal 132; migrant workers
10, 34, 38; practices 72; process 84
refugees 89; Support Centres 91;
Vietnamese 177
register(s) 184; Business 187n5; with
GMAC 174n1; with Penang Textile
Trade Union 29–30; unions 26, 37;
village 165n9
registered 33; as adult workers 164; capital

inflows 44; clothing manufacturers
187n7; clothing and textile factories 28,
30; factories 62, 86, 144; federations 67;
garment unions 23; outworkers 187n6;
trade unions 60, 68; *see also*
deregistered; non-registered
registration impossible to obtain 76;
records 187n6; refused 71; residential
(*hukou*) 101; unions 16, 25–6, 60
relocation 2, 109; strategies 10, 24, 29
residents' rights *see hukou*
restrictions 82; on hiring and firing 119;
MFA 4, 145; phasing out 146; on trade
unions 37–8, 56, 66
Robertson, R. 143, 146–7, 153
Ross, L. 66, 70
Rowley, C. 24, 27, 38n2
rural 97, 101, 123, 144; areas 2, 12, 24, 28,
69, 127, 133, 148; Chinese migrant
workers 18n2; Chinese workers 16;
female migrants 64; homes 100, 102;
labour force 99; provinces 1; rubber-
production estates 87; sending
communities 143; town 14; villages 25
rural-to-urban migrant workers 97;
Chinese 102–3; second generation 99

*Sahabat Wanita* (Friends of Women) 87
security 81, 124; employment 102; forces
71–4; job 147; measures 26; national 75;
social benefits 125, 177; of tenure
removed 36; worker 82
Security Offences Special Measures Act 26
Senate Economic Reference Committee
(SERC) 173
sending countries 37, 91
Sibbel, L. 146, 153
Siddiqi, D. M. 16, 62–3, 66, 68, 72
Singapore 12, 23, 30, 39n5
Singaporean companies 30
Singh, A. 46, 56
Sluiter, L. 124–5
small to medium enterprises (SMEs)
29–30, 34, 36, 39n7, 122–4, 135
small-scale enterprises (SSEs) 122; cottage
industry 17, 119, 124; home-based
working women 171; production 134;
units 123, 125
Smith, C. 6, 14
Social Accountability International (SAI)
34
solidarity 32, 55, 61, **68**, 73, 86; Centre
68–9; class 74; external 47; internal
46–7; worker 12, 124

Sonnenberg, S. 147–8
South Korea 7, 15, 62, 64–5, *131*
South Korean conglomerate 62; LG plant 110
South Pacific Regional Trade and Economic Cooperation Agreement (SPARTECA) 170
Southeast Asia labour: migration of foreign workers 127; movements 23
Southeast Asian garment workers 142; rural development 164; states 23
Sri Lanka 2, *5*, 34
state-sanctioned 163; anti-unionism 27; exploitation 81–2; Industrial Police 75; print media 98; repression 70
strike 26, 43–5, 66, 73, 76, 111, 137, 160; action 38, 54, 56, 98, 108; hunger 65; illegal 16, 32, 39n10, 55; labour 50; leaders 86; migrant worker 104, 106, 114; right to 48; rolling wave of 105, 110; sit-in 85; wildcat 10, 49, 52–5, 69, 72
striking 57; women workers 127; workers 52, 72, 74
suburban: block of land 185; home 90, 182
supply chains 32–3; global 142–3, 147; hierarchies 8; subcontracting 15; workers 31
surveillance 71, 75–6, 133
Sutherland, E. 18, 175
sweat 53, 112
sweat-free 17; labour 142; products 77, 146
sweatshop workers 63, 99

Taiwan 15, 23, 43–4, 89, 164n2
Taiwanese companies 50; FDI in Vietnam 44; owned 49, 106; trading corporations 8; transnational companies 31
Technical and Further Education (TAFE) 185
*Tenaganita* (Women's Force) 87–9, 94n8; report 94n6
Terry Prai 29
Tewari, M. 123
textile, clothing and footwear (TCF) 98, 125; businesses 187n5; homeworkers 173–4; industry policy 170 Clothing and Footwear Union of Australia (TCFUA) 173
Textile Workers Asia-Pacific Regional Organization (TWARO) 31, 33, 39n8
Thailand 11; AAFLI representatives 65; CAMSA 89; clothing export value *5*;

factories 32; foreign investment 57; labour militant movement 10; migrant workers 8
third world migrant labour force 64
Todd, P. 24–7, 39n6
Trade Agreement on Textiles and Apparel (TATA) 145, 148
Trade Union Constitution 1993 47–8, 54
trade union(s) 23, 26–7, 32, 37–8, 38n1, 45–6, 48–9, 53, 567, 66, 89, 94n7, 106, 136, 145; Act 1959 36; affiliation 25; Bangladesh 39n10, 60–1, 64, 67; Cambodian 148; conventional 76; demise 8; density declines 10, 29; federations 38n2, 38n3, 65; ITGLWF 39n9; labour 12; Laws 44, 47, 51, 54; leaders 52; marginalized position 24; movement 126; Nepalese council 92; not gender sensitive 28; official 50; organizing 147; provincial 55; registered 68; registrar 75; traditional 125; workplace-based 13
trade union(s) activities: allowed 125; decline 136; restricted 25–6, 37–8, 56, 66
trade union(s), clothing and textile 15–16, 24, 44; Penang Textile 29–30
trade union(s) member(ship) 10, 24, 35, 77n5, 125; declining 27, 38n1; migrant right to join 35; migrant workers 35
trade union(s) rights 33; of migrant workers 35; to negotiate 36; to represent workers 74
trade union(s) role 49, 51; supportive 55; undermined 31
Tran, A. N. 7, 10–11, 13, 15–16, 43–4, 82
Tsing, A. 6, 8
turnover business 173, 187n5; labour 64, 70; personal income 182; worker 104, 109; workforce 102
TW Co1 *50*; worker 52; workers' strike 53
TW Co2 *50*; worker strike 52–3
TW Co3 *50*; worker strike 53
TW Co4 *50*

UNCTAD 121
union 3, 9, 16, 24, 26, 37–8, 47–9, 52, 54; activity 25, 46, 64, 66; based activism 80, 86; Cambodian militancy 145; chairperson 55; Chinese administrators 106; demands 74; demise 8; density 10, 28–9, 146; elections 76; federations 31, 39n11, 65, **68**, 72; fees 51, 56, 69; figures 172, 174, 187n7; formation

## 202   Index

union *continued*
60–1, 71, 75; Jeans Factory Workers 137; migrant worker movement 93; movement 32, 38n2; organizations 30, 136, 147; organizing 27; PTGWU 29; rights 33, 35; structure 57; struggle 11; TCFUA 173; textile and garment 23; white collar 38n1; *see also* trade union(s)

union leaders 30, 51, 57; assassinations 147; bypassed 45; Chinese 38n1; incarceration 32, 38; Indian and Malay 27; male union leadership 28; mass arrest 65; sided with the managers 52; unofficial 54; Vietnamese 55

union members/membership 38n2, 52; decline 28, 38n1, 125; employees relinquish 36; low 30–1; rights 35; undermined 24

union movement 23, 48–9; activists 126; anti-communist 65; call for solidarity 32; Cambodian 145; Chinese distanced from 38n2; cultural gender divisions 38; in Malaysia 24; migrant worker 93

unionism 14, 23; clothing industry 171; political 65; social movement 38; trade 10, 27, 60, 124, 136, 138

unionists 26, 37; clothing and textile trade 81; Indian 27–8; trade 134

unionized workers 36, 71; garment 10; Malaysian 38n1; workforce 39n6; workplace 6

United Kingdom (UK) 32, *131*

United Nations (UN) 101; Development Fund for Women 2

United States (US) 2, 32, 63–5, 110, 121, *131*, 145, 159; Department of Trade 4; government 148; NGO 68; recovery 107; US$ *5*, 33, 36, 39n10, 43–4, 52–3, 62, 74, 83–4, 114, 120, 129–30, 132–3, 137, 142, 144, 150, 152, 163

unskilled 23; female workers 7, 27, 62; migrant workers 81; peripheral workers 8; workers 99

urban 101, 111; areas 24, 103; cost of living 109; need 99; non-Malays 25; residents 108; semi-urban industrial centres 123; urban–rural divide 13; working class 11; *see also* suburban

urban-based 99; medical services denied 101

urban-rural income gap 101

van der Meulen Rodgers, Y. 124, 146

Vietnam 2–3, *5*, 7–8, 18n1, 34, 43, 50, 48, *190–1*; AAFLI 65; boatpeople 88–9; disputes 45; evangelical ministry 90; FDI 56; industrial relations 46; labour unions 55; migrant workers 81, 83, 87; migrant workers strike 85; socialist state 10; strikes 44, 49; textile and garment industry 53–4; trade unions 47, 57; War 177

Vietnamese 48–9, 80, 85–6, 89–92; Communist government 43; home-based worker groups 175; IR system 45, 55; Ministry of Planning and Investment 44; mobility 16; refugees 177; Trade Union Law 1990 47; trade unions 54, 56; Update conference 94n2; women 84–5, 169, 172, 178, 180; workers 7, 13, 53, 83, *190–1*

Vietnamese American 80; Boatpeople 88; Ministry 90

Vietnamese General Confederation of Labour (VCGL) 43–4

Vietnamese Ministry of Planning and Investment (MPI) 43–4

Vietnamese workers 13, 49, 83; collective action 53; ethnic tensions 86; interviews *190–1*; male 80; male and female 90; repatriated without compensation 85; VGCL 47; working in Malaysia 92

VietnameseAustralians 177

vigilante group RELA 88

Vijayabaskar, M. 120, 122

violence 73–4, 86; domestic 87; racial 25, 84; state 11, 75, 92; threats 69, 71

Vo, A. N. 43–4

voices 70; against exploitation 134; heard 49; interests 48; labour 76; no voice 23; radical 71; raised in protest 70; silenced 66; silent 54; of women 169, 175–6, 185; of workers 18

vulnerable workers 2, 11, 130, 134;

Warner, M. 57

welfare 11, 46; benefits 177; of migrants 89, 91; payments 174, 177, 181, 185, 187n8; provisions 49, 177; service provision 81; shelters 91; social 173; workplace 23

Weller, S. 2, 6, 8

Wills, J. 3

women 2, 33, 73, 85, 103, 129, 132, 142, 157, 165n8, 172, 177–8; Aid Organization (WAO) 87, 94n8; attitudes of perseverance 133; backward 39n4;

career prospects 144; caring responsibilities 160, *161*, **161–2**; Chinese 179–81, 187n11; clothing industry 11, *131*; cyclic replacement 163; employed in clothing industry 77n4; exploitation 124; from Hong Kong 178; inclined against join unions 136–8; income 137, 175; informal labour 17–18; low-paid labour 6; Malay 16, 28, 93; migrant 63, 81–2, 174, 176, 186; MTUC Women's Committee 38n1; NGOs 87, 94n7; participation in unions 31; pregnant 147, 153, 162, 164; sewing machinists 171; sewing skills 7, 27; third world 64; unpaid domestic labour 17; Vietnamese 80, 90, 169; young 97, 102, 109–10, 149

women workers 12, 31, 110, 125–6, 127, 129–30, 157–8, 163, 169, 172, 174; in factories 12; garment workers 1, 10, 163; health-care costs 129; home-based 128, 169, 171–2, 175–6, 180, 185–6; informal 130; leaving 143–4; migrant 174; pool available 14; started early 153; striking 127; support group 37; workforce 160; worldwide 33–4

Women Working Worldwide (WWW) 33–4

worker organizations 23, 46, 93; solidarity 12, 69, 124

worker rights 49, 60–1, 66, 76, 125, 136; citizenship 75; Consortium 3; labour 37, 48, 69; rights-based movement 93

workers 2, 4, 7–8, 10–14, 16, 23–4, 27, 29–32, 34–7, 47, 53, 62, 67, 77n6, 80–2, 85–7, 89–90, 92–3, 94n2, 106, 108, 112, 126–7, 130, 137, 142, 150, 154, 156–7, 160, 164n3, 171; assembly line 179; Bangladeshi 64; Cambodian 18n1; clothing 33; collecting 149; commuting 165n5, 165n6; competition among 128; control 75; disposable 15; employment age **154**; entitlements to maternity leave 159; ex-factory 166n15; expert 132; exploitation 124; factory 166n13; first generation 70; foreign 94; formal sector 129, 131, 133; garment industry 135; home-based 169–70, 172–4, 176, 185; Indian 119–20; industrial 144; informal sector 123, 125; insecurity 147; interests 3, 55; lift out of poverty 94n9; in Malaysia 38, 82; Malaysian 28, 38n1, 39n12; male 77n4; mobilized 65, 73; Nepalese 83, 91; older 103; organization

of 46; organize 26, 72; outsourced 88; plantation 25; protecting 48, 163; recruited *131*; representing 51; RMG 77n2; rural 97; searching 52; shortage of 17, 98, 109–10, 121; skilled 104; SKOP 66, 74; solidarity **68–9**; in sweatshop 63, 99; textile 39n8, 136; union elections denied 76; unionized 36, 71; uprising 61; Vietnamese 49; vulnerability 134; young 105, 107, 153, **155**, 166n12; *see also* child labour; disposable workers; female workers; women workers

workers abused 91, 87, 97, 145; collapsing 134; inhumane treatment 49; labour abuse 93; violence against 92

workers contract 11, 24, 30, 34–6; break 84

workers deaths 33, 134; killed 1, 73; suicide 107

workers discharged or dismissed 29, 35, 71, 76, 103; job cessation **161–2**; lay off 133; lost jobs 100–1, 146; return to sending communities 143; sacked 72

workers education 90, 114; into citizenship rights 75; trained 121; training 146

Workers Employees Unity Council (SKOP) 66, 74

workers strikes 39n10, 45, 52–7, 72–4, 85; organized 16, 44

workers underage *151*, 152–3, **155–6**, 157; child 165n11, 166n12; registered as adult 164

workers wages 35–6, 100, 107, 114; dissatisfied with 111; excluded from economic rewards 138; lower 102, 105

working class 23, 57, 65; Malay 27, 35; urban 11

Workman's Compensation Act 1952 35

workplace 3, 6–7, 15, 18, 44, 54, 81, 85; accidents 88; Chinese unions 106; control 39n4; divisions 38; economic and welfare matters 23; exclusion of trade unions 13; injustices 16; mechanisms 47; mobility 70; relations 45, 48; support 71; trade unions 56; union role 10; worker turnover 109

World Bank 9, 63, 94n5, 151, 155–6

World Confederation of Labour (WCL) 38n3

World Federation of Trade Unions (WFTU) 38n3

World Trade Organization (WTO) *5*, 34, 97–8, 113, 119–20; Agreement of Textiles and Clothing (ATC) 4, 9, 145

## 204   Index

Yangtze River Delta 98, 101–2, 104, 108, 110, 113
Yin, R. K. 50
young workers 155, 157
Yu, X. 106, 112

Yuen, T. 25, 27
Yunus, M. 62

Zhu, Y. 46, 48–9, 56–7